Walk This Way Tenerife

Trails of the Unexpected

By

Andrea and Jack Montgomery

Copyright © 2015 Andrea and Jack Montgomery

All rights reserved. No part of this publication may be reproduced, stored in a retrieval system or transmitted in any form by any means, electronic, mechanical, photocopying, recording or otherwise, without the written consent of the authors.

ISBN-10:1511498811
ISBN-13:9781511498814

Front Cover Photograph: Chinamada to Punta de Hidalgo path.
Rear Cover Photographs: View across the Teno Massif and Jack and Andrea Montgomery.

All photgraphs in Walk This Way Tenerife were taken on the walking routes included in the book.

ACKOWLEDGEMENTS

Brief quotes borrowed from some famous names who have walked this way in past times include German naturalist Alexander von Humboldt whose waxing lyrical about the Orotava Valley does get rolled out a lot, but deservedly so. Also in there is Olivia Stone whose book Tenerife And Its Six Satellites made it clear which she considered the most important island in the Canaries. Last but definitely not least is, Lady Isabel Burton whose musings about Tenerife in her book The Romance of Isabel Lady Burton are a right hoot.

CONTENTS

	Acknowledgments	i
1	Walk this Way - Introduction	Page 1
2	The Weather on Tenerife	Page 6
3	Hints & Tips	Page 11
4	Walks in the North of Tenerife – Anaga Mountains	Page 17
5	Walks in the North of Tenerife – The Orotava Valley	Page 45
6	Walks in the North of Tenerife – Santiago del Teide	Page 67
7	Walks in the North of Tenerife – Teno	Page 91
8	Walks in the North of Tenerife – Garachico	Page 117
9	Walks in the North of Tenerife – Coastal Routes	Page 126
10	Walks in the South of Tenerife – Adeje	Page 150
11	Walks in the South of Tenerife – Arona	Page 166
12	Walks in the South of Tenerife – Guia de Isora	Page 180
13	Walks in the South of Tenerife – San Miguel de Abona	Page 196
14	Walks in the South of Tenerife – Coastal Routes	Page 205
15	Walks in Central Tenerife – Teide National Park	Page 216
16	Walks in Central Tenerife – Vilaflor	Page 244
17	Appendix 1: Walks under 10km	Page 255
18	Appendix 2: Walks 10 - 20km	Page 258
19	Appendix 3: Walks under 2hrs	Page 259

20	Appendix 4: Walks 2 - 4hrs	Page 260
21	Appendix 5: Walks over 4hrs	Page 262
22	Appendix 6: Mountain Walks	Page 263
23	Appendix 7: Forest Walks	Page 265
24	Appendix 8: Coastal Walks	Page 266
25	Appendix 9: Caminoes Reales	Page 267
26	Appendix 10: Family Friendly Walks	Page 269
24	Appendix 11: Routes Near Resorts	Page 271
28	Appendix 12: Vertiginous Routes	Page 273
29	Appendix 13: Our Favourite Routes	Page 275
30	Appendix 14: GPS Coordinates	Page 276

To the Guanche and their goats whose ancient feet and hooves carved the myriad paths that cover Tenerife so that, five centuries later, we can follow in their footsteps.

WALK THIS WAY TENERIFE

"Combined with slopes bedecked with regal carpets of wild flowers and a shimmering Atlantic at their base, this was surely my favourite walk on Tenerife…"

Introduction

Tenerife is an island of incredibly varied landscapes which are criss-crossed by ancient paths dating back to the island's first inhabitants, an island completely unknown as a walking destination and yet, one that offers some of the most unique, varied, challenging and rewarding walking in Europe.

Unlike the neighbouring island of La Gomera which has long been a magnet for predominantly Germany's walking cognoscenti, Tenerife is thought of by millions of northern Europeans as nothing more than a winter sun destination for those in search of a budget break and a suntan. But the presence of the planet's third largest volcano set within a 17km (10 mile) wide crater of surreal landscape, encircled by a dense forest of pine and red earth, lifts its diversity of walking even beyond that of La Gomera.

Lace up the boots on Tenerife and strike out from its resorts and you'll discover rain forests which have survived the Ice Age and which edge deep ravines where communities still live in caves; tiny hamlets whose inhabitants tend precipitous terraces by hand, and beautiful coastal paths which weave through palm groves. And because it's not yet known as a walking destination, you can walk through mountains and valleys for hours and never meet another soul.

As seasoned walkers, Jack and Andy Montgomery have enjoyed hiking in terrain as challenging as the Atlas Mountains, the Swiss and Italian Alps, Cape

Verde and the Pyrenees, as well as the gentle hills of Provence, the coastline of Croatia, the rich meadows of Austria's lakes and the hills, lakes, and lanes of the UK. With thousands of trekking miles behind them, Jack and Andy maintain the Canary Islands offer some of Europe's finest walking trails in weather that allows you to pull on the hiking boots all year round.

From coast to coast and sea level to the summit of Mount Teide, Andy & Jack walk Tenerife, and indeed all of the Canary Islands, regularly and extensively. They want you not only to read about what a unique walking destination Tenerife is but also to discover the joys of walking on this island for yourself. That is why they have written Walk This Way on Tenerife which incorporates all their favourite walks and tells you everything you need to know about getting the most from walking on Tenerife.

Andy and Jack are certain it won't be long before the secret's out of the bag that Tenerife is one of Europe's best walking destinations. So come and enjoy it while you've still got it to yourself... and them.

Happy trails!

Individual route directions
At the start of each route you will find the following information:
- Total distance
- Time taken based on a walking average of 4km per hour, 3km per hour on ascents.
- Whether the route is circular, linear or partially circular.
- Type of terrain.
- Level of difficulty on a scale of 1 to 5 (see key below).
- Scenery to expect.
- Places to get refreshments.
- Downside, if any.
- How to get to the start of the route, by car and public transport
- Parking

Indexed walks
Routes are listed by their geographical location for ease of presentation and fall into north, south or central Tenerife, the north/south dividing line being Mount Teide, and central Tenerife covering Teide National Park and its immediate environs.
Using the appendices, walks can be identified by specific location, by proximity to resorts, by length, difficulty, terrain etc.

General information and advice
At the start of Walk This Way is a comprehensive section of general information about walking on Tenerife – climate, terrain, types of paths, directional signs etc. Advice is given about clothing and equipment and important advice about weather warnings which should be heeded in order to reduce the chances of personal injury while walking on Tenerife.

Getting to the start of routes
There are generally two ways to get to the start of most walking routes; driving or by public transport. We provide guidance on both. The public bus service, TITSA, is very good with services covering much of the island. However, the more rural the location the less frequent the buses (known locally as guaguas pronounced wah-wah) are. We include suggested services for each route from the south, south west and north of the island. But the TITSA website (www.titsa.com) has an excellent route planner which each person can use to work the route they want.

Vertiginous Sections
We've included information about routes we think may have parts that could be a problem for anyone with vertigo. One of us was a vertigo sufferer until a

kill or cure situation on Sigirya Rock in Sri Lanka resulted, thankfully, in a cure. So we understand only too well that there isn't always a definitive answer to what is vertiginous. Where we mention a route as being vertiginous, it's more to highlight the fact that it has potential to be seen as vertiginous.

Caminos Reales
The earliest known inhabitants of Tenerife were the pastoral Guanche, moving their herds from lower to upper lands to access grazing grounds. It's thanks to them that many trails in the Anaga Mountains were first carved out by feet and hooves. With the Spanish conquest of Tenerife in 1496 came the need to construct roads. Building on paths created by the Guanche and initially owned by the Spanish Crown, the highways were known as Caminos Reales (Royal Roads) and were constructed across the island to improve communications and trade between villages. These historic highways form part of many of our routes, their ancient cobbles now supporting hi-tech hiking boots where once only bare feet trod. If you want to get to know some of the island's best Caminos Reales, we've listed which routes include them in Appendix .

Route difficulty rating:
Level 1: More of a stroll than a hike.
Level 2: Some ascents and descents but predominantly flat, and good terrain.
Level 3: Good thigh muscle workout with some strenuous ascents and/or descents but within the range of reasonably fit walkers.
Level 4: Invigorating and demanding with some tough ascents and/or descents and some rough terrain.
Level 5: Only recommended for experienced and fit hikers.

Walk This Way Hotel Recommendations
We include some personal hotel recommendations for each walking area. These are mainly rural hotels we've usually stayed at and like thanks to things such as friendliness, service, good looks and generally because they simply have bags of character.
Price Key: Budget <€80 (£57); Mid-range €81 to €180 (£58 - £128); Expensive >€180 (£128)

Disclaimer
The authors of Walk This Way Tenerife have made every effort to ensure the information given in this publication is full, clear and accurate. Your safety is our concern but it is your responsibility and we accept no responsibility for any injury or loss sustained when using our walking routes.

THE WEATHER ON TENERIFE

"The Canarian Archipelago rejoices in the most magnificent climate in the world, and Orotava is the most excellent of the excellent."

Olivia Stone 1887

The 'island of eternal spring' tag is a bit misleading and not entirely accurate. For a start, whose spring are we talking about? It's hot in summer months but not oppressively so and it's warm to hot in winter months although occasional cold weather fronts can drag the temperatures down during winter, but usually only for short periods.

There's a lot of misinformation written about the weather on Tenerife, usually by people who don't know all of the island or who have a vested interest in directing tourists to certain areas.
The sun doesn't shine every day as some would have people believe, but Tenerife and the Canary Islands enjoy about as good a climate as you can get. You can sunbathe every month of the year which means you can also walk every month of the year in hiker friendly conditions.

However, there are variations and weather patterns do change during the year, so an understanding of the weather on Tenerife is useful before heading into its hills.

The South is Sunny, the North is Cloudy
The south is sunnier, drier and warmer than the north, that's a fact. But it's all relative. The bulk of settlers, noblemen and artists chose the north of Tenerife as home following the conquest in 1496. When Victorians were sent to a temperate climate for the benefit of their health, they were sent to the north of Tenerife. Temperatures in the depths of winter don't normally drop much below 20C (68F) in the shade and it stays in the upper 20s to low 30s in summer. The north of Tenerife can be cloudy and it can rain at certain times of the year but it isn't the default setting. The bottom line is that all of Tenerife enjoys a wonderful climate.

The Sun Shines Every Day on Tenerife
Actually often the sun is shining somewhere on Tenerife. Blue skies are almost a given in Las Cañadas del Teide but everywhere else will experience their share of cloudy days. Even on a cloudy day on Tenerife, the sun can often break through at some point.

Rainy Days in Tenerife
It does rain on Tenerife, even in southern parts but not much and usually not for long. In the north, where there is more rain, it often falls in winter, at night and doesn't last long. Most rain falls in the hills. The most likely time for seriously bad weather is during seasonal changes. November is a prime candidate for stormy weather at some point as is February/March.

Microclimates

There are numerous microclimates across the island which means that the weather can be different from the coast to the hills to the mountains; from one valley to the next and on north, east, south and west coasts. It is why when anyone says Tenerife is an island of contrasts it is not a cliché. It is also why any weather website which has only one forecast for the whole of Tenerife, or even two (e.g. north and south) is not to be trusted.

Weather Alerts

One of the most important things that any walker should do before setting off on a hike is check the weather. Most of the time the weather is wonderful, but there are times when weather alerts are issued by the Spanish Meteorological Office and walking when one is in place can be extremely dangerous.

Alert Levels
- **Green** is the normal state of affairs. Basically this means everything in the garden is rosy.
- **Yellow** means bad weather, but not necessarily seriously. Take care and keep an eye on the situation.
- **Orange** is where things start to get worrying. Simply do not go walking if an orange alert is in place.
- **Red** is... well 'extreme risk' is how the Spanish Met Office puts it. Thankfully that one is extremely rare. Again, it would be madness to go walking if a red alert is in place.

When weather alerts are issued, they don't always affect the whole of Tenerife and the Spanish Met Office also issues quite detailed advice about where could be affected most.

Types of Weather Alerts

Although sunshine is the default setting, in winter months weather alerts are more common than in summer. Mostly they are yellow level.

Rain

There can be monsoon like downpours on Tenerife during the change of seasons. This can lead to dangerous conditions and flash floods. Because of the shape of the island, heavy rainfall can result in raging torrents coursing down from the mountains.

Wind

Mostly the strongest winds blow way up in the hills, so walkers need to keep an eye out for alerts even if it's calm and sunny at the coast. Atlantic storms that stray too close can sometimes bring serious winds to coastal areas.

Thunder and Lightning
Thunderstorms are often more spectacular than anything else. But they are usually accompanied by rain or wind.

Heat
Some visitors see soaring temperatures and rub their hands together. Don't be fooled. Any alert means potential danger and walkers have died of heat exhaustion because they ignored warnings.

High Seas
Simply classed as 'costeros' on the Spanish Met Office site, in some ways this is one of the most dangerous as an alert for wild seas doesn't just mean potential danger for mariners. The sea can look calm, it can be hot and sunny and there might not be a breath of wind. Suddenly huge waves crash against the shore, sweeping away everything in their path. Unfortunately this can include people who didn't know about, or ignored, warnings.

Calima
When the sand from the Sahara is blown across the sea to turn the air a hazy yellow. As well as blotting out the scenery, the dust filled air is potentially dangerous, especially for anyone with respiratory problems.

Where to find out about weather alerts
Hotels often post notices about the weather taken from the Spanish Meteorological website and these show weather alerts. Rural hotels often have a good knowledge of what's happening weather wise and will advise guests accordingly.

To keep an eye on the weather we recommend using AEMet (www.aemet.es) Spain's Agencia Estatal de Meteorología. The website breaks forecasts down to municipality level and shows the forecast for morning, afternoon and evening. If there is an alert, it explains what it is and where is likely to be affected. In ten years we've found it to be far more accurate than any other source. If you have a smartphone enter your location on the AEMet site and it will give you a forecast for where you are.

When is Best for Walking on Tenerife?

The main hiking season for Northern Europeans is between October and Easter. There are far fewer walkers in summer months even though the temperatures aren't as high as mainland Spain; mainlanders descend on the Canary Islands between July and September to escape the searing heat at home.

In reality, any time between late September and June is usually great weather for walking. Only July and August are potentially uncomfortably hot and even then shaded forest trails are comfortable enough.

September and October usually offers wonderfully sharp visibility and is an ideal time for walkers who are also photographers; although in some parts there is a distinct lack of greenery after a long, hot, dry summer.

Our favourite time is spring, when the countryside is lush and green and ablaze with wild flowers.

HINTS & TIPS

Clothing and Equipment

Clothes
A hat is an essential item any time of the year for walking on Tenerife. The subtropical sun will leave its mark whatever the air temperature feels like.

Clothes are a bit more complicated. Layers are the best option as Tenerife's numerous microclimates mean on some routes you can be walking in sweltering hot sunshine for one section, cool exposed windy slopes on another and shrouded in damp bruma (low cloud) in yet another. As a result, clothes can be on and off on an annoyingly regular basis.

As a general rule, in winter months we wear a t-shirt, base layer type long sleeve top and a light waterproof/windproof jacket and find that this combination has kept us dry and warm, or not too warm as the case may be whatever weather conditions we've encountered.

For example, a January walk in Teide National Park can mean an air temperature of 2C. Setting off and the combination of t-shirt, base layer and jacket is perfect. After a short time walking in the sunshine and the jacket comes off. Add in a shadeless ascent and the long sleeve base layer is also too warm, so it comes off as well. As far as trousers go, we favour light walking ones that dry quickly if drenched.

In summer months it's different. Then shorts and a t-shirt are usually ideal. But it depends on the route. It can be hotter at altitude than at the coast in summer, especially around the 1000m mark, but, on the other hand, low cloud in forested areas can bring an unseasonal chill to the air. We were caught in both the Anagas and upper Orotava Valley in August, the hottest month, during early walking days on the island. We've also been caught in sudden and unexpected heavy rain (weather forecasts showed a cloudless sky with no possibility of rain) that raced in from the west. By then we were a lot wiser to Tenerife's weather foibles and had packed a light jacket, just in case.

Even in the dry summer months it can still be a sensible addition to the rucksack.

Footwear
Over the years we've tried walking sandals, light walking shoes/boots and heavy boots. The walking sandals were wonderful in summer months, until one of Jack's fell apart halfway around the Los Órganos route in the Orotava Valley.

The light walking shoes seemed heavenly in warm temperatures for a while, but didn't offer a lot of protection on uneven surfaces such as lava fields or even *caminos reales* (merchant trails). In the end we returned to mostly wearing heavier boots with thick soles perfect for absorbing the sort of rocky surfaces you often encounter on walking routes on Tenerife.

Ultimately, the best shoe to wear depends on individual routes. We have the luxury of being able to choose walking sandals or light walking shoes for coastal routes, or forest paths that are foot friendly, and heavier duty footwear for the likes of Teide National Park. But with airline luggage allowances being what they are, most people won't have the luxury of choice, so a good pair of lightweight boots with thick soles is an ideal all rounder for tackling Tenerife's diverse terrain.

Walking Poles
Canarios have used long poles for walking in the Tenerife hills for centuries, sometimes using them to 'jump' small ravines, a technique known as *salto de pastor* (there's a nice little sculpture of the salto de pastor in San Miguel de Abona). However, we wouldn't recommend anyone goes quite as native as that.
The question of whether to use walking poles or not is very much down to personal preferences.

We initially used one walking pole each but found that when we were regularly stopping to take notes and photographs etc. they became more of a hindrance than a help. Now we rely on balance and the use of whatever nature provides on bits of paths that could be described as 'dodgy'. We especially like to be 'hands free' when it comes to narrow sections of path.

However, many people feel more comfortable using them and there's no doubt poles can help with ascents and descents, of which there are many on Tenerife.

Knee Supports

Descents on some Tenerife routes can be on the steep side. Add a hard and uneven *camino real* into the mix and there can be a lot of stress on knee joints. After experiencing 'twinges' when walking across La Gomera for a week, where ascents and descents are constant, we took to wearing knee supports for the most challenging descents as a precautionary measure. We'd definitely recommend them to anyone who has experienced discomfort when walking downhill.

Maps

Our routes focus on detailed directions for a number of reasons, one of them being we haven't seen a map of Tenerife which is 100% accurate, and neither has anyone else we know who is involved with walking. The best map we are aware of regularly let us down when we were trying out new routes, with some paths shown not actually existing and paths that do exist not being included. All of the Canary Islands suffer from the same problem.

But having a decent map acts as a good safety net, although ours rarely leaves the rucksack these days. We use Kompass Teneriffa when we need to use a map. It's not perfect but it is better than most.

A Compass

If you're someone who likes to use a compass, pack it. We rarely need to use ours, but then we obviously know the landscape very well. In the early days of walking on Tenerife, a compass did come in handy on a couple of occasions when the directions we had were misleading to the point of being dangerous. These were officially produced directions which we realised very quickly were more what should be termed 'vague guidelines'.

But people do get lost regularly on Tenerife. The forests can be dense and paths difficult to make out. Bruma can strip the terrain of landmarks. There was a case where a family of Canarios who lived near Anaga were lost in the ravines and forest for a couple of days after trying to walk to a remote cove.

Incredibly people even get lost in Teide National Park which seems amazing given it has one of the most obvious landmarks you're likely to find anywhere. When this happens it causes both bemusement and amusement amongst locals, who make comments like 'it's not the Amazon or the Siberian Steppes, it's an island. Whatever way you walk, you'll reach the coast at some point.'

Control of Mouflon

At various times of the year there are authorised culls on mouflon which can result in the closure of some walking routes in Teide National Park for part of some days. These elusive wild sheep were introduced for hunting purposes in 1970, a scheme that didn't take off, and now they damage protected flora in the park. Even knowing that, we still feel a bit sorry for the island's relatively small mouflon population. The cull happens twice a year on designated days between the start of May and mid June and again between the beginning of October and mid November. Only some paths are affected.

The National Park's facebook page (Parque Nacional del Teide) is a good source for checking when paths are affected. It is in Spanish but if you see anything about 'control de muflón' with times then it usually means on the day the information is posted certain paths will be closed in the park.

Take Sensible Precautions

Tenerife is a safe island. But petty theft does occur occasionally, mostly where there are large groups of tourists. We leave our car in remote villages without any worry. However, there have been cases of theft from cars at popular spots such as the car parks at the Roques de Garcia and at Cruz del Carmen. Common sense prevails here. Don't leave any valuables in cars and don't leave anything in the car that looks as though it might have something valuable in it. Best of all is to remove the parcel shelf so that potential thieves can see there's nothing to attract their beady eyes.

Map Icons Used

→	Walking Route	🏠	Village/Hamlet
🍴	Restaurant		Hill
P	Parking	🏊	Beach
⛱	Picnic Zone		Marina
■	Place of Interest	⛺	Campsite

Walks in The North of Tenerife
Anaga Mountains

"We climb slowly, maintaining a steady pace, stopping in shallow caves for a drink and some relief. One has Coto de Caza (hunting area) painted on the wall..."

Walking in the Anaga Mountains

Covering the north east tip of Tenerife, the Anaga Mountains have provided pasture, water, shelter and food for centuries. One of the most populated areas of the island in pre-Hispanic times, the abundant rainfall and vertiginous valleys offered deep caves in which to shelter and good grazing land for stock.

Moving their herds from upper to lower reaches, Tenerife's first known inhabitants, the Guanche, created a matrix of trails through the peaks and valleys, trails which today provide the best walking on Tenerife.

Exploring the Anagas is akin to stepping into a living museum and discovering a taste of what life in Tenerife was like before tourism. Atmospheric ancient laurisilva forests (some of the only remaining ones on the planet as the Ice Age destroyed most); tiny remote rural communities who scratched a living by working the back-breaking narrow terraces which cling to the side of steep ravines and lush undulating hill country. Beautiful, dramatic, breathtaking, challenging and rewarding; the Anagas have all the ingredients for classic walking.

Weather

A frequent visitor to the Anaga Mountains is the so-called 'sea of clouds' that roll in like a dense fog bringing moisture and a drop in air temperature. Hikers may find themselves emerging from dense cloud into sunshine as trails descend, or leaving hot sun to experience a sudden drop in temperature as they climb towards the 900 to 1000 metre mark. It's best to check out the weather forecast before setting off or, even better, look at web cam images on www.meteosurfcanarias.com. If the mountains are covered in a thick grey cotton wool carpet, postpone until another day.

Flora

These forests are known as Monteverde or Laurisilva forests and contain many species of laurel, myrtle, Canary holly and heathers which thrive on the average annual temperatures of less than 15C and high moisture content caused by the 'sea of clouds' that characterise them.

Woodlands like these were once prevalent in Europe but the Ice Age pushed their habitat back. Now they only remain in the Canaries, Madeira, the Azores and Cape Verde. Beneath the mantle of trees and shrubs are found many species of wild flowers including foxgloves, campanula, Canary geranium and daisies.

Call of nature

There are toilets at the Visitor Centre at Cruz Del Carmen and at the restaurant Cruz Del Carmen. In Las Carboneras there are two bar restaurants and there's a cave restaurant in Chinamada, appropriately if unimaginatively named 'La Cueva' – the cave. There are a couple of little restaurants and cafes in Taganana that are worth detouring to for a bite or a coffee as well as a natural break. In Roque Bermejo there's a little shop and bar which you can use as long as you buy something and providing they're open, not always a given, and there's a bar in Chamorga.

Eat me

A good value local speciality that's also found all over traditional Tenerife is *escaldón*. In Canarian homes *escaldón de gofio* often accompanies Canarian stews and broths like *pucheros* or *cazuelos* but in some traditional restaurants it turns up on the starters menu.

It's a dish that has links with Tenerife's original inhabitants, the Guanches as the main ingredient is *gofio*; a flour that pre-dates the conquest. It's made from various roasted grains and is still immensely popular across the Canary Islands (if you've never heard of it, just check the flour section next time you're in a Canarian supermarket).

Escaldón in it's most basic form is a very simple dish; consisting of gofio mixed with fish stock (usually) to make a thick paste. The better the stock, the better the *escaldón*.

Restaurant La Cueva in Chinamada is particularly proud of their *escaldón*.

Where To Stay When Walking in the Anaga Mountains
The singularly most difficult part of Tenerife to access, there is no easy option for where to stay in order to access routes in the Anaga Mountains. That's why they have remained so unspoilt.

It's a 20 minute drive and 40 minutes by bus (every 90 minutes) to Cruz del Carmen (Forest to Cave) and 40 minutes by car and 1 hour by bus (5 times a day) to Afur (Hamlets & Hillsides) from La Laguna. A UNESCO World Heritage Site and former capital city of the island, La Laguna has a good choice of restaurants; historic buildings, art galleries and excellent shopping.

Hotel Nivaria, La Laguna
A restored and recently refurbished 16th century mansion set on Plaza del Adelantado in the heart of La Laguna's old quarter. Rooms are spacious and comfortable with contemporary furnishings and a small kitchenette with fridge but you have to pay extra for cooking utensils. The spa is €12 a day for guests and there's a gym which is free for guests. [Mid-range]
Plaza del Adelantado, 11, San Cristóbal de La Laguna; (+34) 922 26 42 98; www.lagunanivaria.com

Hotel Aguere, La Laguna
A cheaper alternative to the Nivaria, the Aguere is a characteristic hotel set on one of the main shopping streets close to the Iglesia de la Concepcion. It has 22 rooms set around the interior patio, each quite sparsely furnished with period furniture and lacking in character but clean and bright. There's a lovely coffee shop in the patio which is open to the public. [Budget]
Calle Obispo Rey Redondo, 57, San Cristóbal de La Laguna; (+34) 922 25 94 90; www.hotelaguere.es

Known as Tenerife's greenhouse due to its humid climate and because it's where most of the ornamental tropical plantings that adorn hotel lobbies across the island are grown, Valle de Guerra is a rural area on the boundary of the Mercedes Forest and Anaga Mountains.

Hotel Rural Costa Salada
A delightfully quirky, rural hotel whose terraces tumble down the cliff side in splendid isolation from anywhere. Secluded corners with sun loungers; patio tables and a swimming pool look out over the ocean which crashes onto the

rocks below. Rooms are all decorated in traditional rural style and furnished with antiques. The hotel dining room has panoramic views and serves traditional Canarian dishes. It's a 30 minute drive to Cruz del Carmen (Forest to Cave) and 50 minutes to Afur (Hamlets & Hillsides) from the Costa Salada. [Mid-range]
Finca Oasis, Camino de la Costa, San Cristobal de la Laguna; (+34) 922 69 00 00; www.costasalada.com

Forest to Cave - Cruz Del Carmen to Chinamada

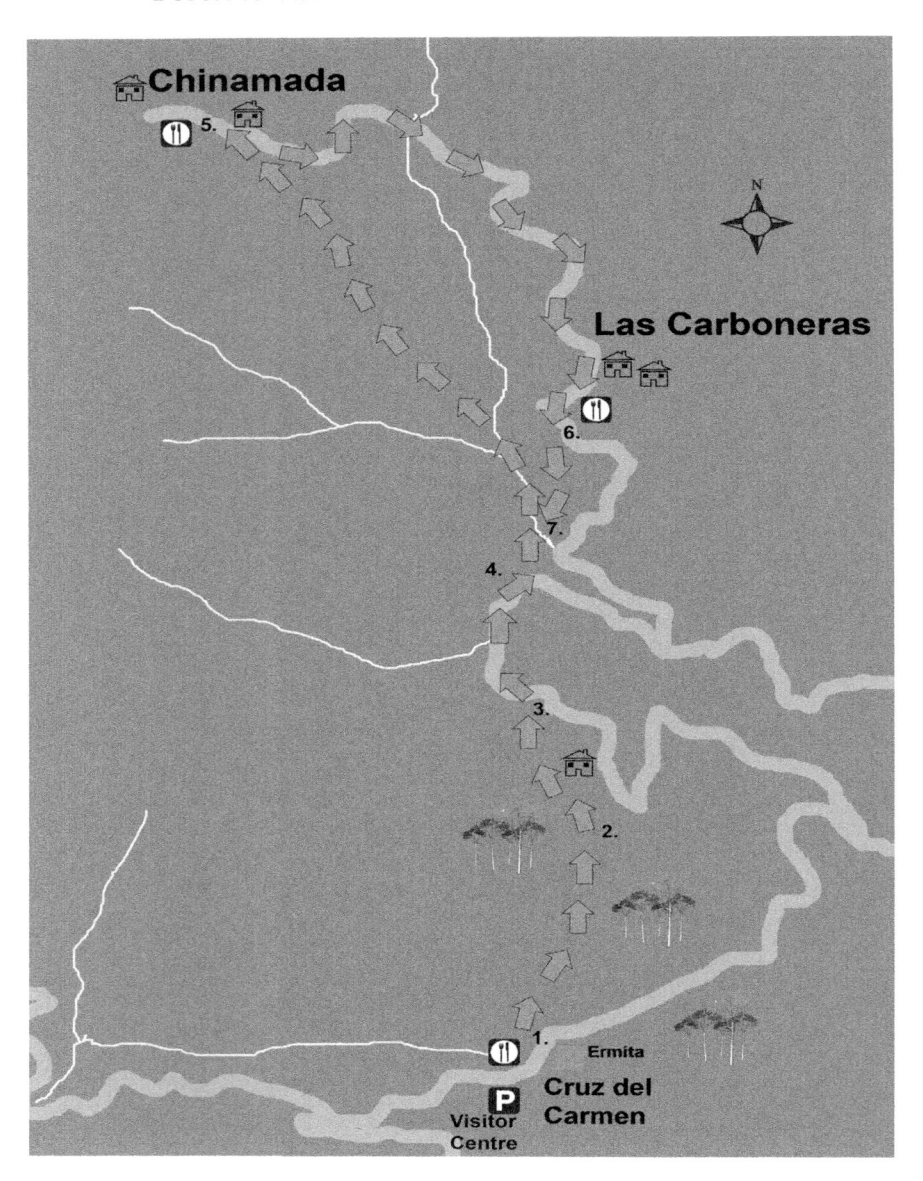

Forest to Cave - Cruz Del Carmen to Chinamada

Location	North east tip of Tenerife.
Circular Route?	Yes.
How Long?	Approx 3.5 hours.
How Far?	12.4 kilometres.
Vertiginous?	The Anaga Mountains are characterised by the ravines that hide quaint hamlets. Where there are ravines, there are generally vertiginous sections. There are no 'hairy' sections as such but there are parts that might pose a problem for vertigo sufferers.
Route Difficulty	Level 3: Good thigh muscle workout, but within the range of reasonably fit walkers. Adding on the Punta del Hidalgo detour brings it up to a level 4 walk.
Wow Scenery	In our view it's hard to beat this walk for diversity and some excellent views.
Underfoot	Forest paths, mountain trails and roads through tiny villages – nice variety for the feet
Watering Holes	Good selection of local hostelries, every hamlet has at least one.
Downside	When the *bruma* (low cloud) rolls in, the temperature drops and views disappear.

This walk takes you from the Mirador Cruz del Carmen, through ancient forests and along mountain trails with views to the tiny village of Chinamada where electricity is considered cutting edge technology. A circular walk, returning via the village of Las Carboneras, it shows you a face of Tenerife unchanged for centuries and a million miles away from the tourist developments of the south coast.

Chinamada lies at 620 metres above sea level on the tip of a ridge flanked on one side by the impressive peak of Roque de Taborno which stands at 706 metres above sea level keeping guard over its namesake valley and settlement, and on the other by a series of slender terraces hewn into the sides of steep barrancos, testament to the heritage of back breaking farming in the mountains.

The residents of Chinamada still live in caves as their ancestors, the Guanche, did for centuries prior to the Spanish conquest at the end of the 15th century. Up until the 1990s, Chinamada had neither electricity nor a road; now hikers and visitors come by mini bus to see the cave houses and to begin the walk to Punta Del Hidalgo or to Las Carboneras.

How to Get There

By Car
Head to La Laguna on the autopista (it doesn't matter where you're driving from) and take the 8B exit from the motorway following signs for Tegueste TF13. The road bypasses La Laguna. Follow signs for Anaga at three roundabouts. After the third you'll be heading straight towards the Anaga Mountains. From there on it's simply a case of looking out for the signs for Cruz del Carmen.

Parking
There's a big free car park at Cruz del Carmen. It gets very busy at weekends when finding a space can be quite difficult.

By Public Transport
The Anaga Mountain's remoteness is a double edged sword. Its distance from the main resorts keeps it unspoiled making it perfect for hikers but it's quite a trek to get there by public transport.

Puerto de la Cruz
Take the 102 to La Laguna and change to the 076/077/273/275 to Cruz del Carmen. (Approx total bus time – 75 mins)

Playa de las Américas/Los Cristianos
Take the 110/111 to Santa Cruz change to the 015 to La Laguna, then the 076/077/273/275 to Cruz del Carmen. (Approx total bus time – 135 mins)

Los Gigantes
There's no easy way, but the best route is to take the 325 to Puerto de la Cruz, change to the 102 to La Laguna and then take the 076/077/273/275 to Cruz del Carmen. (Approx total bus time – 180 mins)

The Route

1. Stepping Out
Follow the trail which begins at the right hand side of the restaurant Cruz del Carmen, signposted 'Chinamada and Punta del Hidalgo'.

The path descends along red earth through dense laurisilva forest with trees covered in lichen. Keep on the path, ignoring false trails which run off to the left and are marked with a yellow and white 'X', until you reach a wooden barrier where the trail crosses a wide forest path.

Cross the path and follow the direction of the pointing finger down the steps on the far side. The winding, root-strewn path descends to the bottom of the forest floor where in winter, small waterfalls run down the rock face. The path begins to ascend and eventually the trees thin until finally, you emerge from the forest into the light and (hopefully) sunshine. From here you can see across the rugged terraced barranco (ravine) of Batán.

2. Remote living (1.44km/35mins)
Take the left fork, keeping the pink house on your right, and follow the trail alongside these remote smallholdings. The hedgerows are thick with brambles and wild flowers and are a haven for bees and butterflies. If you're tempted to pick some berries, stick to the ones on the right or you may find yourself detouring rapidly down the barranco. In the distance you can see the covered banana plantations and the lighthouse at Punta del Hidalgo on the coast.

Stay on the path until you reach the barrier where the trail makes a short incline, marked with a yellow and white stripe, to the right. Follow it up to the road and turn left onto the road.

3. Highway (2km/45mins)
Follow the road past the houses and the bus stop and look over towards the distant red tiled roofs of your destination; the small settlement of Chinamada which sits at the end of the road on the ridge to the right hand side. On your left, you'll come to a series of steps signposted 'Chinamada and Las Carboneras'. Leave the road and follow the steps down to continue the trail.

4. To Chinamada (2.7km/55mins)
Admire the views over the valley and to the peak of Roque de Taborno (2,315 ft, 716 metres) as you zig-zag down the path to the ridge and the signpost. Follow the 'Chinamada and Punta del Hidalgo' direction to the left, past the small wooden cross, with the electricity pylon on your right. Ignore the path to the left (marked with a yellow and white 'X') and continue along the trail which tells you you're in rabbit hunting territory (Coto privado de caza). Try not to step on a hen as the path skirts around the old farmhouse and descends back into woodland. On your right hand side you'll pass a small calvario (Christ on the cross), ignore the path off to the right beside it and continue down the trail until you emerge onto the ridge overlooking Chinamada with views down to the coast at Punta del Hidalgo and back over the steep barrancos.

The path drops down to the left and then switches back on itself taking you into the hamlet of Chinamada.

At this stage, you may like to take a short detour to the viewpoint of Mirador Aguaide (0.6km/15mins) for views back across the Anagas and of the rugged north coast. Follow the path to the right behind the small church in Chinamada. The path weaves between the last two 'cave' houses and over the hill to a viewpoint perched right on the edge of the plunging cliffs.

5. Chinamada to Las Carboneras (6km/1hr 50mins)

For the masochists, a trail begins from behind the Plaza de San Isidro which takes you a further 4.7 kilometres to the coastal resort of Punta del Hidalgo – see 'Detours'.

Leaving Chinamada, walk back up the road out of the village but this time stay on the road following the sign for 'Las Carboneras'. The road undulates alongside Barranco de La Angostura and after 15 mins or so passes a pretty little picnic site set into the rocks; the perfect place to get out the egg sandwiches or just to rest awhile and admire the view.

As you enter the village of Las Carboneras a large garage door announces the Bar Restaurant Tesegre, where the inside is almost as unwelcoming as the outside. Smaller but friendlier is the Bar Restaurant Valentín at the far end of the village where you can sit on their sunny bench and enjoy an ice cream before the uphill slog back to Cruz del Carmen.

Continue along the road out of the village, past the football/basketball court and the last house until you see a blue pipe trailing down the rocks to the road. Just beyond it, on the bend, are steps marked with a yellow and white stripe.

6. All Uphill (9km/2hrs 15mins)

Leaving the road, take the steps and endure the rocky uphill slog, taking frequent stops to catch your breath under the pretence of admiring the view which, incidentally, is well worth admiring.

The path eventually levels out, passing a water fountain and a small shelter in a cave before arriving back at the signpost where the trail to Chinamada began.

7. Homeward Bound (9.7km/2hr 30mins)

Turn left at the signpost and retrace your steps to the road, turning right onto the road and continuing past the houses and the bus stop until you reach a yellow and white marker at a large electricity pylon. Turn right alongside the pylon, leaving the road and entering the forest.

Follow the trail back through the forest, remembering to take the right hand fork below the pink house (marked with a yellow and white stripe on a post).

More uphill forest slog will take you back to the forest path and across, through the wooden barrier with the yellow and white stripe, to the final stretch up to the restaurant Cruz del Carmen where you can *'Unlace the Boots'*.
12.4k/3.5hrs

Detour to Punta del Hidalgo (4.7 kilometres)
The sign at Chinamada advises "90 minutes" to the coast…maybe if you're wearing your underpants over your trousers.

In reality it's downhill all the way for over two hours. However it is an exhilarating experience. The path clings to the side of ravines traversing a volcanic landscape of constantly changing hues as the verdant slopes give way to amber rock faces pockmarked with caves. The laurel forests and potato terraces change to wild lavender and tabaiba as the terrain becomes more arid nearer the coast. In winter the bottom of the barranco floor sparkles with a rare sight; a trickling stream.

At times the descent is steep; ancient steps, cut into the rock make progress that little bit easier, but sap energy if travelling the other way.

Our preferred end to the route is to follow the coastal path to Punta del Hidalgo (almost obscured amongst the undergrowth leading from the cobbled lay-by marked by three small pillars opposite the banana plantation) and to stop off for refreshments and some hypnotic wave watching at the Charco de la Arena restaurant overlooking the rock pools.

We'd only recommend adding this detour onto our main route if you're travelling by public transport; trekking all the way from Cruz del Carmen to Punta de Hidalgo and back again is really only for the super fit.

In truth, this trail really deserves to be treated as a separate walk in its own right. The ascent from Punta del Hidalgo to Chinamada takes about 2.5 hours; the descent slightly less.

There's no real need for specific directions as there is only one path snaking upwards... the only way to go wrong is to try to climb up near vertical rock faces, or to walk off a ravine.

Discover More - Llano de Los Viejos
The old merchants' trail of Llano de Los Viejos, which linked the area with Mercedes and La Laguna, begins at the Cruz del Carmen car park. A twenty minute trek through the laurel forest, along a path worn smooth by centuries of traders taking their goods to Las Mercedes, emerges at a recreation zone (perfect for a picnic). The best of the walk is found a short distance from the start, where a short detour takes you to Llano de Los Loros and superb views towards Santa Cruz, Part of this path has been developed to make it suitable for people with mobility problems and is known as the 'Sendero de los Sentidos'.

Visitor Centre
There's a decent visitors' centre at Cruz del Carmen *(open 09.30-16.00)* with information about the area's flora and fauna; however exhibits are in Spanish.

A place to unlace the boots
The Restaurant Cruz Del Carmen offers an ideal place to rest at the end of your hike and a warm refuge from the bruma (low cloud). Frequented by local farmers as well as by hikers, the bar is welcoming, the food is traditional, the cakes are mouth-watering and there's a good selection of chocolate behind the bar. What more could a weary walker want? La Cueva at Chinamada (closed Monday and Tuesday) is also a great half way spot to enjoy local dishes on the terrace or the interior dining area which includes a small cave. Another option is the jazzy La Gangochera café opposite the Visitor Centre at Cruz del Carmen which has all sorts of local goodies.

Hamlets and Hillsides - Afur to Taganana

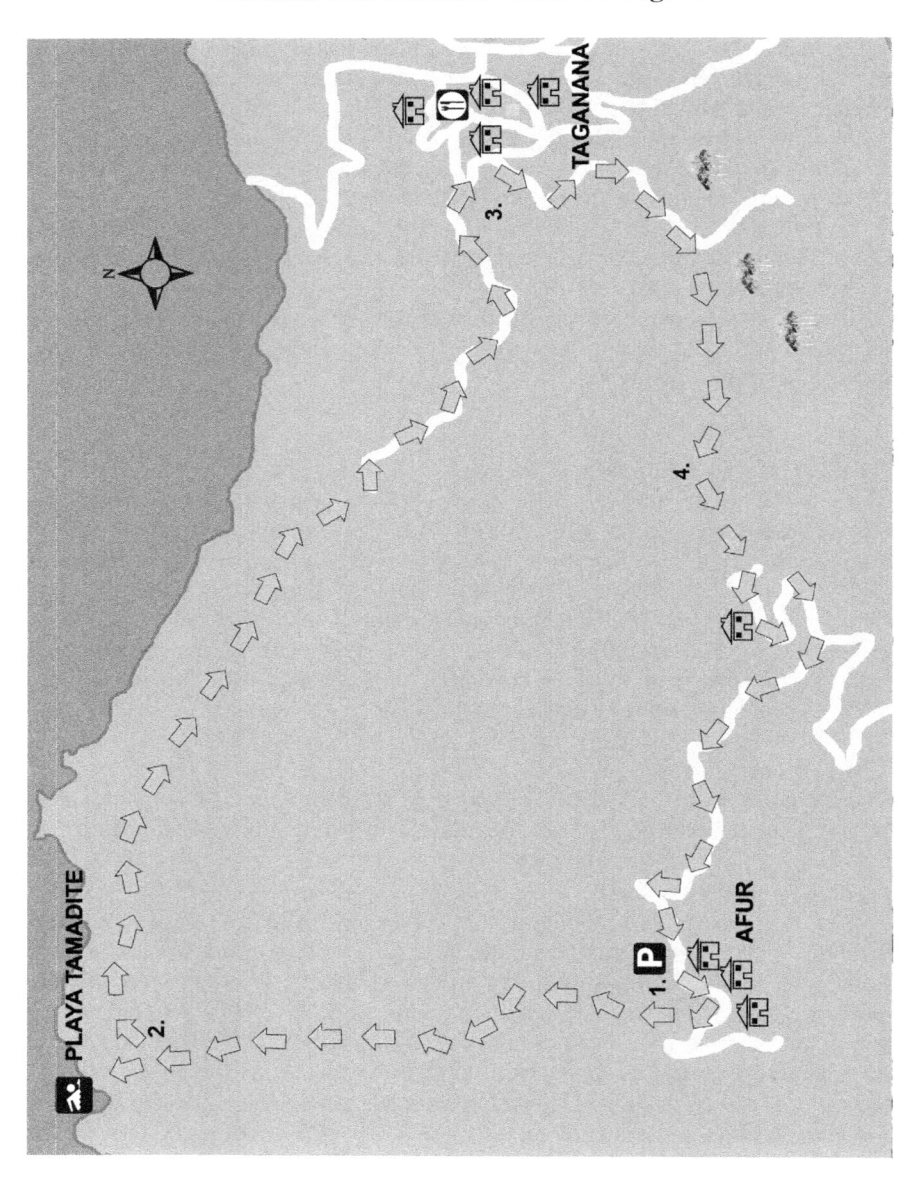

Hamlets and Hillsides - Afur to Taganana

Location	North east tip of Tenerife.
Circular Route?	Yes.
How Long?	Approx 4hrs 50mins.
How Far?	13.3 kilometres.
Vertiginous	The section that runs along the hillside above the coastline may cause problems for anyone with vertigo.
Route Difficulty	Level 3 - There is a lot of ascending and descending. None of it is overly strenuous apart from a stretch into the forest after reaching Taganana.
Wow Scenery	This route has views along the untamed north coast that not many visitors will see.
Underfoot	A good path throughout with a mixture of surfaces ranging from an uneven ravine at the start to a camino real into the forest and concrete tracks.
Watering Holes	There's no longer a restaurant in Afur so Taganana is the only option along the route whilst it's a bit of a drive to the closest watering hole at the end. It's not ideal but a great bar makes the wait worth it.
Downside	There is little shade for most of this route. More of a problem in summer months than winter ones when the temperatures are more walker friendly.

From the little hamlet of Afur with its extraordinary bullet-shaped rock with two, seemingly impossible-to-access houses lodged in the top, this walk takes you through the water rich Barranco Afur de Tamadite where a seam of cane brings year round green to the ravine floor. Following the barranco all the way to the sea you arrive at the secluded, black sand beach of Tamadite before climbing to the ridge and following a coastal path to Taganana with splendid views of the unspoilt north coast.

Passing small allotments of vines, into the hamlet of Cruz Vieja in the upper reaches of Taganana and across a ridge overlooking Barranco Salte del Encerradero, this route takes you to one of the most remote areas of Tenerife where communities exist on subsistence farming and the local church is the centre of village life. The first third of the walk takes you through a barranco which has surface water practically all year, a rare sight on Tenerife with only a handful of barrancos being able to boast the same.

How to Get There

By Car

Head to La Laguna on the autopista (it doesn't matter where you're driving from) and take the 8B exit from the motorway following signs for Tegueste TF13. The road bypasses La Laguna. Follow signs for Anaga at three roundabouts. After the third you'll be heading straight towards the Anaga Mountains. From there on it's simply a case of looking out for the signs Afur and follow them to the end of the road.

Parking
There's a good car park at Afur, right at the start of the route.

By Public Transport

Puerto de la Cruz
Take the 102 to La Laguna and change to the 076 Afur. (Approx total bus time – 1hr 20mins)

Playa de las Américas/Los Cristianos
Take the 110/111 to Santa Cruz change to the 015 to La Laguna, then the 076 Afur. (Approx total bus time – 2hr 40mins)

Los Gigantes
There's no easy way, but the best route is to take the 325 to Puerto de la Cruz, change to the 102 to La Laguna and then take the 076 Afur. (Approx total bus time – 3hrs)

Detour to Taganana
Although the route only skirts the outskirts of Taganana, it's worth taking a detour into this historic rural community that still has the air of past times about it. As you arrive at Cruz Vieja, a path drops down to the left that leads to the charming cobbled streets in the centre of the village. Once there look out for the great old Singer sewing machines sign near La Pianola fountain, where the townsfolk used to collect their water, and the little Church of Nuestra Señora de las Nieves which dates back to the 16th century and is one of the oldest in Tenerife.

An info board at the Ermita de Santa Catalina informs that as well as being a church, the building has been used as a warehouse, morgue and cinema over the years. All around is evidence of an agricultural heritage – cane and vines revealing glimpses into Tenerife's treasures before tourism.

Another good reason for detouring to Taganana is that there are a couple of little restaurants and cafés in the village and, as there aren't any elsewhere on the route, it's a good excuse to take some time out.

A walking information board in Taganana shows that the Camino de las Vueltas route joins up with the Afur route but it's more straightforward to head back to Cruz Vieja and rejoin the route where you left it.

The Route

1. To The Beach.

The route begins in the little car park at the very end of the road in Afur. From the car park, the path descends down the hill, marked with a walking information board and signposted in yellow to 'Playa Tamadite'.

Follow the path as it winds down the hill and in just 178 metres, watch for a small yellow and white tipped post on the right, signposted 'Tamadite'. Turn right and drop down the dusty, skittery path, going straight across the small junction of paths and continuing to follow the yellow and white striped waymarks as you descend into the barranco.

After 550 metres and around 10 minutes you reach a signpost to Playa Tamadite pointing to the right. Go up the rocks and follow the path which you'll see leading off to the right on the other side, clearly marked with yellow and white stripes. Steep, uneven steps cut into the rock take you down and along to reach another ridge 400 metres and 10 minutes later where you continue straight across, following the yellow and white waymarks.

The path now descends to the bottom of the barranco and crosses the permanent stream that feeds the clumps of cane along the ravine floor. Climb up the far bank where wooden railings provide a welcome hand, to reach a ridge where the beach of Tamadite comes into view.

Continue along the path as it winds its way down the barranco towards the sea, passing shallow ponds and small waterfalls en route. The volume of water you encounter will depend on the time of year you're walking; in winter the water may be flowing at a pace with several small waterfalls whereas in high summer much of the floor will be dry with occasional still pools of water. The path is a little unclear at times but remain on the left side of the stream, walking in the direction of the sea.

An hour and 2.5 kilometres after you set off, you'll see a large, red rock on the right hand side of the stream with a path climbing up the bank behind it. This is where you will retrace your steps to, and continue the route to Taganana after you have visited the beach. For the moment, remain on the left side of the stream and follow the path to arrive, 100 metres later, at Playa Tamadite.

2. Along the Coast to Taganana (2.6km/1hr 5mins)

From the beach, retrace your steps to the red rock and, keeping it on your left side, turn left up the path marked with yellow and white stripes as it winds its way to the top, ascending 100 metres in 450 metres distance along the dry, skittery path.

In 15 minutes you arrive at a natural viewpoint on the top of the cliff where you can see along the coast to Roque de las Bodegas, known for its fish restaurants, and beyond to Roque de Fuera (the furthest rocky outcrop you can see out to sea), Tenerife's most northerly point. Follow the coastal path for the next 45 minutes and 2 kilometres until you reach T junction at a vehicle path where a small stone monument sits.

Turn left along the path and follow it as it traverses smallholdings of vines and climbs steeply towards the upper reaches of Taganana, passing occasional buildings. After one kilometre and half an hour, you will see a pink faced cottage above you to the right, Bodega de Queque. A few steps beyond it, take the narrow path which leads up to the right, marked with a yellow and white stripe. Step over the water pipe and rusty wire and continue along the slightly precarious path with the water pipe running along your right hand side.

In 10 minutes and 300 metres the path descends to rejoin the road. Turn right and walk into the little hamlet of Cruz Vieja where you may like to detour to Taganana.

3. The Only way is Up (4.3km/3hrs)

Take the right hand fork, ascending the concrete path in the village, following the signposted direction of 'Casa Forestal, Las Vueltas' and 'La Cumbrecilla, Afur', passing Casa Noni on your right hand side.

At the next fork continue straight ahead on the left hand fork, again following the signposted direction of 'Casa Forestal, Las Vueltas' and 'La Cumbrecilla, Afur', climbing up above the hamlet.

At the junction turn left, again following the signposted direction of 'Casa Forestal, Las Vueltas' and 'La Cumbrecilla, Afur'. In 280 metres, turn sharp right up the stone steps following the signpost direction of Afur. You now have a one kilometre, steady climb up the cobbled, zigzag path for an ascent of almost 300 metres, following the line of the telegraph pylons (don't be tempted to use them as handholds!).

Arrive at the top of the ridge at a crossroads of paths where a signpost hand points the way to Taganana back the way you have just come. Standing with your back to that sign, take the path that runs off to the right (at a quarter past the hour if you were looking at a clock face), to the left hand side of the rock with the crucifix on it.

4. Home descent (6.7km/4hrs)

Views immediately open up on the left hand side over the Barranco Salte del Encerradero and in a couple of steps, on the right hand side is a signpost showing you are heading in the direction of Afur.

The path becomes intense red as you descend steadily into the woods, reaching a higgledy-piggledy finca whose buildings straddle the path and whose washing line fronts the cliff top. Continue on the yellow and white waymarked path through the finca and onto the concrete path that zigzags down.

Emerge onto the TF136 road at the bus stop, turn right and follow the road for 1.6 kilometres to arrive back in the car park at Afur. Unfortunately, since the restaurant closed, there's nowhere in the immediate vicinity in which to *Unlace The Boots* but a short drive back towards Cruz del Carmen takes you to the ever popular Casa Carlos where the beer's chilled, the barbecue's hot and the views are splendid... provided they're not in cloud.

13.3km/4hrs 50mins

To The End Of The Island, Chamorga to Roque Bermejo

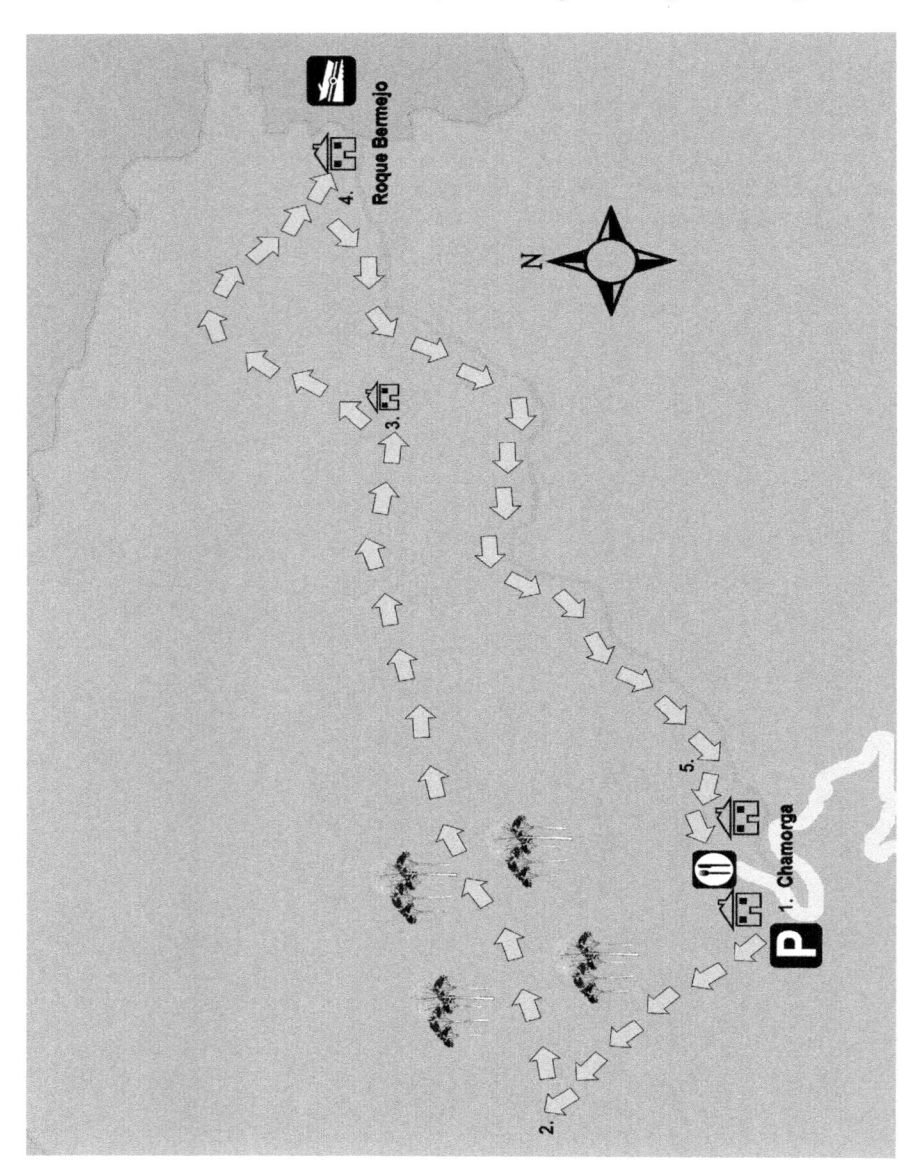

To The End Of The Island, Chamorga to Roque Bermejo

Location	North east tip of Tenerife.
Circular Route?	Yes.
How Long?	Approx 4hrs 50mins.
How Far?	11.7 kilometres.
Vertiginous	There are vertiginous sections along this route. Some of the best views are from sections above sheer drops.
Route Difficulty	Level 4 - It's not a particularly long walk, but the long steep descent from the ridge to Roque Bermejo and ascent back to Chamorga make it worthy of a 4 rating.
Wow Scenery	If the weather is right you'll be treated to quite incredible vistas along the dramatic north east coast as well as of the lighthouse at the end of Tenerife's eastern world.
Underfoot	Mostly a good path throughout with a mixture of surfaces ranging from forest paths, merchant trail and dirt tracks. The descent to Roque Bermejo can be slippy due to small loose stones.
Watering Holes	The bar at Chamorga is one of the most unattractive you'll see, but it's great with an infectious community spirit.
Downside	If the *bruma* (low cloud) rolls in, the views on the first half of the walk can be lost.

This testing route takes you through some of the most remote parts of the Anaga Mountains and of Tenerife. Setting out from the end of the road, you ascend through the forest with views over the north east coast before making a steep descent to the Anaga Lighthouse. The route then continues to the village and little harbour at Roque Bermejo, accessible only on foot or by water taxi from Santa Cruz, before returning to Chamorga along the deep ravine of Barranco de Roque Bermejo.

NB Make sure you take plenty of water (1.5 litres per person), sunscreen and a hat for this route.

How to Get There

By Car

Head to La Laguna on the autopista (it doesn't matter where you're driving from) and take the 8B exit from the motorway following signs for Tegueste TF13. The road bypasses La Laguna. Follow signs for Anaga at three roundabouts. After the third you'll be heading straight towards the Anaga Mountains. From there on it's stay on the road that heads east, following signs for Chamorga when the road splits and the main road continues to Taganana. It's still a long drive through the forest to the very end of the road.

Parking

There are usually places to park on the road right at the start of the village.

By Public Transport

Puerto de la Cruz

Take the 102 to Santa Cruz and change to the 947 to Chamorga. (Approx total bus time – 1hr 20mins)

Playa de las Américas/Los Cristianos

Take the 110/111 to Santa Cruz and change to the 947 to Chamorga. (Approx total bus time – 2hr 40mins)

Los Gigantes

The best route is to take the 325 to Puerto de la Cruz, change to the 102 Santa Cruz and change to the 947 to Chamorga.

Water Taxi

From Marina Puerto Chico at the top end of Santa Cruz harbour (near San Andrés), pick up the Nautica Nivaria water taxi which will drop you at Roque Bermejo beach where you can begin the walk, following the route directions from the beach (page 43) and either going clockwise as in the notes, or anticlockwise via the Anaga lighthouse, following the notes in reverse from the beach. You must book the Nautica in advance (www.nauticanivaria.com).

The Route

1. Stepping Out

There's a walking information board at the bus stop by the little parking area just before the church in Chamorga. Walk towards the church and in 40 metres there's a second walking board from where the path is clearly signposted to Igueste de San Andrés 9.9km on the PR TF5. Follow the path as it ascends into the trees.

Ignore the steps that lead off to the right almost immediately and continue straight ahead. You'll see a yellow and white striped waymark on your left. This zigzag path will ascend gradually through the forest for 2.2km. Stick to the main path which is clearly visible and don't deviate onto any paths running off to the side.

After almost 500 metres you reach a signpost and you stay right following the direction to El Draguillo 2km. The rain forest is an ancient laurisilva forest whose like has not existed in the Mediterranean since the Ice Age but as the Macaronesian islands are so far south, they escaped the icy clutches of the big freeze and have survived to this day. Depending on the season and how much rain has recently fallen, you may traverse an occasional brook via its stepping stones.

2. To the ridge (1.24km/30mins)

After half an hour of ascent, you reach a small crossroads where the path to El Draguillo heads left towards the coast. Stay right and continue to ascend towards the ridge. In another 200 metres the vegetation will thin and you will get views down over the north east coast from Punta de Hidalgo lighthouse in the west to the hamlet of El Draguillo almost directly below you. You may even be able to see the outline of Mount Teide appearing above the cliffs. Alternatively, you may be looking down over a sea of clouds or worse still, be in one and see nothing.

Another 700 metres of ascending takes you to a fenced area where you enjoy a view over the two rocks that represent the most northerly points of Tenerife – Roque de Fuera (the one furthest away from the shore) and Roque de Tierra (better known as Roque de Dentro). These two rocks are actually of great geological and geomorphic importance as they are such good specimens of one of the most characteristic ecosystems of the Canary Islands.

In another 100 metres or so the views open up to your right side and you can see back down over the village of Chamorga.

A small fork in the path takes you left to one last viewpoint before returning to take the right fork and now beginning what will be a 700 metre descent to Anaga Lighthouse.

As you emerge out of the forest above the ridge, you can see a derelict building on the ridge below which is where you will pick up the path to the lighthouse.

3. To the lighthouse (3.4km/1hr 20mins)

Arriving at the derelict Casas de Tafada, turn left immediately before the derelict house and follow the path that runs around to the left of the building and begins to descend the cliff. In 200 metres a path will join from the right (the path that drops more steeply down from the ridge), and continue straight ahead, passing a yellow and white waymark on the left.

The path now zigzags its way down the cliff for 1.5km towards the Anaga Lighthouse which soon becomes visible on the headland below. Stick to the main path which is clearly visible, and don't deviate onto any paths running off to the side. When we walked this route at the end of October there had been heavy rains the week before which had brought a lot of loose scree down causing the surface to be slippery in parts. Take care and take your time.

1.7km and almost an hour after you left the ridge, you will arrive at a signpost just above the lighthouse. Continue to descend towards the lighthouse, taking a break on the little wooden bench beyond the signpost to admire the views before arriving at the green fence of the lighthouse. The Anaga Lighthouse was built in 1863 and stands 235 metres above sea level. One of the most remote lighthouses on Tenerife, it is currently operated by three workers who share 24/7 shifts but up until the turn of the 20th century it was manned by families who lived in the large accommodation attached. Beyond the lighthouse the surface becomes even more skittery as the path continues to wind its way down towards the coast until 20 minutes and 1 kilometre later, you reach a junction with a signpost showing Chamorga 3.2k heading up cobbled steps to the right. This is the route you will take to return to Chamorga.

Continue straight ahead in the signpost direction of Roque Bermejo and follow the path as it leads down towards the village. At the green crucifix of the little church, turn left between the church and the house and follow the path as it winds its way around the headland above the village to the little harbour where you can enjoy a rest.

The sea taxi Nautica Nivaria deposits and collects hikers from this little harbour throughout the day and takes them back to Santa Cruz. When you've rested, leave the harbour and retrace your steps back up the headland. If the little shop and bar are open you can divert left along the path that takes you into the village of Roque de Bermejo and then continue up the headland path as it climbs steeply to emerge at the little church.

NB You have a hot and unshaded 4km slog up Barranco de Roque Bermejo ahead of you so make sure you have enough water before you leave the village.

Continue to retrace your steps to arrive at the junction you passed on the way into Roque Bermejo and this time, turn left up the stone steps following the signpost direction to Chamorga 3.2km.

4. That damn barranco (8km/3hrs 10mins)

From here you have an hour and a half and 4 kilometres of gradual but unrelenting ascent back to Chamorga along the Barranco de Roque Bermejo. When we did this route at the end of October, the heavy rains the week before had caused a part of the lower path (at the stream bed) to collapse which meant a scrabble over rockfall and up boulders to progress, energy-sapping but easily doable. There are no real directions necessary for the barranco, there's only one way to go, but it will seem interminable if it's a hot day.

5. Homeward Bound (11km/4hrs 45mins)

Arrive at the partial concrete vehicle path which denotes you are reaching the end of the route and finally getting out of that damn barranco. Continue to follow the path until it becomes tarmac at the beginning of the village and in another 90 metres you arrive at the little bar Casa Alvaro to *'Unlace the Boots'*. It may not look very welcoming from outside but the locals are friendly, the drinks are chilled and it's one of the best places in the world after a long, hot walk.

Continue to follow the path through the village for another 500 metres to arrive back at the bus stop where you began.
11.7km/4hrs 50mins

Walks in The North of Tenerife
The Orotava Valley

"...having traversed the banks of the Orinoco, the Cordilleras of Peru, and the most beautiful valleys of Mexico, I own that I have never beheld a prospect more varied, more attractive, more harmonious in the distribution of the masses of verdure and rocks, than the western coast of Teneriffe."
Alexander von Humboldt 1799

Walking in La Orotava Valley

Forming a major part of the lush, fertile, north of Tenerife, La Orotava Valley has long been prized for its rich soil and abundant flora. In the upper reaches en route to Teide National Park, dense pine and laurel woodland provide a maze of paths that skirt the island's spine beneath the ever present gaze of Mount Teide. Views extend right across the valley to Puerto de la Cruz on the coast and on clear days to La Palma on the horizon.

In the middle reaches, the rich, red soil is still farmed the way it has been for years and villages like Aguamansa, La Florida and Pinolere have existed off the land for centuries. Meadows of grasses, hedgerows of wild flowers and green tapestry hills create a rural idyll for walkers.

Weather

Weather conditions in the north of Tenerife are known in botanical terms as the perfect climate and when you hear the term 'land of eternal spring' being used to describe Tenerife, it was to this part of the island that the original quote referred. Less prone to low cloud than the Anagas, La Orotava is accessible for wonderful walking all year round and if dappled forest paths, red earth and the scent of fresh pine are your thing, you'll come back time and again to enjoy these woodlands.

Flora

In the pine forests you'll find an abundance of heathers and laburnums, leggy clumps of yellow parsley, the delicate lilac flowers of rock roses and scented yellow broom. Trees are cloaked in the long tresses of fine lichen and in the woods boulders wear a bright green coat of moss. In the hedgerows of the open countryside you'll find profusions of wild daisies, forget-me-nots, geraniums, lavender, thyme, sage and lilies as well as the rampant vestiges of cultivated fuschias and sweet peas.

Call of Nature

There's a bar restaurant at La Caldera but you have to ask for the key so you'll need to buy something. Alternatively there are some at the picnic zone at the far end of the crater, down the short path opposite the horse 'car park' but they're only likely to be open at weekends and Bank Holidays. There are several restaurants in Aguamansa.

Eat me

Recommending a freshwater fish on an island in the Atlantic might seem an odd thing to do. However, the log cabin restaurant at La Caldera is not far from the trout farm in Aguamansa. The idea of tucking in to pan fried trout with almonds after a long walk is too tempting to resist.

Where To Stay When Walking in La Orotava

Rural Hotel Victoria, La Orotava

A beautiful, restored, 16th century, traditional manor house in the heart of La Orotava, just around the corner from the famous Casas de los Balcones. Rooms are set around a lovely interior courtyard where the bar and the excellent restaurant are located. Décor and furnishing is all traditional, including beautiful tiles, and rooms have views over the old quarter to the sea or to the mountain. There's a rooftop sun terrace but other than that, amenities are thin on the ground. Think character rather than facilities. [Mid-range]

Calle Hermano Apolinar, 8, La Orotava; (+34) 922 33 16 83; www.hotelruralvictoria.com

Northern Exposure, Los Órganos

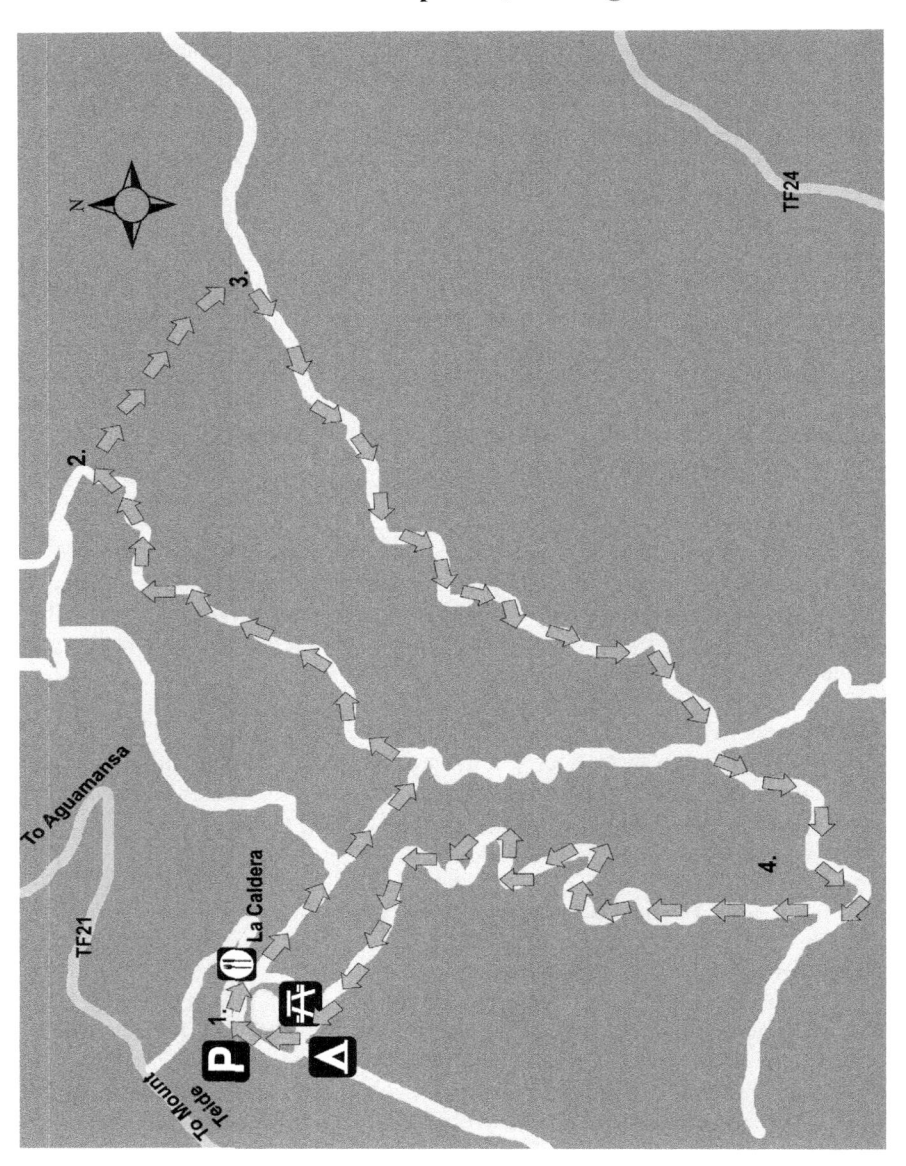

Northern Exposure, Los Órganos

Location	North west Tenerife.
Circular Route?	Yes.
How Long?	Approx 4hrs 20mins.
How Far?	11.8 kilometres.
Vertiginous?	Mostly not, but there are a couple of vertiginous sections as the path weaves in and out of ravines.
Route Difficulty	Level 4 - Much of this route is along gently undulating forest paths. However, thirty minutes into the walk, there's an almost straight up ascent, the most testing part of the route. But isn't it great to get the hardest part over and done with early?
Wow Scenery	Absolute stunning views of Mount Teide and the Orotava Valley. This is scenery which inspired Victorian adventurers.
Underfoot	Good forest paths on the even stretches. A carpet of pine needles and dry water channels can make for slippery ascents and descents in some places.
Watering Holes	A couple of real gems of places to unlace the boots.
Downside	The walk starts around the 1000 metre mark; a magnet for clouds if there are any.

This walk begins at the picnic zone of La Caldera which sits in a small crater 1200 metres above the coast in the most fertile part of Tenerife. Climbing 355 metres through ancient pines you reach a spectacular forest trail around the perimeter of a deep valley with views over the La Orotava Valley to Puerto de la Cruz. Emerald forests carpet the mountainsides below Mount Teide adding the final touch to this lovely vista. This is a circular walk where you get most of the hard work completed in the first third and can then relax and enjoy the dappled shade of an enchanted forest trail that twists and turns through a perfumed wilderness high above Tenerife's north west coast.

How to Get There

By Car

From Puerto de la Cruz, it's straight up the hill toward Mount Teide on the TF21. The turn off to La Caldera is on the left shortly after you leave the town of Aguamansa. From Los Cristianos, unless you want to take the scenic route, it's quickest to take the TF1 and TF5 north and take the exit signposted for La Orotava and El Teide. From Los Gigantes take the TF82 via El Tanque to reach the TF5 to Puerto de la Cruz and then the TF21 to La Caldera as above.

Parking
There is plenty of parking at La Caldera Zona Recreativa. If the car park is full people leave their cars on the road that circles the picnic zone.

By Public Transport

Puerto de la Cruz

The 345 service runs regularly directly from Puerto de la Cruz to Aguamansa and even La Caldera itself.

Playa de las Américas/Los Cristiànos

Take the 343 to Puerto de la Cruz and change to the 345 in Puerto de la Cruz.

Los Gigantes

Jump on the 325 to Puerto de la Cruz and change to the 345 in Puerto.

The Route

1. Stepping Out

Follow the tarmac road which begins at the left hand side of the car park where the bus stops. On the left is a sign showing 'Siete Fuentes 19.7km, La Esperanza 30.6 and a walking routes information board for 'Camino Natural de Anaga-Chasna'. Follow the path in the direction of Siete Fuentes, past the log cabin bar/restaurant La Caldera on your left and the picnic zone sitting in its crater on your right.

[You might want to make a call of nature at the picnic zone toilets which are at the far end of the crater, down the short path opposite the horse 'car park'. Only likely to be open at weekends and Bank Holidays.]

After 183 metres the tarmac road swings round to the right. Leave the tarmac road and continue straight ahead on the wide forest pista (path) signposted: 'Pista Norte Del Pino' on the left hand side and with a little sign saying 'Los Organos' on the right hand side. Beyond the giant pines you can see the fertile ridge which you'll be traversing and below it, slightly to the left, the organ pipe rock formation known as Los Órganos.

After 8 mins and 815 metres you arrive at a small seat in a wooden shelter. Stay on the main pista which bears round to the left, ignoring the path up into the forest. A chained path on the left leads to a private finca but we continue on the main pista, past the steps leading up into the forest until, 27 mins and 2.3km into the walk, you reach a stone house and a small bridge.

Just 6 mins further, the path forks with the left fork dropping steeply downhill. Stay on the right hand path and in 300 metres you see the steps on the right leading up into the forest, signposted 'Siete Fuentes 17.0km, La Esperanza 27.9km' and 'Camino El Topo, Llanos de Chimiche 7.4km' which is where you begin your ascent.

2. The Climb (2.7km/40mins)

Follow the path up through the forest, climbing steadily all the time. At first it's a little confusing as small water courses run off into all directions but stick to the well trodden ground with fewer pine needles, always climbing, and the path becomes clearer as you continue. This is a steep ascent so take your time and rest to take in the views that appear tantalisingly through the trees.

After 12mins and a 100 metre climb you reach a flat forest pista, turn right and then take the steps on the left hand side that lead up into the next section of forest which winds mercilessly up hill for a further 50 metres of elevation to a small seat below a pine tree.

Another 18mins and 55 metres of elevation and hard slog and the path flattens out with Mount Teide appearing on the horizon and views back over La Orotava behind you.

More ascending past a large pine tree with a pixie-sized hole in its trunk and along a dappled forest path where, on your right hand side, you'll pass a signpost showing 'Pinolere 3.7km' back the way you've come and 'Casa Del Agua 0.4km' straight ahead and a very confusing 'Arona 57.5km' sign also in the direction we're heading, before a final thigh stretching push takes you through a rock gate and the end of the hardest part of the walk, having ascended 355 metres over a distance of 1.54km. Climb onto the rocks at the left side of the gate and reward yourself with a breather overlooking the vista. If you've timed it right, this is a great spot for lunch.

3. Little Red Riding Hood (4.2km/1hr 40mins)
Turn right from the stone gate and where the path forks at the Caminos Forestal signpost, continue to the right following the direction of 'Llanos de Chimiche', along the dappled path as it gently twists and turns through the pine scented forest. Breathe in the perfume of hot pine needles and try not to miss your footing as you gawp at the scenery that's accompanying you.

After 1 hour and 1.57 km you pass a rocky outcrop which is another great spot for lunch provided you've got the head for it. As you begin to traverse the rim of a steep barranco (valley) notice how the vegetation thickens. If the yellow broom is in blossom, stop to smell its heady perfume. Marvel at the stark beauty of the bejeques, or stonecrops, that grow in yellow-headed spikes from their rosette bases and the delicate lilac flowers of rock roses.

Take care traversing the narrow hand-railed and fenced section of ledge that juts out over the side of the valley and emerge on the other side to the vistas once again opening out over the coast.

20 mins beyond the narrow ledge you arrive at 'Tree Beard'; a huge old pine tree festooned with hanging lichen. The path continues past another rocky outcrop where you can walk across the rocks for sheer views over the ledge, best not attempted if the cloud has rolled in and obscured the sheer drop below you!

The path reaches the confluence of 3 barrancos from where you have a 10 minute ascent from the valley floor until the trees begin to thin a little and you reach a crossroads of paths.

4. The Homeward Slalom (9.3km/ 3hrs 36mins)

Take the path to the right which runs steeply down hill on the equivalent of a dry ski slope. The loose scree here is lethal so take care and try tacking, keeping feet sideways-on to the path. Lots of smaller paths lead off in all directions, tempting you to take short cuts, but you do so at your own peril; my buttocks are overly acquainted with this particular section of the walk!

After just 17 minutes of defying gravity you emerge onto a wide pista. Turn left.

Continue straight along the wide path for 25 mins until you reach the tarmac road. Go straight across and follow the path that runs behind the ONE WAY sign with the fence on your right hand side. In 4 mins you arrive back at the La Caldera car park and you can head to the log cabin bar/restaurant of 'La Caldera to *'Unlace the Boots'*.
11.83km/4 hours 23 minutes

Unlace the Boots
The log cabin La Caldera restaurant (closed Wednesday) is perfect for a post-walk refreshment. If it's cold, there's usually a blazing fire inside. Service can be slow, but the restaurant is full of character and a good place to spot some local birds. The restaurant serves basic Canarian cuisine, including trout from the nearby fish farm.

Camping at La Caldera
Anyone wanting the full 'great outdoors' experience can pitch the tent at La Caldera's camping zone (near the end of the Los Órganos route just off the tarmac road which circles the zona recreativa). Camping zones in Tenerife literally mean an area designated for camping, there are few facilities. At least in this case there are the facilities of the zona recreativa nearby.
Camping is free on Tenerife.
See www.todotenerife.es for more information.

La Caldera Zona Recreativa
Eating al fresco in the woods is almost a national pastime for Canarios. On Sundays and public holidays, the picnic benches dotted around the trees on the slopes of La Caldera (the cauldron) overflow with whole families and displays of food that are more 'banquet' than picnic. There's a great buzz at these times and it's not uncommon for the woods to be filled with the sound of picnickers bursting into impromptu song, but parking can be a nightmare.

At other times, the zona recreativa is relatively quiet except when school trips arrive and turn La Caldera's basin into a giant football ground for scores of budding Ronaldos and Messis.

A Glimpse of Rural Life, La Caldera to Aguamansa

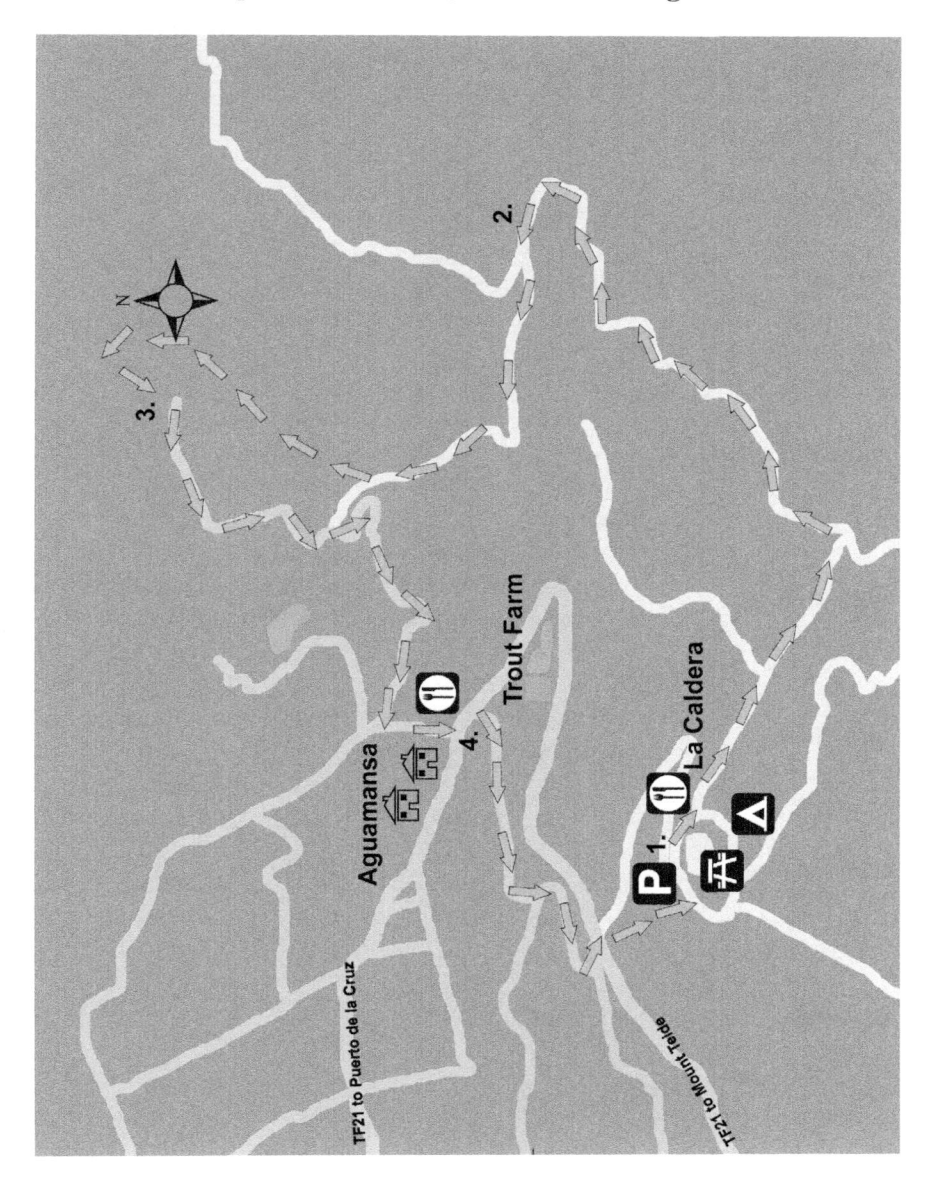

A Glimpse of Rural Life, La Caldera to Aguamansa

Location	North west Tenerife.
Circular Route?	Yes.
How Long?	Approx 2hrs 20mins.
How Far?	7.6 kilometres.
Vertiginous	No.
Route Difficulty	Level 2/3 – This is a relatively gentle country walk but there are a couple of short, steep ascents and the climb back to La Caldera should work those lungs.
Wow Scenery	Worth it for the views back across the forest to Mount Teide, but also interesting are the scenes of country life. Get lucky and you'll see potato pickers at work in the fields.
Underfoot	Much of the route is on firm forest paths with a section on tarmac.
Watering Holes	You have to pass through Aguamansa, where there are a few distracting Canarian restaurants serving robust country fare, to reach the final section back to La Caldera. Plus there's the cabin at La Caldera.
Downside	The walk is all around the 1000 metre so if there are clouds, there's no climbing above them.

This is a gentle walk which takes you through open countryside as well as woodland. It may not have the spectacular views of the Los Órganos route but it traverses beautiful country meadows filled with wild flowers and gives you a glimpse into the stunning rural landscape of Aguamansa. With a trout farm and birds of prey sanctuary set in woodlands and gardens to throw into the mix, this makes for an interesting and varied half day ramble.

How to Get There
See information for the Los Órganos route on page 51.

The Route
1. Stepping Out
Follow the tarmac road which begins at the left hand side of the car park where the bus stops. On the left is a sign showing 'Siete Fuentes 19.7km, La Esperanza 30.6 and a walking routes information board for 'Camino Natural de Anaga-Chasna'. Follow the path in the direction of Siete Fuentes, past the log cabin bar/restaurant La Caldera on your left and the picnic zone sitting in its crater on your right.

[You might want to make a call of nature at the picnic zone toilets which are at the far end of the crater, down the short path opposite the horse 'car park'. Only likely to be open at weekends and Bank Holidays.]

After 183 metres the tarmac road swings round to the right. Leave the tarmac road and continue straight ahead on the wide forest pista (path) signposted: 'Pista Norte Del Pino' on the left hand side and with a little sign saying 'Los Organos' on the right hand side. Beyond the giant pines you can see the fertile ridge which you'll be traversing and below it, slightly to the left, the organ pipe rock formation known as Los Órganos.

After 8 mins and 815 metres you arrive at a small seat in a wooden shelter. Stay on the main pista which bears round to the left, ignoring the path up into the forest. A chained path on the left leads to a private finca but we continue on the main pista, past the steps leading up into the forest until, 27 mins and 2.3km into the walk, you reach a stone house and a small bridge.

Just 6 mins further, the path forks with the left fork dropping steeply downhill. Take the left fork as it descends into the forest.

2. Forest Descent (2.8km/40mins)
Descend down the path through the forest, treading carefully to avoid the 'evidence' that this path is also used by local caballeros (horsemen). Ignore paths running to the right and then to the left, staying on the main path in a gentle and gradual descent. After 15 mins you arrive at a junction where a signpost at the top of a left turn tells you that you're leaving a protected area.

Ignore the turn and continue straight ahead for another 10 mins until you reach another junction with paths off to left and right and a broken down wooden picnic shelter on a mound to the right. Take the path on the left opposite the picnic table and descend sharply to the tarmac lane.

3. Flower Lovers' Lane (4.5km/1hr 13mins)

Turn right onto the lane ignoring the path on the right hand side that runs back into the woods. Continue for 10 mins along this delightful lane bordered by allotments filled with potatoes and vines in red earth and hedgerows brimming with a kaleidoscope of colour from wild flowers including crimson poppies, delicate blue forget-me-nots, jaunty yellow daisies and soft pink geraniums. On the left you pass Camino de Las Castañas (Chestnut Tree Avenue) before reaching the crossroads at the shrine. Turn left up the hill and 4 mins later take the right hand turn at the crossroads sign posted 'Aguamansa'.

This is Camino de Mamio and it takes you through the heart of Aguamansa's rural idyll past houses with ramshackle outbuildings and rusting trucks in the yard, meadows of tall grasses and wild flowers, stone cottages with thatched roofs and the occasional eagle riding the hot air currents overhead. Less than 200 yards later the path forks at a signpost showing 'Casa Del Agua 1.3km' straight ahead and 'Casa Forestal 0.9km' to the right. Go right.

Ignore the path that runs off to the left hand side and stay on the main path until it eventually reaches the floor of the barranco (valley) where the Casa Forestal path leads off to the left alongside the barranco. We stay on the path as it bends around to the right and uphill past the first houses of the hamlet's centre and finally arrives at a main street. Turn left for a calf-stretching climb uphill past the Paso Del Teide Restaurant to the main road.

4. A Woodland Return (6.4km/2hrs)
Turn left onto the main road and walk along to the Aguamansa Restaurant, cross over the road and take the tarmac path that runs uphill alongside the 'Las Fuentes 1000 metres' sign. The path winds up into the woods past the closed gate of the trout farm and bird of prey sanctuary (see 'detour' for the 15 min walk to the centre which is well worth visiting – open every day 10am to 3pm) for 7 mins until you reach a sign for La Caldera on the left hand side. Follow the sign up the steps into the woods.

*Stay on the path as it bends around to the right and takes you deeper into the woods. After some 200 metres you reach a signpost showing 'Camino de la Orilla .5k' to the right. Stay on the left hand, upper path going straight ahead in the direction of 'Lomo Chillero 1.2k' which leads to a wide pista. Turn left onto the pista, go straight across and under the bridge which takes you beneath the road, signposted 'La Caldera 0.4k)

Up the steps to the signpost and follow the path to the right into the forest through moss covered trees and boulders for a 10 minute calf stretcher back to the car park and a *'Place to Unlace the Boots'* (see the Los Órganos route on pageX).
7.6km/2hrs 20mins

A Fishy Detour
If you've got the time and energy, take a short detour to see the trout farm and bird of prey sanctuary at Aguamansa. Instead of staying on the path through the woods (*above), go straight up to the road on the path that hugs the fence, turn left and follow the road for 7 minutes to the trout farm. On your return, re-trace your steps along the road and when you get to the 'TF21 16km' sign, drop down into the woods on your right and continue left along the path from * above.

The Guanche Way, La Caldera to Cruz del Dornajito

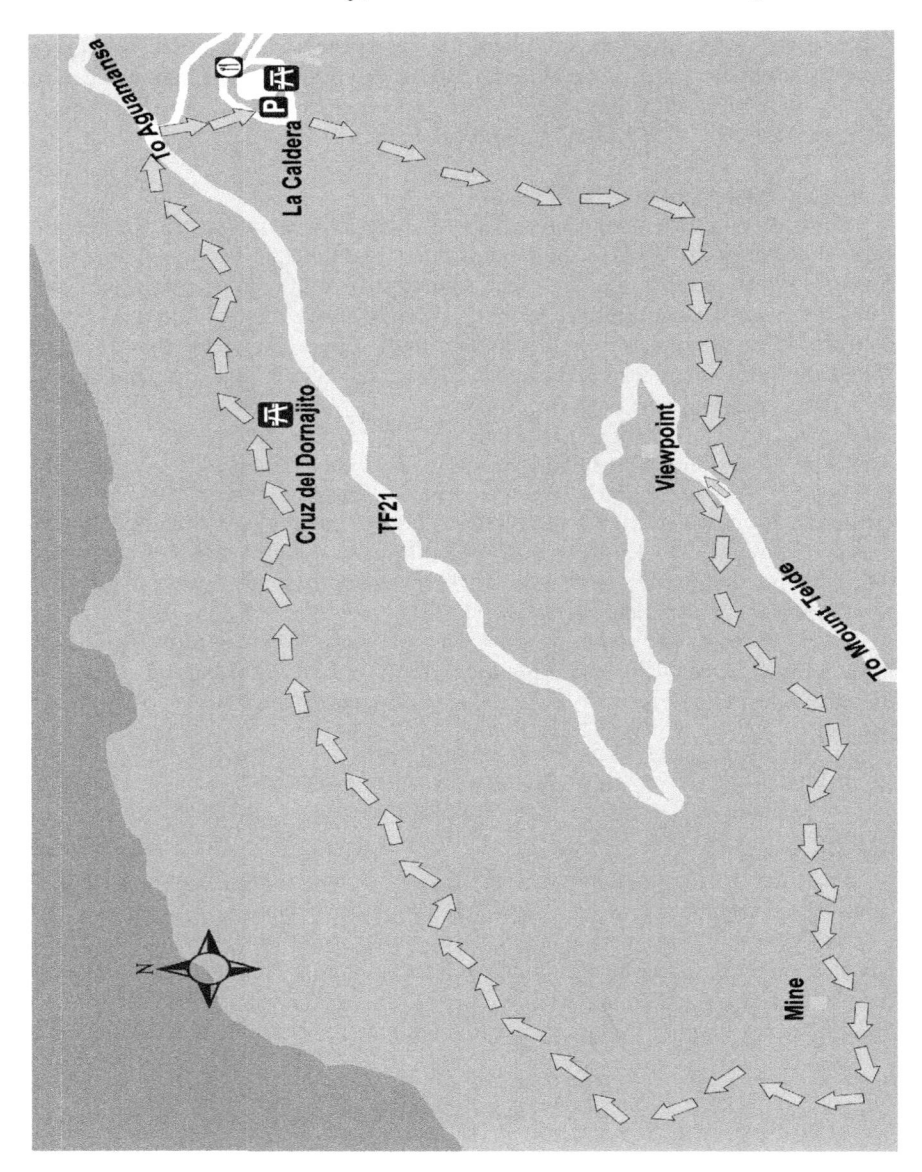

The Guanche Way, La Caldera to Cruz del Dornajito

Location	North west Tenerife.
Circular Route?	Yes.
How Long?	Approx 4hrs 45mins.
How Far?	15 kilometres.
Vertiginous?	No.
Route Difficulty	Level 3 - Apart from a couple of ascents and descents, much of this route is on relatively level forest paths. This means that it offers some of the WOW type of scenery you get with the Los Organos route but for less effort.
Wow Scenery	The storm that destroyed part of the pine forest in the valley left bare stretches on the hillside. The upside of this is that the views of valley, Mount Teide and the north coast are even more stunning than before.
Underfoot	A quite steep ascent through the forest near the start and at the end, but in between are relatively flat forest trails with only slight ascents and descents. Almost perfect walking terrain on foot friendly forest paths.
Watering Holes	The rustic cabin at La Caldera is a great place to end a walk with a cool cerveza.
Downside	If the cloud rolls in, the best views may be obscured.

Another wonderful walk in the upper La Orotava Valley, this time heading east from the recreational area of La Caldera, following the old Guanche way which would originally have been created by the indigenous population of the island to drive their goats from lowland pastures to highlands for summer grazing. Later, the route became connected with the Camino de Chasna which took pilgrims from La Orotava to Candelaria to worship at the feet of their Patron Saint, and merchants to markets in Vilaflor.

This varied and relatively gentle circular trail is off the more popular routes that emanate from La Caldera so you are unlikely to encounter many more walkers, making it a peaceful and beautiful trail to follow. It begins with a steady but not gruelling, 200 metre ascent through the pine forest before levelling out and crossing the La Orotava to Teide National Park road to sweep the top of the valley with views to the coast, La Palma (if visibility is good enough) and possibly over a sea of clouds. More gentle forest walking leads to the ancient spring of Cruz del Dornajito where you can enjoy a tranquil picnic with ocean views before gradually ascending back through the forest to La Caldera.

How to Get There
See information for the Los Órganos route on page 51.

The Route
1. Stepping Out
At the bus stop end of the La Caldera car park, on the right hand side, is an information walking board showing the route for 'Camino Natural de Anaga-Chasna'. With that board at your back, walk left and cross the car park, keeping the sea on your right hand side. After 100 metres turn left up the steps signposted: 'Camino de Los Guanches' and Llanos de Chimiche, PRTF-35.
In 60 metres stay right at the small fork and in another 50 metres, continue straight ahead on the Camino de Los Guanches, signposted Llanos de Chimiche.

150 metres later, at a small Y junction, stay right and straight ahead following the 'Sendero' direction on the sign on the tree. Continue straight ahead at the next small junction, 340 metres later, following the yellow and white striped waymark and in 100m you cross over a fat, old water pipe and continue to ascend gradually.

In 640 metres, half an hour after setting off from the car park, you reach a small T junction with a rock cairn in its centre. This is where you leave the TF-35 and take the unmarked path going right. Ignore the yellow and white X.

2. Forest Ascent (1.45km/30mins)

In just 90 metres you reach a wide forest pista where you turn right and descend down it for 1km until you reach the main, La Orotava to Teide National Park road, emerging at a junction which signs 'Pista Chimoche' back the way you've come.

3. Coastal Views (2.6km/55mins)

Carefully cross over, turn right and walk along the road for 80 metres until you reach a wide, orange dirt path leading off to the left signposted Ruta 13, Pista La Bermeja y Pista Almagre y Cabezón. Turn left down this path.

The path skirts the hillside for 1.6km, staying left and straight ahead at a fork 15 minutes and 1 kilometre into the path, with Mount Teide ever watchful ahead and to your left, and views over Puerto de la Cruz, La Quinta and Punta Brava. These vistas only opened up in 2012 following a tropical storm which devastated the forest here, snapping trees as if they were matchsticks. Nature will recover but in the meantime, enjoy the views until the path enters the forest.

4. Woodland Trails (4.4km/1hr 25mins)

400 metres into the forest you reach a small x-roads where you continue straight ahead on the wider path. A kilometre and 15 minutes later you reach the junction of La Gorita where you continue straight ahead, to the right of the Y-junction, and descend slightly. After 70 metres ignore the gated entrance to a

small mine working on the right, and continue straight ahead on the path.

In 520 metres you reach an inverted Y-junction at which a signpost on a tree on the left points the way left to Las Cañadas. Continue straight ahead and to the right and in just 60 metres, turn right at the T-junction.

5. Onto the GR131 Chasna Way (6.7km/2hrs)
180 metres later arrive at a junction where the GR131 path (denoted by small wooden posts with a burgundy stripe top and by red and white striped waymarks) crosses your path. Turn right onto the narrow GR131 path marked on the small post as Camino Natural Anaga-Chasna.

This is the GR 131 path which you will be following all the way back to La Caldera. The path ambles through the forest, sometimes becoming indistinct as it crosses dried stream beds. Keep a watchful eye out for the red and white striped markers which will keep you on the right track.

Over the course of the next 25 minutes, the path crosses three x-roads. Continue straight ahead each time, following the red and white markers and the signpost direction to La Caldera and La Esperanza.

After 1.3 kilometres you reach a wide vehicle path. Once again, cross over it and continue straight ahead on the other side, passing a lone bench in 10 minutes and 600 metres. From here, the path crosses another set of three x-roads, each time continuing straight ahead, clearly marked in the, now familiar, red and white stripes and continuing to follow the signpost direction La Caldera and La Esperanza until you emerge, 1.4 kilometres and half an hour later, into a clearing with glorious views over the La Orotava Valley and down to the coast.

6. The Hinterland (9.4km/2hrs 55mins)
At this point the path turns right, to the right of the large pine tree and continues along the GR131, accompanied by red and white waymarks. From here you notice a difference in the flora that accompanies the path. You are now skirting the boundary between Teide National Park, on your right, and the agricultural terraces of the upper La Orotava valley on your left. Dense pine forest and thick carpets of dried needles have been replaced by brezal (tree heather) and young laurel trees laced with broom, foxgloves and spurges. You'll also encounter several brambles, so watch for the occasional, ankle slashing, stray stem. When we walked this in late summer we were accompanied by a buzzard, circling overhead on the lookout for lunch.

In 180 metres at a fork, stay right following the signposted direction to La Caldera 4.8km and in a further 200 metres reach a junction where you turn left following the red and white waymarks.

Continue straight ahead at the next signpost and for another 300 metres beyond it until you reach a concrete path. Turn left and descend, keeping right at the Y-junction, for 100 metres and down the wooden steps to reach Cruz del Dornajito.

A natural spring and fountain (it was dry when we were here in late summer), Cruz del Dornajito has been mentioned in historic chronicles for four centuries as it is the only natural water source to be found on the old Chasna route which travellers took from La Orotava to Mount Teide. Now a small shrine, the chozo (shelter) above the spring is an idyllic place to enjoy a tranquil lunch with hypnotic Ocean views.

7. A Woodland Return (10.6km/3hrs 20mins)

From Cruz del Dornajito, climb the woodland steps following in the signpost direction of La Caldera 4km and La Esperanza 34.6km. In 340 metres reach a tarmac road on a bend and continue straight ahead following the red and white waymarks.

Cross straight over the path 260 metres later and continue straight ahead for a further 400 metres until, 15 minutes after leaving Cruz del Dornajito, you reach a signpost, hidden in the foliage on the right of the path but preceded by a small, wooden GR131 post. Leave the path here (there is a red and white X on the path straight ahead) and climb up the narrow path to the right following signpost direction to La Caldera 3.2km.

At the top, go left for 30 metres to the T-junction where you turn left again and follow the path for 15 minutes and 560 metres until you arrive at a signpost where you drop left, back into the forest.

In 160 metres turn right at the junction, following signpost direction La Caldera 3.2km (funny how apparently you haven't made any progress since the last signpost, over 700 metres later!).

Another 760 metres and the path turns left at the x-roads junction, now following signpost direction Aguamansa 1.8km. Take the left turn at the next signpost, 630 metres later, still following the Aguamansa direction, and in a further 200 metres reach a tarmac road.

Continue straight ahead and to the right (the waymarks here are green and white as the red and white GR markings go temporarily absent) and in another 100 metres reach a signpost where you turn right following the direction for our old friend La Caldera 1.1km and Aguamansa 0.9km where once again, you find yourself ascending, but only for 100 metres you'll be glad to hear.

8. The Final Push (14.2km/4hrs 25mins)
At the T-junction with a wider path turn left following signpost direction Aguamansa and continue for 4 minutes and 250 metres to reach a junction where you turn left up the path with the green, white and red stripes on the post and then right, 20 metres later following the signpost direction Lomo Chillero and La Caldera 0.7km.

In 6 minutes and 280 metres you reach a wide pista and go straight across and under the bridge which takes you beneath the road, signposted La Caldera 0.4k.
Up the steps to the signpost and follow the path to the right into the forest through moss covered trees and boulders for a 10 minute, 450 metre calf stretching ascent back to the car park at La Caldera.
4hrs 45mins/15.2km

A Place to Unlace the Boots
La Caldera's bar/restaurant is the perfect walker's venue for unlacing the boots at the end of a hike. Log cabin exterior, roaring fire inside in winter and wooden benches on a terrace surrounded by fuchsias, daisies and the forest create the perfect chill-out zone for hikers. Add a cool beer and some freshly grilled trout and it's unbeatable. Watch out for the cheeky blue chaffinches and Canarian tits which also frequent the bar and who'll be off with food from your plate before you know it.

The Aguamansa Restaurant at the end of the village is a great alternative when La Caldera is closed (Wednesday). A great selection of traditional Canarian country fare (rabbit, goat and trout etc) comes dished up with uninterrupted views of Los Órganos (as long as there's no cloud) and you get the bonus of Shetland ponies in the adjacent field – it's rural heaven.

Walks in The North of Tenerife
Santiago del Teide

"Up here, we feel like Gods. We're standing on the edge of the world looking down on the painfully slow snake of Dinky-sized cars that are threading their way up the TF 82 behind a banana truck..."

Walking Around Santiago Del Teide

Located between 900 and 1200 metres above sea level in the sunny west of Tenerife, geographically the Santiago Valley doesn't lie too far from the major holiday resorts of the south and south west coasts, but in looks and nature, it's a thousand miles away from them.

Untouched by the developments of mass tourism, the Santiago del Teide valley is an unspoilt rural area in the heart of Tenerife. Including the Chinyero volcano, site of the last volcanic eruption on Tenerife in 1909, and the Erjos Pools, the valley provides some of Tenerife's most beautiful scenery. Dotted with tiny hamlets where small communities continue to farm primarily by hand, traditional crafts such as pottery still thrive.

Visit in spring and you'll see the valley's wild flowers burst into life in an explosion of vibrant colours. Choose winter to explore and Mount Teide may provide you with a gleaming white mantle of snow to contrast with the emerald forests and piercing blue sky. Small hamlets where rural handicrafts are kept alive; pine forest trails, lava fields and dragonfly-rich ponds await those who take to the Santiago Del Teide valley.

Weather
On these routes you get two microclimates for the price of one and it's fascinating to see where they join. The starting point for Pools & Pines is in the El Tanque municipality whose north facing aspect is affected by the same trade winds which bring moisture to the north coast. Subsequently at this level, around the 1000 metre mark, there can be low cloud and rain, hence the lushness of the landscape. However, within a relatively short distance you cross to the south west facing side of the ridge where the climate is more arid, as is the now very different landscape. Here, and along the Valle de Arriba to Arguayo route, sunshine is the more likely companion.

Flora
In spring the meadows of Valle de Arriba erupt into a brilliant red, purple and yellow canvas as the wild poppies, tajinaste and buttercups come into flower. On the arid west face of the Chinyero reserve the red flowers of tabaiba and yellow flowering house leeks dominate. But the best time to visit is late

January and early February when the slopes of the valley are awash with the gentle pink petals of almond blossom.

Call of Nature
There are toilets at Bar Fleytas and at Bar Tropical in Arguayo. Apart from that, it's the great outdoors as usual. There are no bars in Valle de Arriba so you might want to visit somewhere in Santiago del Teide before you set off. There's a lovely little picnic zone right at the start of the village and the kiosk has toilets. You have to ask for the key but provided you buy something (water, choc ice or even one of their fabulous arepas), it shouldn't be a problem.

Eat me
Given the fact this area is renowned for its almond trees in bloom in January/February then anything with almonds has to be tried. *Almendrados* are biscuits that come in all shapes, forms and sizes but have one thing in common; almonds. Bar Fleytas has a variety of almond biscuits.

Where To Stay When Walking in Santiago Del Teide

Hotel La Casona Del Patio, Santiago Del Teide
A tranquil hotel in a great location with excellent walking straight from the door and easy reach of Masca Barranco, La Casona is an elegant, contemporary, rural hotel built in the grounds of the 17th century former home of the Lord of the Manor. All glass, wood and stone, rooms are set on two storeys in a quadrangle around an open courtyard and combine traditional ceilings with contemporary furnishings and rustic panache. There's a lovely little tasca on the site of the hotel which offers traditional Canarian cuisine and local wines in a characterful dining room or in the lovely patio. [Budget]
Calle la Iglesia, 72, Santiago del Teide; (+34) 922 83 92 93; www.lacasonadelpatio.com

Into the Valley, Valle de Arriba to Arguayo Circular

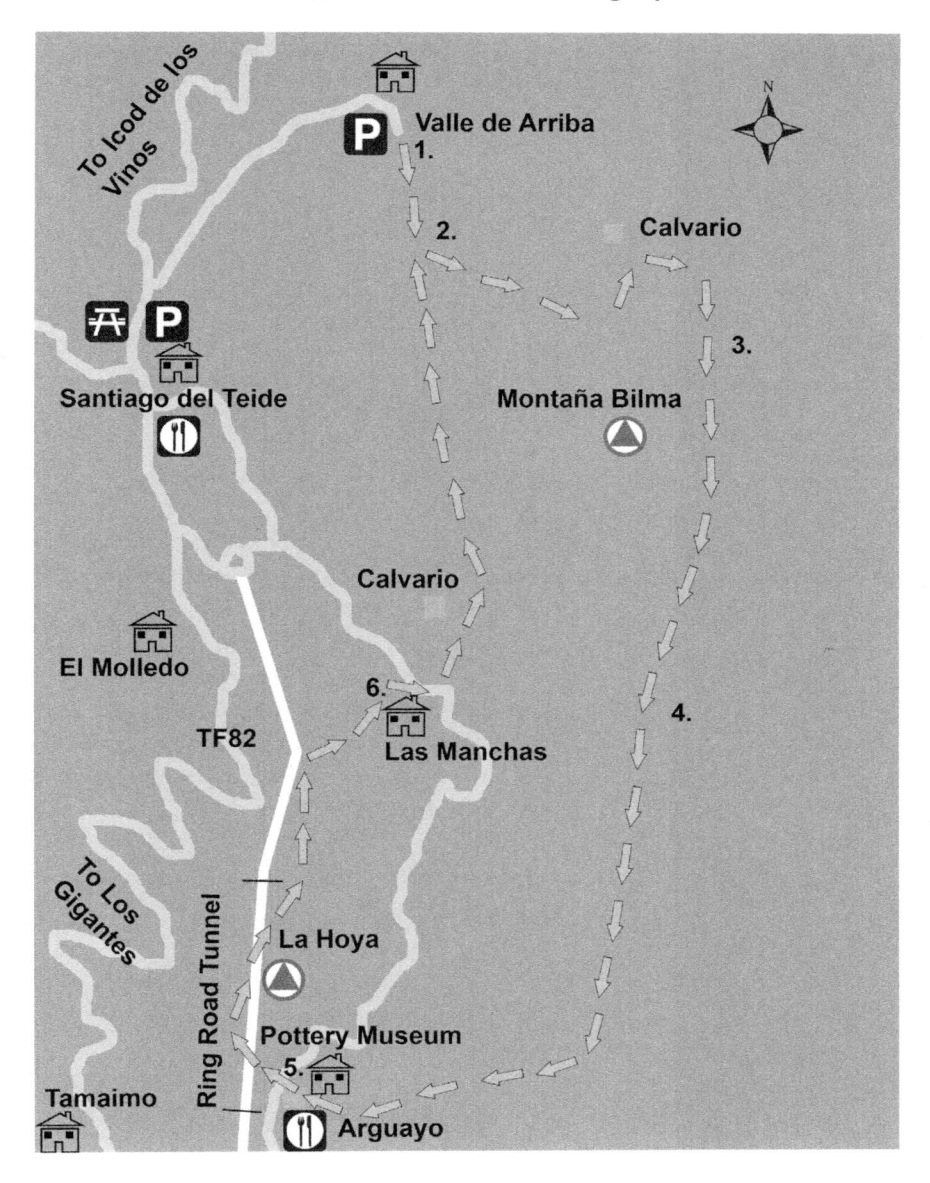

Into the Valley, Valle de Arriba to Arguayo Circular

Location	North west Tenerife.
Circular Route?	Yes.
How Long?	Approx 3hrs 50mins.
How Far?	14.3 kilometres.
Vertiginous?	No.
Route Difficulty	Level 3 - Invigorating in parts; you'll know you've been on a decent hike. Although there are some lung testing ascents, many stretches are relatively level.
Wow Scenery	Enough to fill a newsagent's postcard stand. Beautiful valleys, Mount Teide at its best and even La Gomera, La Palma and if you're very lucky, El Hierro.
Underfoot	Loose volcanic scree in parts means this isn't one for walking sandals. The route is mainly on well maintained farmer's paths and goat trails traversing a sweeping valley, but some crossing of lava fields can cause a bit of nervy ankle wobble.
Watering Holes	Very pleasant hostelries to collapse into at the midway and end points of the route.
Downside	If you're travelling by bus, there's a bit of a walk from Santiago to the start of the route in Valle de Arriba. It is pleasant though.

Hiking in this area takes you through idyllic countryside and offers commanding views over the valley under the ever present gaze of Mount Teide. In winter, when the mountain is cloaked with snow, the pine forest is deep green and the meadows are filled with wild flowers, the landscape becomes positively Alpine.

How to Get There

By Car

Valle de Arriba lies just outside of Santiago del Teide on the TF82 in the direction of Icod de los Vinos. At the turn off to the village from the TF82 follow the sign for Valle de Arriba. Continue along Camino Real passing the small church of Santa Ana on the left. Take the first right onto Calle San Fernando and first right again into Calle El Reventon with the phone box on one corner and fresh water spring on the other.

The water tap on the corner has fresh mountain spring water and is a good place to refresh supplies provided you have a spanner to hand to turn the tap! Ask anyone who's there if you can fill your water bottle and they'll be happy to oblige.

Parking

There's road parking in Valle de Arriba near the start of the route.

By Public Transport

Puerto de la Cruz

Take the 324 to Los Gigantes and get off in Santiago del Teide.

Playa de las Américas/Los Cristianos

Take the 460 to Icod de los Vino and, as above, get off in Santiago del Teide.

Los Gigantes

Easy peasy. Jump on the 325 to Puerto de la Cruz and guess what? Leave the bus in Santiago del Teide.

The Route

1. Valle de Arriba

Continue to the end of Calle El Reventon where the road ends and park. The walk begins on the wide path straight ahead beyond the bench. Continue straight ahead along the wide dirt track (signposted Arguayo 8.6km) as it starts to ascend.

After 186m and just beyond the lone tree with the circle for drying almonds beneath it, look out for a path on the left before the large water pipe. Follow this path and climb up the hill out of the valley entering the Chinyero Natural Reserve.

2. Chinyero Reserve (750 metres/10mins)

Climb to a signpost pointing to Santiago del Teide to the right and follow the path up the hill to the left signposted Chinyero/ El Calvario. Beyond the ridge the path begins to take on the look and feel of a Derbyshire hike as you trudge endlessly uphill between high dry stone walls beyond which, if you're doing this in late January or early February, the almond blossom trees turn the landscape pink. Your efforts are rewarded by the view of Mount Teide which appears directly ahead, perfectly framed on a ridge between the stone walls.

In another 750 metres, at the end of the dry stone walls, continue straight across the small junction in the path, keeping Mount Teide directly ahead and the cone of Mount Bilma to your right.

500 metres later, turn left at the next crossroads (more of a T- junction) and continue until you reach the small 'El Calvario' (cross) housed in its white altar. The three crosses at El Calvario mark the spot where the villagers from Valle de Arriba brought the statue of Christ during the eruption in 1909 and thus 'miraculously' halted the lava flow to save the village. A further shrine has been built into the lava itself opposite El Calvario.

Opposite the shrine is a SP showing 'Chinyero 3.9km' to the left and 'Santiago del Teide 3.6km' to the right. Continue straight ahead with the Calvario on your L in the Chinyero direction as the path veers to the R. Ignore the path to the left and continue straight ahead passing the propped fig trees.

500 metres beyond Calvario, turn right at the T junction keeping Teide on your left and continue until you reach the edge of the Chinyero lava fields where the path splits. Head toward the gate a little way in front of you in the direction sign-posted 'Chinyero 3.4 kilometres. Almost immediately turn right and follow

the path into the lava fields.

3. The Lava Fields (2.8km/40mins)
The foot-sore path follows a low stone wall and crosses a water channel. After 600 metres you reach a junction with a small step up which can easily be missed. The trail looks as if it continues to the right but in fact there are yellow and white crosses to the right and the left. Take the path which goes straight ahead keeping Teide on the left as you pass between two large boulders. In another 250 metres a path signposted Chinyero veers off to the left. Ignore it, and ignore the painted cross on the stone, and continue ahead to the right. Keep an eye on the horizon to your right (whilst avoiding tripping) for the floating shape of La Gomera and, as you continue, the twin peaks of La Palma. The path will eventually skirt the edge of the pine forest until the Chinyero Reserve ends and the Corona Forestal begins.

4. Through the Forest (4.7km/1hr 30mins)
Turn right at the Forestal sign, keeping on the upper path (green and white stripes on rock) and continuing for 630 metres until you reach two stone way-markers, MP79 and MP80. Turn left and follow the path for 450 metres till you reach the stone wall, then turn left keeping marker MP70 on your right.

Continue downhill alongside the wall and after 10 minutes you'll pass between markers MP61 and MP62, ignoring the turn to the left and continuing downhill. After another 10 minutes you arrive at a small, stone wall T-junction with an X on stones to the R. Turn L and continue, carrying straight on at the small crossroads. The vegetation begins to change as you cross climate zones into the warmer, drier west and begin your descent into Arguayo.

The path skitters down a zigzag path to abandoned quarry workings, bearing left over an old water course. At the bottom of the path stay right, walking towards the flat topped mountain of La Hoya until you reach the village road.

5. Arguayo to Las Manchas (7.9km/2hrs 40mins)
Turn right and walk to the tree in the middle of the junction, turn left up Calle San Agustín. Cross over Calle Candelaria and continue to the T junction with the road mirror. To the right you will see an old wine press. Turn left and drop downhill to the lovely pottery museum of Cha' Domitila.

Cross the road at the sculptures of the women potters of Arguayo and climb the concrete slope and steps on the far side.

At the top, follow the path to the left and revel in the views that unfold as you traverse this beautiful path around the mountain. Below you lie the Santiago del Teide valley and the village of Tamaimo and on the coast you can see to the pretty resort of Playa de la Arena. The path descends to the new road where you emerge in front of a blue bridge. Turn right onto the wide pista of red earth and, keeping the large pine tree on your left hand side begin to climb the merciless 100 metre ascent over 600 metres into Las Manchas where you can collapse onto a bench to recover.

6. Back to the Valley (10.9k/3hrs 40mins)

At the top of the slope, turn right and then left onto Calle Los Laureles, past the village church, and continue to the road. Turn right on the main road, cross over and continue to the corner. Leaving the main road, follow the path that begins on the left and takes you up past another small calvario (the white monument with wooden crosses) towards Mount Bilma,

Ignore the path to the left immediately after the calvario and two minutes and 300 metres later, hang left onto the path clearly marked by boulders through the abandoned quarry. On your right is a quite bizarre, mauve coloured canyon with eye-catching rock formations partly fashioned by nature, partly by man.

Follow the path through the lava fields. After 15 minutes the path splits to the left to a small viewpoint overlooking the valley. The view is somewhat spoiled by pylons these days but still impressive enough. Continue on the well marked path until it emerges from between narrow stone walls and re-joins the route you followed out of Valle de Arriba at the signpost for Santiago del Teide, Chinyero/El Calvario and Valle de Arriba.

Go straight ahead, following Santiago del Teide direction, to retrace your steps to the ridge above Valle de Arriba. Cross the ridge, leaving the Chinyero Reserve and descend back into the valley. At the valley floor, turn R at the SP showing 'Valle de Arriba 3.5 km' and walk back to your car.
14.3km/3hrs 50mins

A Place to Unlace the Boots
Bar Tropical in Arguayo is good for some mid-route refreshments. Santiago del Teide town has a choice of places to relax after a long, or short walk. The tasca and courtyard at La Casona del Patio is in a pretty setting as is the little bar amongst the eucalyptus trees in the picnic area on the opposite side of the road. Their *arepas* (Venezuelan filled cornflour pancakes) are as good as we've eaten on Tenerife.

Discover More
Cha Domitila Pottery Centre
Pottery making in this area is a tradition which stretches back to Guanche times. The post conquest settlers continued with the tradition and their descendants have similarly taken up the mantle, ensuring that the craft is kept alive. The little pottery museum is off the normal tourist track and deserves your patronage. Not only is it situated in a charming little building with a lovely leafy courtyard, it's an interesting reminder of life in the area in the not too distant past...and you might get to see potters at work.
(+34) 922 863 465; Carretera General, 34, Arguayo; entrance free; 10.00-13.00 & 16.00-19.00, closed Monday.

Farmer's Market
If you happen to be in the area at the weekend, there's a small farmers' market in Santiago del Teide; these are good places to stock up on local fruits, vegetables, herbs and some of the valley's quaffable wines. Open Saturday & Sunday mornings.

The Force of Nature

Beauty comes at a price. The Valle de Santiago is one of the most attractive looking valleys on Tenerife, even if Mother Nature has done her best to transform it on at least two occasions. Tenerife's last volcanic eruption from Chinyero in 1909 sent bubbling streams of lava towards the hamlets of Valle de Arriba and Las Manchas. Disaster seemed inevitable until in desperation the townspeople of both villages carried images of Christ and Santa Ana to the edge of the molten rivers and prayed for divine intervention. Lo and behold the lava stopped, a few feet short of Las Manchas' doorsteps. Eternally grateful, the local people hold annual fiestas celebrating this miracle.

Lightning almost struck twice when in 2007, out of control forest fires swept across Tenerife and threatened to engulf the hamlets in the valley. It's unclear if Santa Ana was called on again, but as fires reached the outskirts of Valle de Arriba and Santiago del Teide, the hot winds which had fuelled them dropped and the towns were spared. In 2012, fierce forest fires once again devastated the area.

Pools and Pines, The Erjos Pools

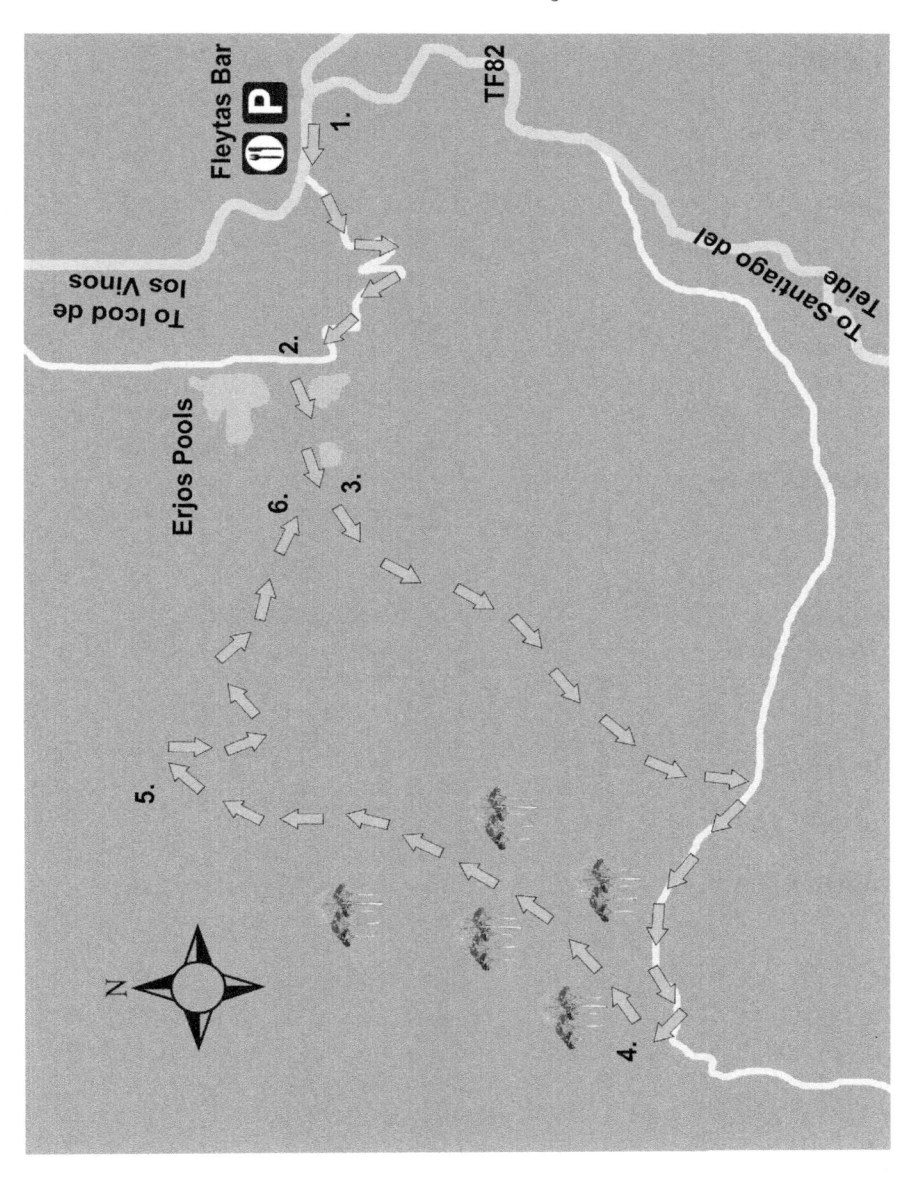

79

Pools and Pines, The Erjos Pools

Location	North west Tenerife.
Circular Route?	Yes.
How Long?	Approx 2hrs 15mins.
How Far?	5.9 kilometres.
Vertiginous?	No.
Route Difficulty	Level 3 - A good workout, but not overly testing. The path involves a couple of ascents, but these tend to wind easily up the hill rather than being straight up thigh testers.
Wow Scenery	This is a stunner of a walk with an overdose of some of the best scenery on Tenerife... and it's got pools.
Underfoot	It's foot friendly country lanes and forest trails all the way.
Watering Holes	The route starts and ends at Bar Fleytas, a great walkers' watering hole... unless you pick the day it's closed (Friday).
Downside	The only downside we can think of regarding this route is that it is such a lovely trail that it's over all too soon. If a cloudy day, the best views of Mount Teide may be obscured.

Beginning alongside the popular Bar Fleytas restaurant (closed Friday) on the cusp of two micro-climates that straddle the TF421 between Ruigómez and the tranquil hamlet of Valle de Arriba, this delightful circular hike takes in the serene beauty of the Erjos Pools, a scented forest trail and vistas over the Santiago Valley.

Created originally by quarry works, the Erjos Pools are some of the few remaining natural lakes on Tenerife and attract a wide variety of bird and insect life. Their existence was threatened by the forest fires of 2007 which dried the lakes up and destroyed the surrounding forests. But Mother Nature has been busy and now the lakes are back to their former glory.

How to Get There

By Car
Fleytas Bar, the start of the route, lies near Santiago del Teide on the TF82 in the direction of Icod de los Vinos.

Parking
There's parking outside of Fleytas Bar, but it is for patrons. There is also rough parking spaces on the verge between the bar and the turn off to San José de los Llanos.

By Public Transport

Puerto de la Cruz
Take the 324 to Los Gigantes and get off at the Bar Fleytas bus stop.

Playa de las Américas/Los Cristianos
Take the 460 to Icod de los Vino and, as above, get off at the Bar Fleytas bus stop.

Los Gigantes
Easy peasy. Jump on the 325 to Puerto de la Cruz and guess what? Leave the bus at Bar Fleytas.

The Route

1. Stepping Out
From Bar Las Fleytas, walk along the main road to the right in the direction of Ruigómez for 3 mins and 157 metres until you reach the first right hand bend. At the start of the bend you will see a wide dirt path which drops down to the left in a zig zag towards the Erjos Pools below. Follow the cobble and sand path, ignoring an indistinct turn off to the right, as the path curves around to the left and reaches a T junction.

2. The Erjos Pools (703 metres /3mins)
Turn right and in 80 metres you reach a signpost which shows San José de Los Llanos to the right and Punta de Teno and Cumbre de Bolico 4.5 km to the left. Go left. There's a yellow and white striped marker on the right hand side of the path. Drop down the dip and then begin to climb alongside the brambles between the pools, making a mental note to return when the berries are ready for picking.

After 150 metres, ignore the path off to your left which has a yellow and white X, stay right and in a couple of steps the path splits three ways. The path to the right hand side leads to the pools (see 'detour') which we will explore on the return leg of the walk. Straight ahead is marked by a yellow and white X and will be our return route. Take the path to the immediate left marked with a yellow and white stripe. Follow the path, watching out for crickets which play chicken across the path in front of you, until you see a yellow and white arrow which shows that the route goes up to the left hand side over a small ridge signposted 'Cumbre de Bolico'.

3. To the Bolico Ridge (1.3km /30mins)
Go left, following the signpost direction for Cumbre de Bolico, and climb through a narrow, rocky gully lined by small dry stone walls and bordered by fire-blackened trees. The path continues to climb steadily through shady patches of tree heather and Canary Willow for 700 metres and 20 minutes until you arrive at the peak of the ridge beside a signpost and emerge onto the wide path with views over Valle de Arriba and Santiago del Teide. On the horizon, Mount Teide and Pico Viejo shimmer. Here, you're on the cusp of a micro-climate changeover and you can see the arid slopes beyond Valle de Arriba which contrast starkly with the lush Erjos Pools behind you.

Turn right on the ridge, ignoring the yellow and white X which marks the way, and climb for 500 metres and 10 wheeze and gasp minutes until you reach a turn off to the right hand side where the road is barred by a gate. Follow the turn off to the right and squeeze through the gap at the side of the gate and onto the wide forest path. Turn right on the path and follow it for 460 metres and 10 minutes down the skittery descent until you see a path leading off into the woods on the right hand side. Stones mark the entrance and there's a 'no cycling' sign at the beginning of the path. Turn right and follow this path into the woods.

4. Into the Forest (3km/1hr 10mins)

Descend the narrow zigzag path, after 5 minutes passing a stone marker on a left hand bend and carefully negotiating the boulder-strewn gully as you cast glances at the views which open up over the north west coast and the open air swimming pool complex of Los Silos. A rocky outcrop juts out over the headland from which you can see the Los Silos coastline easily. A path descends giddily down to the left here; ignore it and stay on the more sensible path which leads off to the right hand side.

Continue your descent, noticing how the fresh green shoots are stemming from the base of petrified, blackened trunks. After a kilometre or so of forest trail you emerge onto the ridge with the most incredible vista ahead of you.

Dominating the scene is Mount Teide and the lower peak of Pico Viejo. Below and to the left are the low buildings of the eco-museum at El Tanque. To the right of Pico Viejo you can see the frozen black lava river from Mount Chinyero – Tenerife's last volcanic eruption - and ahead of it and to the right is Montaña Bilma which you circumnavigate on the Arguayo walk.

5. Ridge above the Pools (4km/1hr 35mins)

Turn left and walk along the ridge for 60 metres to see the path that drops down to the right hand side which will take us back down to the Erjos pools. (For some more views over the north west coast, continue along the ridge to the pine thicket at the end and climb onto an outcrop to look over to the left.)

Follow the path as it makes a skittery descent towards the valley floor, in 500 metres passing a low chain fence with plastic hoops on and ignoring the path which leads off to the right hand side.

After almost a kilometre and 20 minutes of descent you arrive at the crossroads where we took the right hand path up to Bolico Ridge. (At this point you may chose to take a small 'detour' and explore the Erjos Pools and their wildlife.) Ignore the turning to the left and follow the wider path straight ahead. Ignore the path to the right hand side and continue around the curve, keeping the large lake on your right hand side.

5. Homeward Bound (5.1/2hrs 5mins)

In 160 metres and 3 minutes you arrive at the San José de Los Llanos signpost and turn right for 70 metres before turning left, then immediate right and swinging round to the right to get back onto the zigzag path that leads up from the Pools to the ridge. Re-trace your steps up the path to the ridge, turning right on the main road and walking back to Bar Fleytas.
5.9km/2hrs 15mins

A Place to Unlace the Boots

Bar Fleytas (closed Friday) at the start of the Pools and Pines route is the oasis for walkers in this area. It's a refuge when the bruma rolls in and the ideal place to collapse into at the end of a long walk. It's warm and welcoming whether you want liquid refreshments, to sample some tasty Canarian home cooking, or need a sugar boost courtesy of the pastries and almond cakes on the bar.

Discover More

Camino de la Virgen de Lourdes (1km/30 mins)
For a short walk with a surprise, in the centre of the village of Santiago del Teide is a white bridge over the little barranco, fronted by an archway above which is a statue of the Virgin Mary. Cross the bridge and follow the crosses as they climb up the narrow, rocky path to a flower covered shrine and a little fountain. This is a lovely spot from which to enjoy great views back over the village of Santiago del Teide before descending back the way you came.

An Explosive Landscape, Chinyero Circular

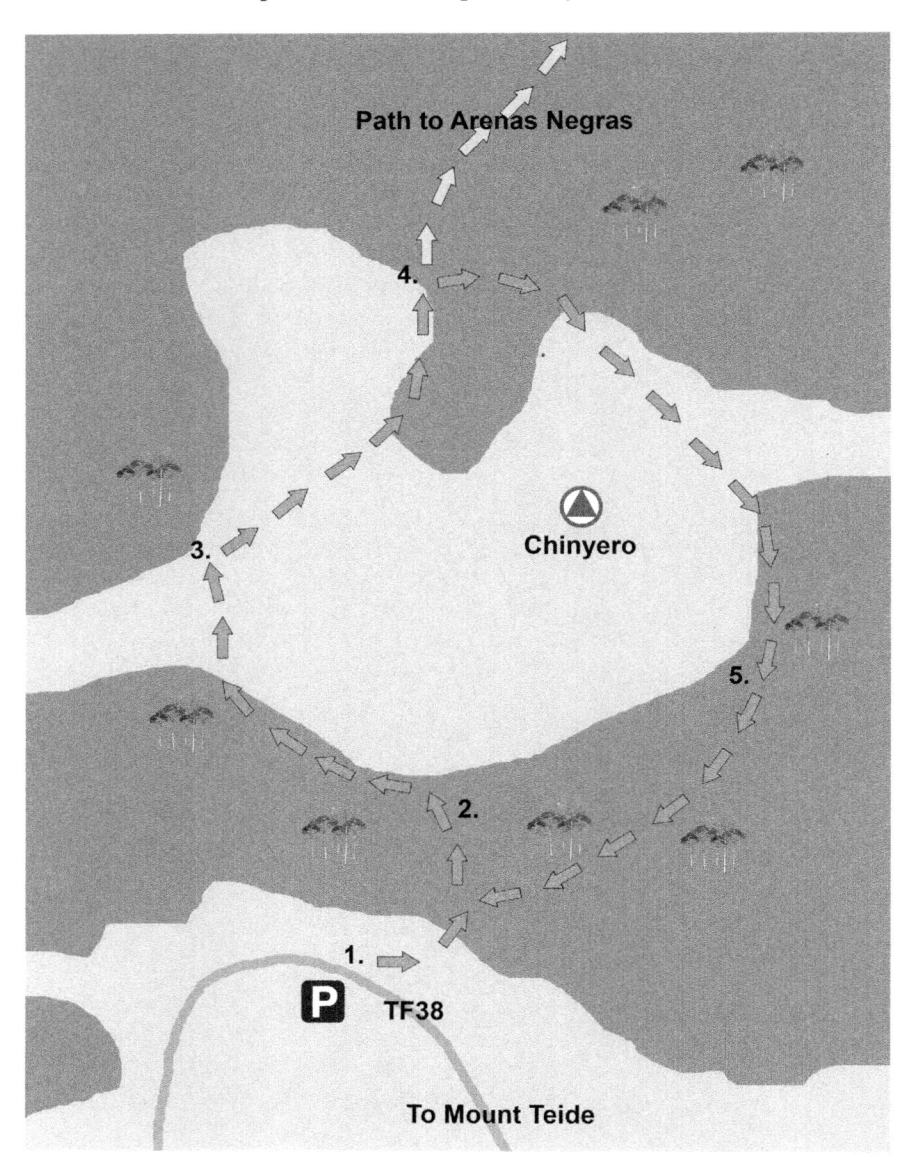

An Explosive Landscape, Chinyero Circular

Location	North west Tenerife.
Circular Route?	Yes.
How Long?	Approx 2hrs 10mins.
How Far?	7 kilometres.
Vertiginous?	No.
Route Difficulty	Level 2 - With a good path for company all of the way along reasonably flat terrain, this isn't a difficult walk. It's not a stroll in the park though thanks to the sections which cross the lava fields.
Wow Scenery	You get views across the sea of clouds in the north, Mount Teide and Pico Viejo rising above the sweeping pine forest and Chinyero's ruddy volcanic cone.
Underfoot	Mostly a very pleasant and well constructed path and forest trails, but a section crosses a rough volcanic landcsape and the loose lava can be tiring on the feet and ankles.
Watering Holes	There aren't any establishments nearby. There is a picnic site at the northern access to the Chinyero route which has wonderfully sweet spring water on tap.
Downside	The fact that there's no place to unlace the boots at the end of the walk.

This relatively easy, level walk is around the site of Tenerife's last volcanic eruption. For 10 days in November 1909 lava and ash spewed from Mount Chinyero, burning up the pine forests as it crept inexorably towards the little hamlet of Las Manchas. Popular folklore maintains that the villagers brought a statue of Santa Ana, placed her at the outskirts of the village and miraculously, the lava flow stopped. Today the area is a magnificent landscape of frozen lava rivers, emerald pine forests and golden earth beneath the benign gaze of Mount Teide.

How to Get There

By Car
The path begins between markers 14 & 15 on the TF38 Chio to Boca Tauce road alongside the 'Montaña Chinyero 1410 metres' signpost.

Alternative, anyone driving from the north can access this route from the Arenas Negras Zona Recreative outside La Motañeta on the TF373. (see additional directions at the end of route).

Parking
The road flattens out on either side of the dirt track at the start of the route and there is adequate room for parking.

By Public Transport
As no bus runs along the Chio/Boca Tauce road, there is no access to this route by public transport. However, the route can be accessed from its northern side via the picnic zone at Arenas Negras and the 630 service from Icod de los Vinos to Puerto de Erjos passes the track leading to the zona recreative.

The Route

1. Stepping Out
Follow the wide path leading clearly off through an open barrier and past 'Espacio Natural Protegído' signs. After 5 mins the path swings round to the left, narrows and becomes stonier. 2 mins later a 'Reserva Natural Espacio' sign denotes the small crossroads at which the circular walk begins. Yellow and white striped markers on stones show we can go either right or left. We're going left.

2. To the Centenary Site (946 metres/14mins)
The clearly laid out path reaches a crossroads with a wide, dusty pista and

continues straight across, following the yellow and white stripes, skirted in spring and summer by banks of wild grasses. 6 mins further on you reach the crossroads with the Santiago del Teide and El Calvario routes.

Take the path to the right clearly signed 'Circular Chinyero 5.7 km'. Now surrounded by the solidified wasteland of the 1909 eruption, the path traverses lava and in another 6 mins arrives at the junction with the Los Partidos route.

3. To The Half Way Point (1.9k/27mins)

Take the path to the right, signposted 'Chinyero Circular', up the steps and through the lava fields. After 5 mins you'll arrive at a small plaque on the right hand side of the path which commemorates the centenary of the eruption and was laid in November 2009.

Crossing lava fields makes for uncomfortable walking, the feet have a respite when the path reaches the pine forest and morphs to soft sand. Passing trees petrified by forest fire, the route reaches another small crossroads by a 'Reserva Natural Espacio' sign and continues straight across, once more subjecting feet to the trials of lava walking.

Along this section in spring, Mother Nature presents a spectacular palette of frozen lava river banked by tides of candy floss pink Rumex Maderensis. 20 or so minutes after passing the plaque, the route reaches a T junction and turns right onto the wider path. Shortly afterwards the Arenas Negras and Garachico routes join from the left hand side denoting the half way point in the walk.

4. To The Lonesome Pine (3.2k/1hr 2mins)

At the Arenas Negras/Garachico junction, turn right following the 'Chinyero Circular' sign and continue along the path with Mount Teide and Pico Viejo now on the horizon ahead. Some 20 mins and 1km or so further on, the views open out to the right revealing Mount Chinyero and the path reaches a fork. Take the right hand fork passing the yellow and white stripes on the rock and keeping Chinyero directly on your right.

A slog along the side of a lava flow takes the path to a brow beyond which the desolate landscape left by Chinyero spreads, bordered by pine forests and framed by Mount Teide. To the right of Chinyero, the outline of the twin peaks of La Palma can sometimes be seen above the cloud on the horizon.

A 'Reserva Natural Espacio' sign borders a small crossroads and the path goes straight across keeping Chinyero on the right hand side. 7 mins beyond the crossroads the path reaches a T junction signposted 'Chinyero 5.7km' in either direction where a wide pista leads off to the left and two paths go to the right; an upper and a lower path. Take the upper path to the right and climb up for 5 mins until you reach a large, fat pine tree with a charred trunk and widely spreading branches. The views from this vantage point are excellent and it makes the perfect picnic spot; the stones providing comfortable seating and the tree obligingly lending welcome shade.

5. Homeward Bound (5.8k/1hr 50mins)

10 mins beyond the lonesome pine the path divides and a yellow and white 'X' shows that straight ahead is not the way to go. Take the right hand path and drop down through the forest for 13 mins until you reach a crossroads over a wide, dusty pista. Go straight over and in another 3 mins the path again crosses a wider pista which is where the route joined the Chinyero Circular path. This time leave the path and turn left onto the pista, and follow it as it swings around to the right and in 5 mins takes you back to the TF38.
7k/2hr 10mins

Walks in The North of Tenerife
Teno

"Emerald carpets punctuated with rock roses, tabaiba and spurge dropped away into sheer cliffs down to the sea while overhead buzzards circled on the lookout for lizards and rabbits..."

Walking in Teno Rural Park

The west offers fantastic walking opportunities through some of Tenerife's most stunning scenery. The area is characterised by villages and hamlets that feel light years away from the modern tourist developments. Merchants' trails were once the lifeline between these small communities and these now provide ideal paths for exploring an area where traditions and farming practices haven't changed much in centuries. Straddling micro climates, there's a wild and raw beauty to Teno Rural Park which changes its scenery and weather with every twist and turn in the path while affording views across the coasts and the occasional glimpses of Mount Teide if you're lucky.

The second most popular day trip destination of Masca is the scene of one of the most challenging walks on Tenerife - the prehistoric Masca Barranco (gorge) which twists and turns beneath monolithic cliff walls on its journey to the sea. Continue your drive through the valley of Masca to emerge on the other side and you'll discover El Palmar. Defined by the giant 'pie' created by clay quarrying, carpeted with wild flowers and boasting some of the most dramatic scenery on Tenerife, life in sleepy El Palmar couldn't be further away from the tourist tours of Masca if it tried. Here, the changing of the traffic lights passes for excitement in a corner of Tenerife unseen and unknown by the the vast majority of visitors.

Weather
The weather either side of the Teno Mountains can be very different. The south west side (Masca route) enjoys lots of sunshine whereas there's more chance of cloud on the west side at El Palmar. The El Palmar to Teno route bridges both micro-climates. Walks that begin in cloud at El Palmar can enter sunshine at Teno Alto and then find themselves moving between cold wind and hot sun as they traverse the ridge. It definitely pays to dress in layers on that route! We've experienced a phenomena in the hamlet of Los Bailaderos where it was raining at one end of the hamlet and sunny at the other... and it's not a big place. The chances are the weather will be walker-friendly whatever the time of year. On a clear day the views of the El Palmar Valley offer one of the sweetest vistas you'll discover on Tenerife.

Flora

The Masca Barranco takes you from the lush palm groves and fruit trees of the village, down the cactus and euphorbia filled gorge where giant agave leaves combine with prickly pear cactus to create an inhospitable-looking landscape. All along the barranco, underground water courses provide stunning pools and waterfalls which feed dense mini-forests of cane, leggy grasses and palm fronds. By contrast, El Palmar Valley is vibrant with yellow broom, wild parsley, berry-laden brambles, a multitude of wild flowers and forests of pine and tree heath. Walking in the Teno Rural Park in spring gives you an insight into Tenerife's wild flowers rarely seen anywhere else. Entire fields are vibrant with violet tajinaste and white wild radish; hedgerows bow under the weight of Canary Island bell flowers, St John's Wort and wild fennel, and valleys sprout carpets of lilac cistus.

Call of Nature

There are several restaurants in Masca where the owners expect you to either be a customer or to pay a small amount for the privilege and there are public toilets at the back of the beach in Los Gigantes for when you get off the boat. There are several bars in El Palmar and two bars in the village of Los Bailaderos where you can use the facilities as long as you buy something.

Eat me

The goat cheese in Teno is simply explosively good. Try some curado and you'll soon know why we used the term 'explosively'. It's packed with flavour and ideal for anyone who likes their cheese to come with a swaggering personality. An oddity to try in Masca is cactus lemonade. It's much better than it sounds.

Where To Stay When Walking in Teno Rural Park and Garachico

Located in the less populated and far less touristy, north west of Tenerife, access to Teno Rural Park is easiest and quickest from Garachico.

Hotel San Roque, Garachico
Probably our favourite hotel on the island, Hotel San Roque is the perfect blend of traditional and contemporary. A lovingly restored, 18th century mansion which is furnished in Bauhaus and places art house design features alongside tea wood floors and carved balconies to impeccable effect. Rooms are set around the splendid interior courtyard and feature Rennie Mackintosh furniture, whirlpool bath and DVD player. There's an elegant swimming pool around which breakfast and dinner is served, and the rooftop solarium affords views across the town to the mountains and the sea. [Expensive]
Esteban de Ponte 32, Garachico; (+34) 922 13 34 35; www.hotelsanroque.com

Hotel La Quinta Roja, Garachico
Set on the lovely La Glorieta plaza, the 17th century former home of the Marquis of Quinta Roja is another fabulous Garachico hotel where guests are welcomed like old friends. Ochre walls, tea wood carved balconies and an interior patio garden form a stylish retreat. Built to keep a wary eye on the horizon for pirates, the hotel's lookout tower provides a conservatory lounge with 360 degree views. Breakfast on the outside terrace alongside the terrapins includes home made jams and cakes. There's a small solarium on the roof and a tasty tasca for tapas and wine. [Mid-range]
Glorieta de San Francisco s/n, Garachico; (+34) 922 13 33 77; www.quintaroja.com

Hotel Rural El Patio
Set amongst the banana plantations of the north west coast a short drive from Garachico, El Patio is a haven of tranquillity. The home of the Ponte family since 1507, this gorgeous manor house and finca has extensive gardens, including a swimming pool, as well as endless banana groves through which trails run to a small pebbly cove. The hotel's highlight is its beautiful courtyard, adorned by palm trees planted by the owner's grandmother in 1902, in which balmy evenings are spent beneath a star studded sky with only the sound of the cicadas for company. [Budget]
El Guincho, Garachico; (+34) 922 13 32 80; www.hotelpatio.com

Up Country, El Palmar to Teno Alto

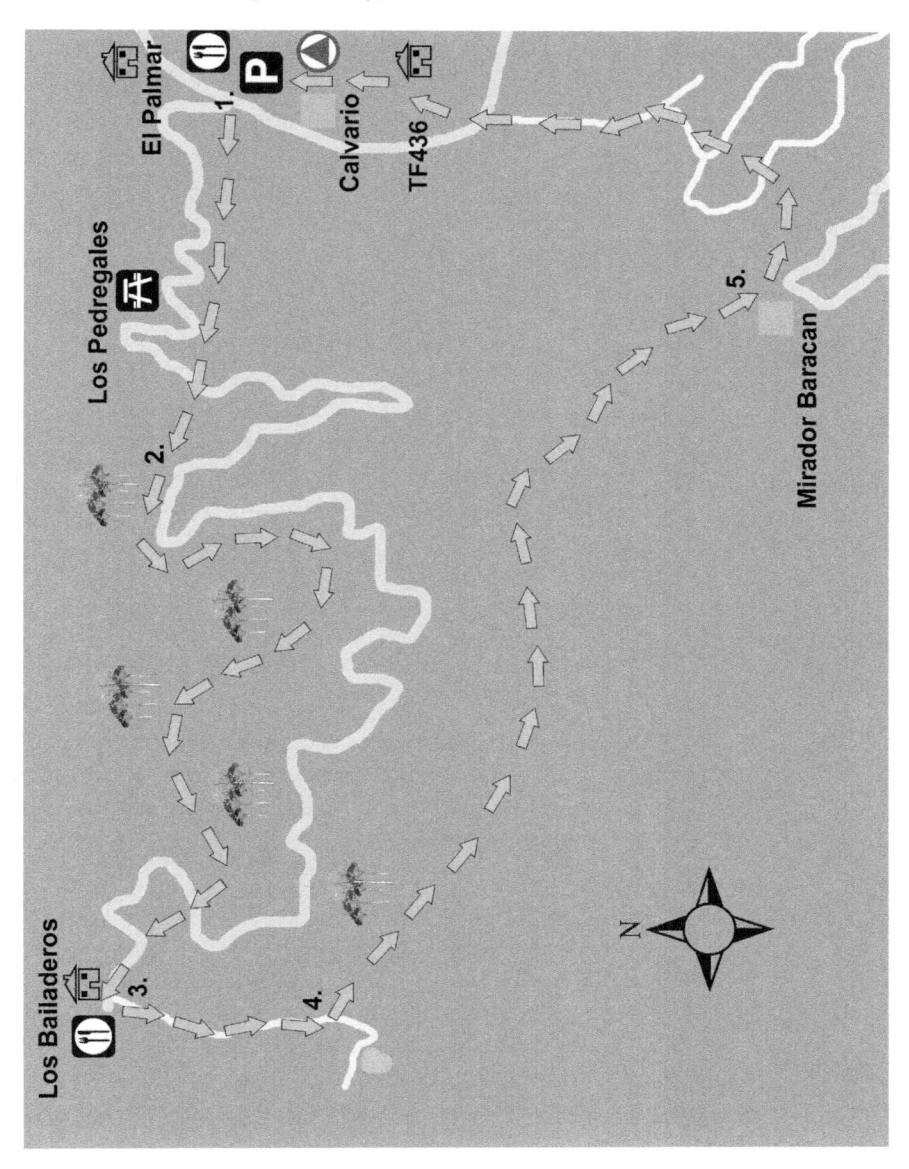

Up Country, El Palmar to Teno Alto

Location	North west Tenerife.
Circular Route?	Yes.
How Long?	Approx 4hrs
How Far?	10.5 kilometres.
Vertiginous?	There is a ridge walk section which could be seen as vertiginous to some.
Route Difficulty	Level 3 - The initial ascent is testing so take plenty of stops to soak up the views. After that it's nice easy paths with a couple more ascents and descents along the way.
Wow Scenery	Walk this route on a clear day and when Mount Teide joins the picture, it's difficult to think of a better scene on Tenerife.
Underfoot	There's a merchants' trail for part of the route but mostly it's solid forest paths and open ridge paths that are a joy to walk on. Tiring on the thighs in parts but a good surface throughout.
Watering Holes	There's a choice of truly authentic Tenerife bar restaurants at either end of the route.
Downside	On a clear day you can see forever as they say, but if the *bruma* descends it's a different matter. This route crosses various micro climates so can change from hot and sunny to cloudy and windy on some winter days.

The magnificent El Palmar Valley in the north west of Tenerife is one of the last, undiscovered beauty spots on Tenerife. Once the site of extensive quarrying, the valley is dominated by what looks like a giant pie with slices cut out of it. No longer being carved up, El Palmar is a lush, unspoiled valley that undulates between the Monte Del Agua and the Teno Mountains. Carpeted in wild flowers in spring and frequently cloaked in low clouds in winter, the sight of the El Palmar Valley in full sunshine can be elusive but when it comes, it's a sight for sore eyes.

This lovely walk is one of our favourites and gives epic views over two coastlines, dappled woodland paths and a glimpse into the rural hinterland of Tenerife. An hour's steady climb is rewarded with views that expand with every few metres until you reach tranquil Teno Alto. Some more climbing and you emerge on a ridge traversing two coastlines with some of the best views to be seen on Tenerife, provided the cloud doesn't descend and spoil the fun. A leisurely descent takes you back to El Palmar, preferably with a block of goat's cheese in the rucksack.

How to Get There

By Car

From Puerto de la Cruz, follow the TF42 to Buenavista del Norte and then inland on the TF436 to reach El Palmar. From southern resorts drive to Santiago del Teide (TF82) and then take the TF436 through Masca to El Palmar.

Parking

El Palmar is a quiet town that not many visitors pass through. There is always plenty of parking spaces opposite the start of the route.

By Public Transport

Puerto de la Cruz

Take the 363 to Buenavista del Norte and change to the 355 or 366, both of which go through El Palmar.

Playa de las Américas/Los Cristianos

Take the 460 to Santiago del Teide where you can catch the 355 to El Palmar.

Los Gigantes

Jump on the 325 to Santiago del Teide where you can catch the 355 to El Palmar.

Places to Unlace the Boots

Restaurant Los Bailaderos in Los Bailaderos is a very typical Canarian restaurant that is good for a midway lunch stop. There are some traditional dishes on the menu for a taste of the hearty local cuisine like rabbit, goat and escaldón de gofio. There's also a quaint little bar/shop opposite. We recommend stocking up on the local cheese at the 'grocery' shop in the village, it is divine and has real attitude - the curado is for true cheese aficionados.

There's more choice back in El Palmar - again all traditional restaurants. If you've got your own transport, head up the road in the direction of Masca to Mesón del Norte (closed Monday) which does a very nice and reasonable menu del dia deal for €10.

Discover More: Teno Cheese

One of the must try and buys for anyone who visits Teno Alto and the village of Los Bailaderos (the name refers to goat farming and has nothing to do with dancing) is the local cheese. The goats' cheese in Teno is said to be flavoured by a diet that includes wild fennel and discarded tomatoes.

Cheese on Tenerife comes in three types – queso fresco, semi-curado and curado. Whilst the fresco is good, it's the semi-curado and curado that excel. These are cheeses with attitude. The semi-curado packs a flavour filled punch whilst the curado is for serious cheese aficionados (so strong it burns).

A good sized chunk of cheese costs around €5. If you can't buy any local cheese whilst you're in Teno, you can't pick up excellent Tenerife cheeses in any good supermarket. For the really strong varieties, farmers' market are best.

The Route

1. The Only Way is Up

The route begins in El Palmar, at the turn off to Teno Alto and Los Pedragales and is marked by a large sign detailing the route which is referred to as 'PR-TF57 Callejón de Teno'. From the signpost, the walk is 4.2 kilometres to Teno Alto. Follow the cobbled path lined by a dry stone wall as it climbs relentlessly up through the valley amidst high bracken, wild parsley and brambles, and stay on it as it crosses the red stone path at Los Pedragales and the zona recreativa (picnic area) signposted to Teno Alto 3.5km.

Emerging from beneath the pines, the path reaches the road where the signpost tells you it's 3.3km to Teno Alto. Cross over and continue up on the other side through the cactus. The path winds its way through shaded groves where you can take respite from the sun and to wonderful viewpoints back across the valley behind you. If it's a clear day, look for the peak of Mount Teide (recognizable by its paler, pumice tip) beyond the Monte del Agua mountains.

The landscape becomes thinner with sparse pine trees as you reach the top of the ridge where the path evens out. Continue along the path, following the yellow and white striped markings on rocks and you will see the signpost showing Teno Alto 2.7 km pointing your route to the left.

2. Forests, Mountains and Goats (1.2km/1hr 5mins)

Double pipes run alongside the path as it descends into a lovely woodland walk which skirts the road. On the right hand side, nailed to a tree, notice the old 'walker' symbol of a strident hiker who looks like Elvis Presley. After 200 metres and 6 or so minutes you emerge from the forest into a clearing where a signpost tells you you're now half way between your setting off point and your destination at 2.4km to go. Follow the sign down the path to the left hand side, marked by yellow and white stripes on a rock.

The path drops down through fir trees, laurel and tree heathers and there's another Elvis on the right hand side, this time bearing the number 6 on his shirt. Climb up the stone steps to the left and follow the path as it begins to skirt the gorge with emerald carpets of tree heathers in every direction. On the saddle of the ridge in the distance you can see white and red buildings and the green roof of a finca that keeps goats, the tinkle of their bells echoing around the valley.

After a kilometre, you emerge into a rocky clearing just past another Elvis, the path drops down to the right hand side where yellow and white stripes on a rock mark the way.

Another kilometre and 25 minutes later, the lane starts to climb up to the left with a yellow and white X on a rock. Stay on the cobbled path to the right hand side and follow it over the wooden footbridge to rejoin the path further on and continue to the right. 300 metres and 5 minutes later, ignore the path as it sweeps up to the left, and continue walking straight ahead on the cobbled way, following the advice of Elvis on a tree on your right hand side.

Another 200 metres and 3 minutes and you're on the up again as the path climbs to meet the road. Go straight over the road and rejoin the path on the other side, signed 'Los Bailaderos 0.3km'. Pass the small shrine and continue straight ahead and down until you reach the road. Turn left and stroll into the village of Los Bailaderos where you'll find a shop on your left hand side which sells excellent, locally produced goat's cheese as well as a good assortment of local jams and sauces. Further on you'll find two bars, both serving food, and beyond them the wide open malpaís, high above Buenavista del Norte.

3. Switching Climate Zones (4.1km/1hr 45mins)
Take the tarmac road that leads left out of the village, opposite the plaza and kiddies playground, marked with yellow and white stripes on a lamp-post on the left corner and follow it uphill past Bar Teno Alto on your left and more yellow and white stripes on the lamp-post ahead on the left.

The quiet road winds its way steadily up out of the village with views back down across the western tip of Tenerife and, if it's a clear day, Mount Teide on the horizon.

As you climb you move from the north westerly facing to the south westerly facing coast and you can begin to see changes in the vegetation to reflect the more arid climate.

In 15 minutes you reach a junction where the tarmac gives way to ridged concrete and a signpost tells you it's 17.2km to San José de Los Llanos and 3km to Cumbre de Baracán. Continue straight ahead in the direction of Baracán passing yellow and white stripes on the rock on your right hand side.

4. Red Steps and Ridges (5km/2hr 5mins)
Less than 200 metres further on, turn left off the wide path and onto a narrow trail, following the signpost direction to San José de Los Llanos and Cumbre de Baracán. The red earth path climbs up towards the woods in a series of steps and between large boulders, looking like the entrance to some ancient temple. On breezy days this is a wind tunnel and can buffer you into the woods.

Continue on the path through the twisted limbs of laurel and tree heath and emerge onto the wide open ridge with views over to La Gomera. The path becomes a little indistinct here as it climbs up through the arid scrub land. If you visit in spring these cliffs will be coated in magnificent displays of wild flowers and if you're very lucky, the horizon will be clear enough to see to Mount Teide and all the way up the north west coast to Tacoronte ahead and over the Buenavista coastline and golf course behind you.

The path continues to traverse the top of Barrancos del Carriza and de Las Aneas with views over Las Portelas with the mighty mountain standing guard at its back. Traversing the ridge between climate zones, from windy to calm and back again, the path eventually descends to the ridge of Baracán where you can see the mirador and car park on the Masca road beyond.

5. Descend to the Valley (7.8km/3hrs 10mins)

Just before you reach the car park at Mirador de Baracán, a path drops down to the left hand side, marked with a yellow and white cross on a rock on the right. This is the old camino real. Follow the path down the hillside towards the distinctive 'pie' of El Palmar Valley ahead of you. In 10 minutes you'll pass a black, volcanic stone building on your right hand side, continue descending and in another 300 metres you'll reach a gate.

Go around the gate onto the wide path and directly opposite you'll see a very narrow path running straight down towards the tarmac road below. This is a little short cut if you want to take it.

When you reach the tarmac road, turn left and in 100 metres or so you'll reach the corner where the wider path emerges.

If you're happy to drink in as much of the valley as you can, ignore the short cut and turn left beyond the gate, following the wide path as it twists its way to the tarmac road. Turn left along the road. In 3 minutes you reach a T junction with a 'Give Way' sign on the far side, turn left and in around 7 minutes you reach the outskirts of El Palmar. Cross the main road and go straight down the concrete lane on the opposite side. The lane descends steeply into a gulley with water pipes running above head height to the right hand side and up again between some prickly pear cactus groves until it reaches a wider concrete road.

Turn right on the road and walk towards 'the pie', passing a traditional Canarian style house on the right hand side, until you arrive at El Calvario – three crosses set onto a concrete plinth on the corner. Continue to the right with El Calvario at your back until you reach the signpost for Monte de Agua and El Palmar where a left turn takes you back to the road, opposite the start of your Teno Alto walk and time to *'Unlace the Boots'*.
10.4km/4hrs

Black Caves and Broken Cottages – Los Silos to Erjos

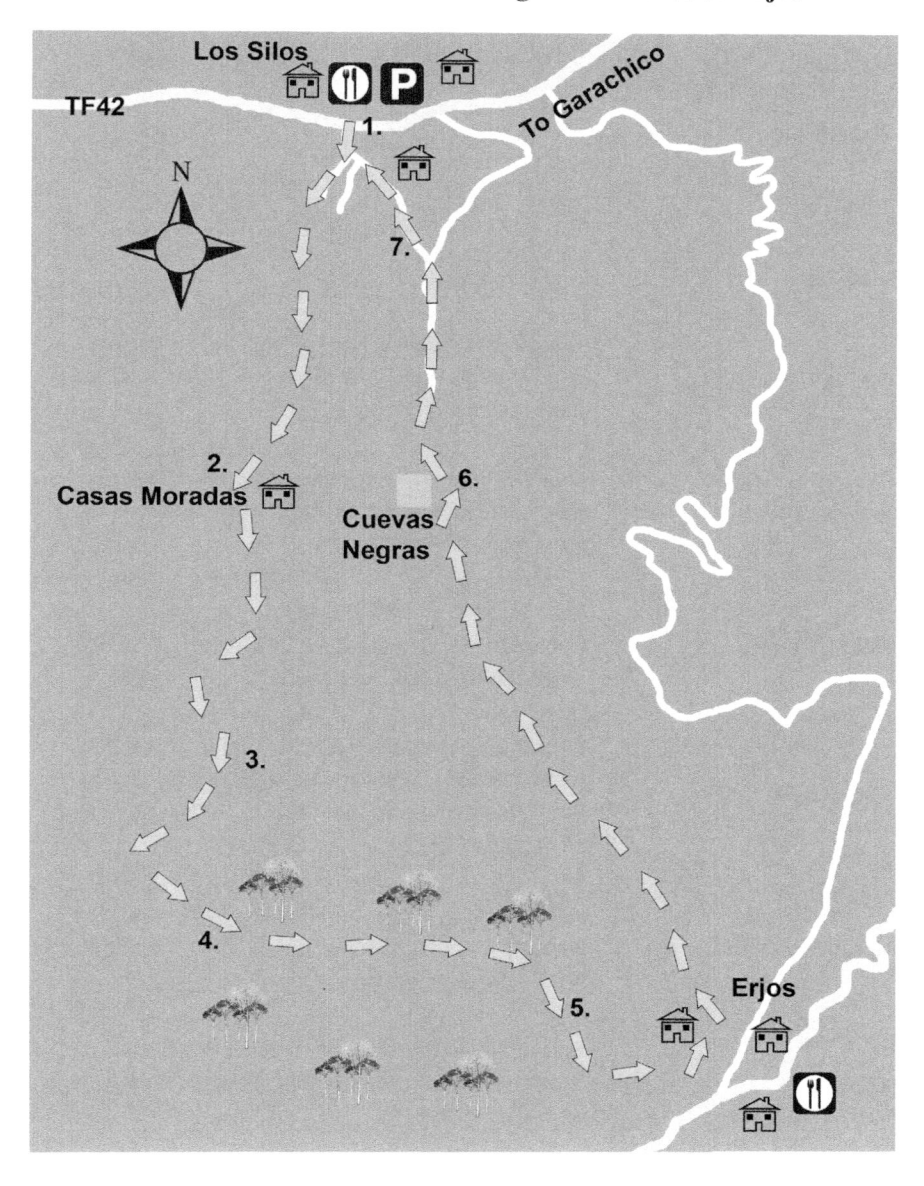

Black Caves and Broken Cottages – Los Silos to Erjos

Location	North west Tenerife.
Circular Route?	Yes.
How Long?	Approx 6hrs 20mins
How Far?	17.6 kilometres.
Vertiginous?	There is some ridge walking involved and a steep descent at the end of the route which may be an issue for vertigo sufferers.
Route Difficulty	Level 4 – There's a long gradual ascent with this route before an equally long section on the flat before a steep and dramatic descent.
Wow Scenery	This route travels into territory where not many visiting walkers venture, so the views over hidden barrancos and thick forest feel quite special.
Underfoot	A good, solid but comfortable path for most of the route. The final section is on a rocky merchant trail whose hard, uneven surface can sometimes be as much a hindrance as a help.
Watering Holes	Apart from the bars at Los Silos, there are a couple of places in Erjos, including (maybe) an unusual cafe that's really off the beaten track.
Downside	Continually watching where to put your feet can become wearisome on the steep descent. But the pay off makes it worth it.

This walk takes you from the pretty village of Los Silos on the north west coast, climbing high above the coast alongside abyssal barrancos, past abandoned villages and through the Monte Del Agua forest to the village of Erjos from where you descend via a spectacular rock face of dark, volcanic caves to return to Los Silos. A circular walk involving some 930 metres of ascent and descent, this route takes in great views, forest trails and ancient gorges in one of Tenerife's least touristy corners.

How to Get There

By Car
From Puerto de la Cruz, follow the TF42 to Los Silos. From southern resorts take the TF82 through Santiago del Teide and drop down to the coast at either El Tanque (very winding road) or outside of San Juan del Reparo (winding road) and then head west to Los Silos.

Parking
There are plenty of parking spaces on the TF42 at Los Silos. You should be able to park close to the start of the route.

By Public Transport

Puerto de la Cruz
Take the 363 which passes Los Silos.

Playa de las Américas/Los Cristianos
Take the 460 to Icod de los Vinos where you can catch the 363 to Los Silos.

Los Gigantes
Jump on the 325 to Icod de los Vinos where you can catch the 363 to Los Silos.

The Route

1. Stepping Out
The route begins at the bus stop on the corner of the TF42 Garachico to Buenavista road and the little side street of Calle Susana, opposite the entrance to Plaza Iglesia and the church. Turn left along Calle Susana following the wooden signpost direction to Senderos/Erjos/T Trigo/Cuevas Negras/Las Moradas and you pass a walking signpost showing Erjos 11.5km on the PR TF54 and 5.6km on the PR TF53 (our return route).

100 metres or so along the lane you reach a junction where the PR TF53 and

the 54 separate. Turn right following the signpost direction to Las Moradas on the 54. Here you'll catch your first sight of a figure we call 'Elvis', a walker's sign on a yellow triangle which shows a chap with a large quiff striding confidently along. Elvis appears at irregular intervals throughout this walk, rarely in a helpful position and often out of eye line but it's fun to spot him when he does make an appearance. Much more helpful are the yellow and white stripes that waymark the route.

In 170 metres there's a small fork in the path, keep left following the signpost direction Las Moradas. A yellow and white X on the right denotes that's the wrong path. The path now begins its gentle but relentless ascent along this tranquil old camino real, initially alongside a cane-filled barranco and gradually climbing to reveal views back over the coast to Los Silos and the ocean.

As you continue to climb, you'll pass a stone bridge on your left and in another 100 metres the path crosses to the other side of the barranco over another stone bridge and continues to wind uphill for a further 350 metres before crossing back again to resume the uphill slog on the right hand side of the barranco. As you continue you'll notice a change in the landscape with more tabaiba (spurge) making an appearance.

2. Casas Moradas (2.3km/1hr)

The path reaches the dilapidated stone houses of Casa Moradas where you can take a breather and admire the vistas over Isla Baja before continuing on the ever-upwards trail, skirting the abyssal barranco and surrounded by the thorny leaves and 'hat stand' flowering spikes of giant agave plants.

After 1.4km of ever-ascending trail, you emerge at a small spur where views open up over the barrancos of the valley to the coast. Onwards and upwards the path continues, in another 340 metres passing small, squat posts bearing the reassuring yellow and white stripes that tell you you're still on the PR TF54. The scenery has now taken on the look of a petrified forest, with lichen draped over branches and wispy tree heath, still with those views over the barrancos, and the ascent has mercifully levelled out.

2.6km and 1hr and 10mins after passing Casas Moradas, the path straight ahead peters out at a small junction and now climbs up to the right on steps cut into the earth. Climb the steps and continue up through the woods to emerge, 140 metres later, at a wider pista by a signpost which shows Los Silos back the way you came and Las Portelas to the right. We go left following the direction of Erjos 6.6km and Monte de Agua 3.8km.

3. Forest trails (5km/2hr /10mins)

550 metres and 10 minutes along this path you reach a junction and go right, continuing to follow the signpost direction to Erjos and Monte de Agua for a 140 metre ascent through the forest before levelling out and traversing a ridge with barrancos on either side.

This path continues ahead for 1.4km and 40 minutes until you reach a large boulder viewpoint and 80 metres and 3 minutes later emerge onto a very wide path.

4. Monte de Agua (7.2km/3hrs)

Turn left, following the signed direction to Erjos 4.5km, and begin your walk through the heart of Monte de Agua where you are surrounded by some of the best preserved laurel forest on Tenerife. Damaged by forest fires in 2011, the forest has regenerated and although you can still see the occasional charred trunk, is as lovely as ever. One kilometre and 15 minutes into the forest you reach a clearing, take the path on the 2nd left, clearly marked with yellow and white stripes on a rock on the right hand side. You will notice that you are still ascending, albeit very gradually, but you will soon reach the highest point on the route and it will be all downhill from there.

Note: When we last walked this route in August 2014 there was some work going on a couple of kilometres beyond the clearing, to install recreation areas and (we think!) areas for access by disabled. If the path is taped off, tell someone on site you are following a walking route ('sendero') and they will let you through.

After almost 4km and an hour traversing Monte de Agua you pass a marker on the left that denotes the end of Teno Rural Park and a path running off to the left. Ignore the path to the left, and continue straight ahead for 150 metres and 3 minutes to reach the foot of some communications masts and a signpost. Don't miss this turn off.

5. Into Erjos (11.2km/4hrs)

Follow the path that drops down wooden steps to the left, signposted Erjos 0.6km and follow it alongside terraces (some still bearing witness to the forest fires of 2011) for 400 metres until it reaches a T junction in a narrow lane, then turn left following in the direction of San José de Los Llanos 4.3km and Plaza de Erjos 0.2km.

In 120 metres you emerge onto the road opposite a signpost. Turn left onto the road and follow it downhill in the direction of Los Silos 5.5km and Cuevas Negras 3km. Continue straight ahead as you pass a zona recreativa (picnic area) on your right hand side, keeping left on the lower path as the path splits, and follow it to what looks like a dead end, past the No Cycling sign, to the last house on the left. Here you'll see a yellow and white waymark on the wall on the right. Drop down the paved path to the left and continue straight ahead following the yellow and white waymarks and ignoring any turn-offs (marked with a yellow and white X).

You will shortly pass a small tea house which has never been open when we've passed, and continue along the path, descending steadily. After 1.4km the path reaches an abandoned house on the left side and 800 metres further, one on the right whose vine-covered arbor crosses the path. When we were here in August, it wasn't clear if someone was still living in this house as there was washing on the line. If so, the place needs a little TLC. 360 metres beyond the vine arbour, stay right at the fork in the path, following the yellow and white striped waymark.

6. Cuevas Negras (14.6km/5hrs 20mins)

Arrive in the abandoned hamlet of Cuevas Negras at a signpost showing Erjos 3.1km back the way you came and Tierra de Trigo 2.2km right. Continue straight ahead in the signpost direction of Los Silos 2.7km and in 350 metres and 10 minutes the views open out over the most amazing landscape of dark cliff walls towering above you, their faces scarred in deep, dark caves. These are the Cuevas Negras (Black Caves) and this view is the main reason we advise doing the route this way round (that, and the killer ascent on the PR TF53 from Los Silos to here!).

A steep descent of 830 metres and twenty or so minutes brings the camino real to an end at the valley floor where the route continues straight ahead for 80 metres to emerge at a signpost on a concrete path where you go straight ahead onto the dirt track, following the signpost direction to Los Silos 1.5km. Ten minutes and 650 metres later the path crosses a wooden bridge and you turn left following the direction of Los Silos.

7. Homeward Bound (16.5km/6hrs)
80 metres after the bridge you reach a second wooden bridge and this time go right, following the yellow and white waymarks and passing the old stone lavaderos (communal laundry) on your right as you continue straight ahead and find yourself on Calle Susana. Continue straight ahead for 530 metres and you find yourself back at the fork in the path where you turned right (now on the left) to begin your walk. Continue straight ahead for the final 100 metres to arrive back at the bus stop and cross over the pedestrian crossing into Los Silos where you can 'Unlace the Boots' at the lovely Art Deco bandstand café in the plaza.
17.2km/6hrs 20mins

Places to Unlace the Boots
The café underneath the bandstand in the main plaza in Los Silos always seems to be open. As well as selling snacks, they sell home made pastries and tarts. It's worth trying a freshly made fig tart, it's completely different in taste to dried figs.

In Ancient Footsteps, Masca Barranco

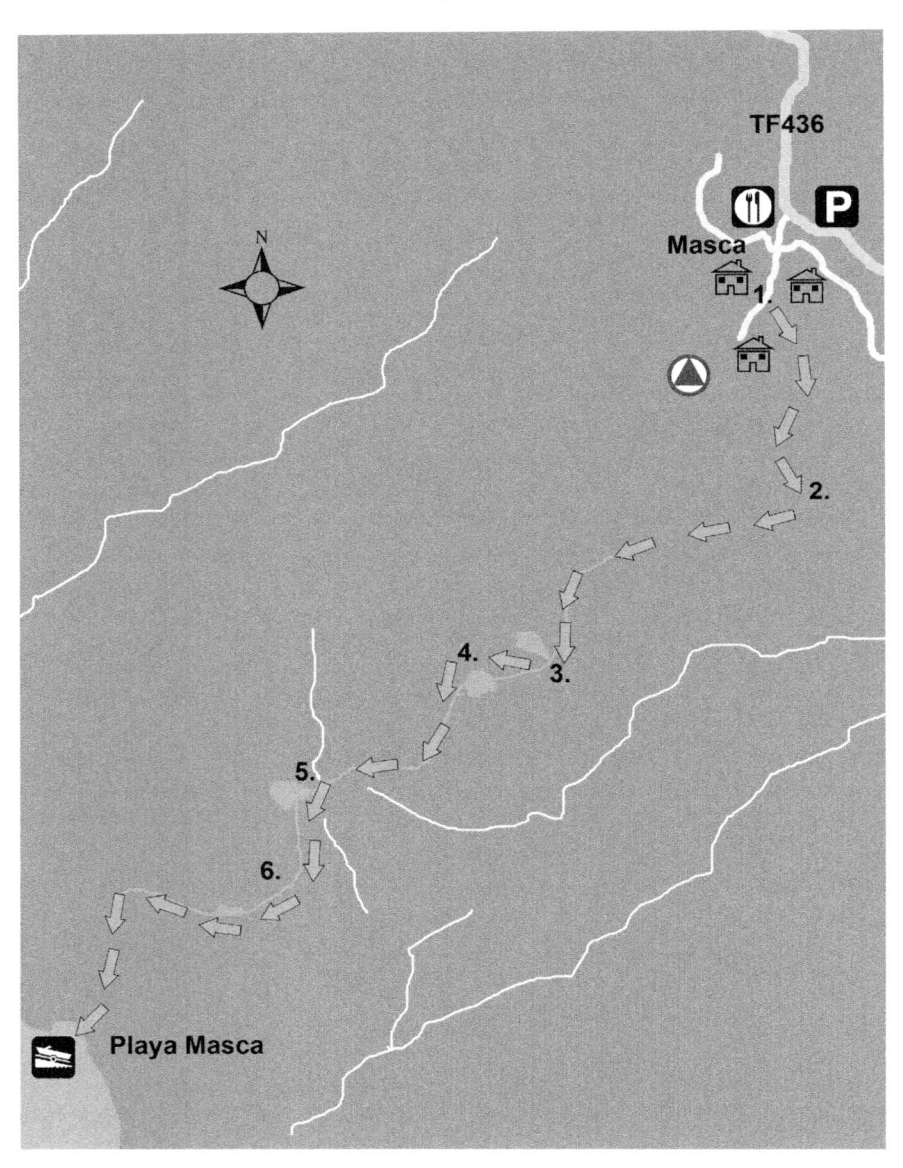

In Ancient Footsteps, Masca Barranco

Location	North west Tenerife.
Circular Route?	No.
How Long?	Approx 3hrs one way, 6hrs return.
How Far?	6.3km each way.
Vertiginous?	No. One very short section involves holding a wire to walk along a ledge. However, it's not far off the ground.
Route Difficulty	Level 4 - Distance isn't the tester here. The ongoing descent on the way down and ascent on the way back isn't that extreme. But the terrain is challenging much of the way with sections that require care and dexterity.
Wow Scenery	You start with one of the scenic splendours of Tenerife, Masca, and then enter one of the most atmospheric ravines you're likely to encounter anywhere.
Underfoot	Ranges from flat tracks to boulders to pebbly river beds to crossing streams. It is hard going in sections so care is required at all times. There are a lot of accidents in the Masca Barranco, mainly because people are unprepared.
Watering Holes	Lots of great places in Masca itself but you need to do the return route to collapse into one at the end of the walk.
Downside	Its popularity means that it's a busy route and organised groups aren't always considerate of other walkers.

After the Barranco del Infierno in Costa Adeje, Masca Barranco is the second most popular hike on Tenerife and one of its down sides is the volume of other hikers you encounter, particularly in large guided groups. But don't let its popularity fool you into thinking it must be easy. Unlike the manicured paths of Barranco del Infierno, Masca Barranco is an adventure hike covering some of the toughest terrain on the island which requires stamina, supple joints and constant concentration to avoid injury and/or losing your way. In our opinion, either undertaking or selling tour-guided hikes in Masca Barranco without taking into account age or health restrictions is nothing less than irresponsible practice. Every year people sustain injury or get lost in Masca Barranco and most of those people should not have been there in the first place.

Experienced hikers with a good level of fitness will find this assault course through Masca's prehistoric gorge to be incredible.

How to Get There

By Car

From all directions, drive to Santiago del Teide to take the wonderful winding road to Masca almost opposite the church.

Parking

There are plenty of parking spaces above the village, but they fill up as the day goes on. Arrive early to be sure of a space.

By Public Transport

Puerto de la Cruz

Take the 325 to Santiago del Teide and change to the 363 to Masca.

Playa de las Américas/Los Cristianos

Take the 460 to to Santiago del Teide where you can catch the 363 to Masca.

Los Gigantes

Jump on the 325 to Santiago del Teide where you can catch the 363 to Masca.

Tips for hiking Masca Barranco

There are multitudes of paths and detours around boulders all along the way. As long as you don't stray too far from the path, it doesn't matter which you take but some are more energy sapping than others. Sometimes you have to look further ahead to see the way. Watch for signs that may help you – daubs of paint on rocks, cairns, white chalk arrows or even trails of discarded tissues. As long as you find the four landmarks (see point 5 below), you'll make it to the beach.

Important advice before you undertake Masca Barranco
1. The majority of people hike Masca Barranco one way only – from the village of Masca to the beach. From there a boat collects them and takes them to Los Gigantes. If you plan to go with just one car, you'll have to do the return hike which is a real thigh-killer.
2. Tickets for the boat can be purchased at any of the bars in Masca village and cost €10 per person. You can also buy tickets at the beach but it's wise to buy them before you set off so ticket sellers can phone to Los Gigantes and ensure enough boats are despatched for the volume of hikers.
3. The last boat from Masca beach departs at 4.30pm in winter and at 5.30pm in summer. Give yourself plenty of time to make sure you don't miss it or you'll have no alternative but to hike back. Camping on the beach is a dangerous option and has resulted in fatalities from rock fall.
4. There are very few landmarks on this hike which makes directions almost entirely dependant on timings. Use the first leg of our directions to time yourself against our guide. That way you'll know if you're faster or slower than us and can adjust our timings accordingly. It took us 2hrs 40mins to do this hike, others have been known to take as long as 6hrs.
5. We have chosen directions in sections – each of which ends in a clear landmark (the gate, the cave, the detour & the rope wire). That way, if you get lost, you only have to backtrack to the last landmark.

The Route

From the car parking zones in Masca village, walk down the steep cobbled path, staying right at Las Fuentes restaurant (where you can buy your ticket for the boat) and follow the narrow descent to the bottom where the path runs to right and left. Turn right and follow the path past the fruit and straw hat sellers towards Bar Blanky.

1. Stepping Out (12mins)
The route begins on the left hand side of the path, just beyond the fruit and straw hat sellers and is clearly marked by a large board and by steps leading down into the barranco. Check your watch and follow the path as it zigzags down over steps, cobbles and dirt, all the way to the bottom of the ravine and the wooden bridge which will take you across the valley floor to begin the hike down the barranco. At the bridge, check your timings against ours and adjust our timings from here on in (see point 4 above).

2. The Bridge (486m/15mins)

Cross the bridge, climb up to the left and follow the path to the right as it skirts the barranco. After 800m and about 8 minutes you'll reach the stream which will accompany you, on and off, for much of your hike. Cross at the lowest and narrowest downstream point. In another 2 minutes you'll find yourself walking a ridge above the stream alongside a wire fence. Another 15 minutes and you'll reach some pools which the dirt path skirts above, below a rock overhang, and emerge onto a platform clearing.

Ahead is a large boulder with a clump of cane growing in front of it. Take the path to the right hand side of the boulder and continue for another 7 minutes until the path drops down to cross the stream again to the far bank. After another 8 minutes of scrambling, you'll see a yellow metal gate wedged into the side of a large rock. Drop down by the left side of the gate.

3. Yellow Gate (2k/1hr)

Once through the gate the path continues to the left but wander onto the level ground ahead to see the small waterfall behind you before you continue. In 10 minutes you reach a pool with clumps of cane and a large boulder on the right. Paths go right and left and you can take either. In another 6 minutes the path and stream converge taking you down over boulders and through a gully. Crossing the stream, there are two large boulders on the left and the path goes between them, leaving the stream to continue to the right for the time being. Stay on the path to the left until you reach the stream again, some 5 or so minutes later.

Slow progress continues over the uneven terrain before the barranco begins to visibly widen out at a large island of boulders in its centre with a clump of cane growing in front. In the barranco wall high above you on the left is a gaping cavern. Go up and round to the right hand side of the boulder island until, 5 minutes later, you reach a cane grove with two tunnels through it. Take either path as they merge anyway, and then cross the stream and go up on the boulders. In 6 minutes you reach more cane and again, the path goes two ways but both lead to a large drop. Instead, go the right hand side and follow the path through the cane tunnel and along the bed of the stream.

Continue along the bed of the stream and in around 6 minutes you'll see that the barranco splits and takes a turn to the right. Continue to follow the path to the right until it seems to disappear into a tunnel descending through a gap in large boulders. Unlikely as it seems, this is the route.

4. Boulder Tunnel (2.2k/1hr 6mins)

Carefully lower yourself down over the slippery and wet footholds through the rock tunnel and continue to follow the path or paths, as some of the many walkers in the ravine have created 'new' routes, taking the one which offers the easiest way to progress.

The route crosses the stream back and forward, passing more cane thickets and small waterfalls (how many depends on which time of year you walk the route). GPS goes missing in this section as the walls of the ravine close in above. Eventually you reach a rock blockade where a sign warns of danger from rockfall. The sign directs you right. There is no easy way down, but it's not a long descent over the large boulders to reach the lower level and rejoin the path once again.

Once safely down, look ahead to see an impressive arch of solidified lava in the cliff face to your left.

5. Rock Arch (4.4k/2hrs 12mins)

From the rock arch, the route continues along the bed of the stream and on the bank. Watch for where the path appears to continue around by the stream to the left of a clump of boulders. A faint, white arrow on the boulders points the way up and over the boulders with the stream below you on the left hand side. Keep looking out for cairns and paint daubs on rocks pointing the 'right' way until you find yourself at a wire rope secured into the rock face to help with balance as you walk over the steep sided rock face.

6. Rope Wire (4.5k/2hrs 20mins)
Within about 5 minutes of the rope wire you should be able to hear the sea which tells you you're getting close to Masca Beach. It's a sound to lift the spirits, but there's still a fair bit of rock climbing and path seeking to do as you trek your way down the stream bed towards the mouth of the gorge. Finally, after interminable turns, the Atlantic Ocean appears in a V on the barranco and the end is in sight for those who are taking the boat to Los Gigantes.
6.3k/3hrs

For the masochists, it's time to find a rock on the beach for lunch and a rest before tackling the return journey and the final, killer climb from the bridge to the village.

Places to Unlace the Boots
If doing the route both ways, there are lots of lovely places to choose from in Masca itself. Similarly, if catching the boat to Los Gigantes (€10, tickets from restaurants in Masca or at the beach) there are plenty of cafés and restaurants in the resort. Those around the marina might have the best views but you'll pay more for the privilege.

Walks in The North of Tenerife
Garachico

"Sometimes the sky is filled with soft lilac hues, at others the sea looks as though an alchemist has turned it to silver..."

Walking in Garachico

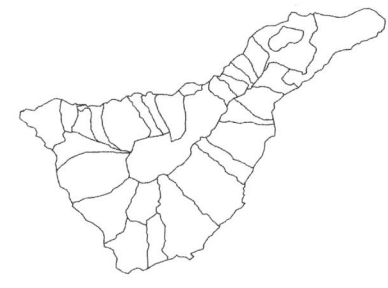

Once the wealthiest town on Tenerife, its deep, natural harbour providing the stepping stone for trade between Europe and the New World, unlucky Garachico has been plagued (literally) by misfortune throughout its history. From fire and flood to pestilence and plagues of locusts the town has seen disaster after disaster. But the one that finally destroyed its wealth was the eruption of 1706 which destroyed the harbour and wiped out 384 neighbourhoods.

Weather

Fanned by sea breezes, the temperature on the coast remains pleasantly warm throughout the year, cooling as you climb higher into the upper reaches of the municipality. Adequate rainfall in winter provides the perfect conditions for the banana plantations you can see covering swathes of coastline and make carrying waterproofs a sensible option when walking. In summer, when the mercury passes 30°, the lava rock pools of El Caletón are a favourite cooling spot with locals.

Flora

The area's history of volcanic eruption may have caused havoc to its buildings but has ensured a lush variety of flora in its mineral-rich, fertile earth. Along coastal stretches you'll find sea lettuce, marine thyme and house leeks; as you climb higher into the hills you'll see clumps of euphorbias, spurges and convulvulus (bindweed). If you were to continue into the upper reaches of the municipality you would find vines and willow before arriving at pine forests.

Call of Nature

There are toilets on Calle Francisco Martínez de Fuentes, tucked in beneath the steps up to the lovely Plaza Libertad where you emerge at the statue of Simon Bolivar and opposite the bandstand café which, incidentally, does nice coffee.

Following the Lava, Garachico to San Juan del Reparo Circular

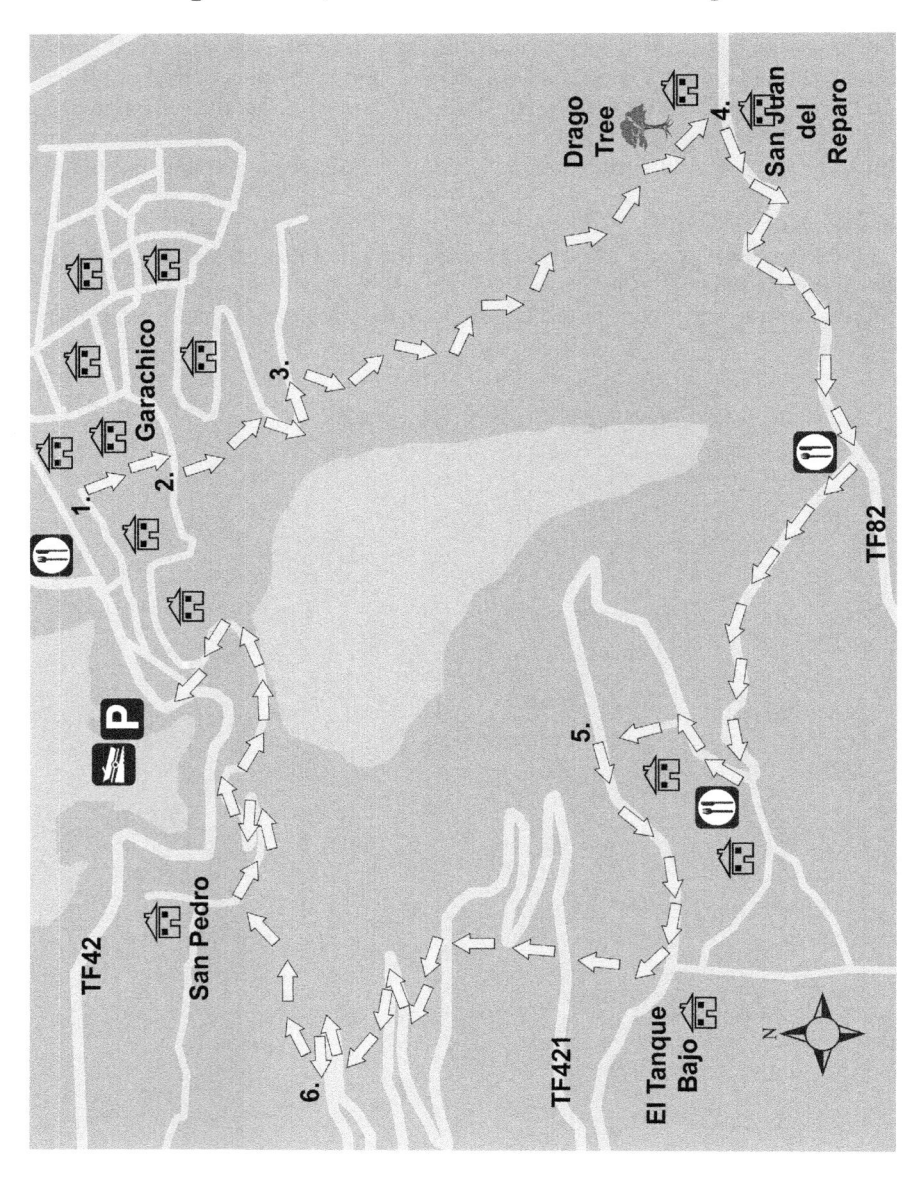

Following the Lava, Garachico to San Juan del Reparo Circular

Location	North west Tenerife.
Circular Route?	No. It's relatively easy to do both ways and finishing in Garachico means a good choice of restaurants.
How Long?	Approx 2hrs return.
How Far?	5.6 kilometres.
Vertiginous?	Although it's a quite steep ascent, there are no vertiginous sections.
Route Difficulty	Level 3 - It's not a long route but it's all uphill which means a decent level of fitness is required, especially in hot weather.
Wow Scenery	Great views over Tenerife's unluckiest town and across the lava streams that ended the town's role as the island's main port and centre of commerce in 1706.
Underfoot	The route follows a merchants' trail which means a decent, if hard, surface most of the way.
Watering Holes	There's a bar in San Juan del Reparo with no signs identifying it as such but there are usually a few locals hanging around outside. Garachico has plenty of cafés and restaurants.
Downside	It's interesting to follow the flow of lava that nearly destroyed a town but San Juan del Reparo is a bit of a non-entity of a place.

This energy-sapping climb above the town gives clear views over one of the frozen lava streams before ambling through the old hill town of San Juan del Reparo and then descending by footpaths rarely used by anyone any more, along the line of the second lava trail, following the ghosts of a never-forgotten nine days in Garachico.

How to Get There

By Car

From Puerto de la Cruz, follow the TF42 to Garachico. From southern resorts take the TF82 through Santiago del Teide and drop down to the coast outside of San Juan del Reparo (winding road) which comes out just outside of Garachico.

Parking

There's parking all along the seafront in Garachico. There are also two car parks; one at the harbour and the other beside the football pitch. The latter has limited spaces as it's also used by coaches.

By Public Transport

Puerto de la Cruz

Take the 363 to Garachico.

Playa de las Américas/Los Cristianos

Take the 460 to Icod de los Vinos where you can catch the 363/107 to Garachico.

Los Gigantes

Jump on the 325 to Icod de los Vinos and then catch the 363/107 as above.

The Route

1. Stepping Out (8 mins)

The route begins behind Garachico's Town Hall, opposite the rose coloured Hotel Quinta Roja in Plaza Libertad. Go down Calle 18 de Julio, the road that runs between the Town Hall and the Casa de Los Gomeros. On the wall on the right hand side is a sign showing Chinyero 12.9k and San Juan del Reparo 2.8k and a noticeboard showing the routes. Continue straight ahead, passing the Casa Los Enanitos (House of the Dwarfs) after 100 metres and continue up the hill where you can see the start of the cobbled path which winds its way up between the banana plantations. Follow the path for 170 metres until you emerge onto the road where there is a small *mirador* (viewpoint) with a picnic table.

2. Upper Garachico (268m/6min)

Across the road, just beyond the mirador, you'll see a path up to the left, signposted towards San Juan del Reparo 2.5km. Follow the path for 300 metres until you emerge onto the wide road. Turn right and walk up the road, past the barrier, until you see the start of the main path which is clearly signposted towards San Juan del Reparo 2km. This is where your big ascent begins and you will ascend 370 metres over a distance of 2km.

3. The Hard Work (800m/20mins)

The path climbs through volcanic debris and twists and turns its way mercilessly uphill with ever expanding views back over Garachico. After 320 metres and 10 minutes of climbing you reach a large pine tree and a barely noticeable path that turns sharp left on itself and runs beneath the branches of the pine tree to a gate. This is the entrance to an old abandoned finca with acres of overgrown terraces and sea views. Watch for the brambles snatching at your ankles if you're going to take a closer look.

Onwards and upwards the path climbs, ascending another 130 metres over a distance of 700 metres until you pass a large crucifix on the left of the path. From here, it's another 137 metres of ascent over 660 metres distance to arrive at the end of the path, on the outskirts of San Juan del Reparo.

Unfortunately, you haven't quite finished punishing those leg muscles yet...

Turn right onto the tarmac and continue to climb for another 330 metres until you can see the glorious crown of a drago tree ahead of you and to the left. Just before you draw level with the drago, turn right along the side street to emerge into San Juan del Reparo on the main road that links Icod de Los Vinos to Santaigo del Teide. Across the road, the church plaza makes a pleasant place to sit and eat lunch while you get the air back into your lungs.

4. San Juan del Reparo (2.8km/1hr 15mins)

From the point at which you emerged onto the road, turn right (left if you've got the church at your back) and walk along the road, passing gardens, allotments and a pretty rockery of lava fronting a cave on left side of the road.

After 620 metres and 10 minutes of road, you reach the large café/restaurant and viewpoint of Mirador de Garachico. Continue straight ahead and follow the road as it curves down to the right following the road sign direction to Tanque bajo on the TF421. Unfortunately, the pavement runs out here and you have to walk on the road itself but it's a relatively quiet road and there is a wide verge for most of the way you'll be on it.

In another 10 minutes you'll pass the restaurant Bar Unión with its proliferation of signs on jolly chefs, and 5 minutes later you'll see a path dropping left off the road where there's a gap in the barrier. The path leads down beside a paddock and above chickens in a yard, to arrive at what looks like a dead end, at someone's garage doors. Right in front of the garage, steps drop down to the right. Follow the steps and continue down, along the concrete path that descends down to the road.

5. Doing the TF Shuffle (4.5km/1hr 50mins)
Turn left and walk along the road for 180 metres, passing a small island of trees in the road with a pretty little fountain in its middle, to reach a paved path that runs down to the right immediately after a mustard coloured house and before you reach the junction where a mosaic sign proclaims that you are now in El Tanque, Casco Histórico (you might want to take a look at the pretty plaza and the church of Santa Ana whose tower you can see directly in front of you, before you continue).

Turn right down the paved path and follow it for 50 metres to a small road. Turn right along the road and follow it all the way to the end where there's a sports stadium. The path continues straight ahead from the left hand corner of the end of the tarmac and winds down to emerge onto the road.

From here the route will take a more direct route down, crossing over the TF421 several times as the road zigzags its way down to Garachico.

Go straight across the road and the path continues down from just beyond the wooden railing on the other side. Follow the path for 300 metres as it descends to meet the TF421 where the road bends to the right, and continues straight ahead, dropping down to the left of Casa Maria before arriving at the road again.

Once again go straight over the TF421 and continue on the path which drops down by a house from the other side of the road on the left and then becomes a pleasant, grassy trail that runs alongside a wooden fence and continues to descend.

Reach the TF421 again and this time, turn right along the road, following it for 280 metres as it bends sharply to the left and then straightens out again and you'll see the path drop down to the right. Views are now right across the coast to the lighthouse of Los Silos in the west and along the north coastline beyond Garachico.

6. Homeward Bound (6km/2hrs 40mins)

Now finally free of the TF421, turn right off the road and follow the path as it makes its final descent back to Garachico, passing an old, stone water trough, slightly raised on the right side of the path, en route, before arriving at a green railing and alongside the church of San Pedro. Turn right onto the road and follow it as it winds down the hill, lined by wonderful eucalyptus trees, to arrive, almost a kilometre later, opposite the harbour in the centre of Garachico where multiple choices of places in which to *'Unlace The Boots'* await.
7.44km/3hrs 15mins

Places to Unlace the Boots

You're spoilt for choice in Garachico. We particularly like the local buzz around the kiosk in Plaza de la Libertad and it's probably the prettiest plaza on Tenerife.

Walks in The North of Tenerife
Coastal Routes

"The past lies heavily in the air along a flower-lined, cobbled camino real that links old haciendas..."

Way Out West, Buenavista del Norte

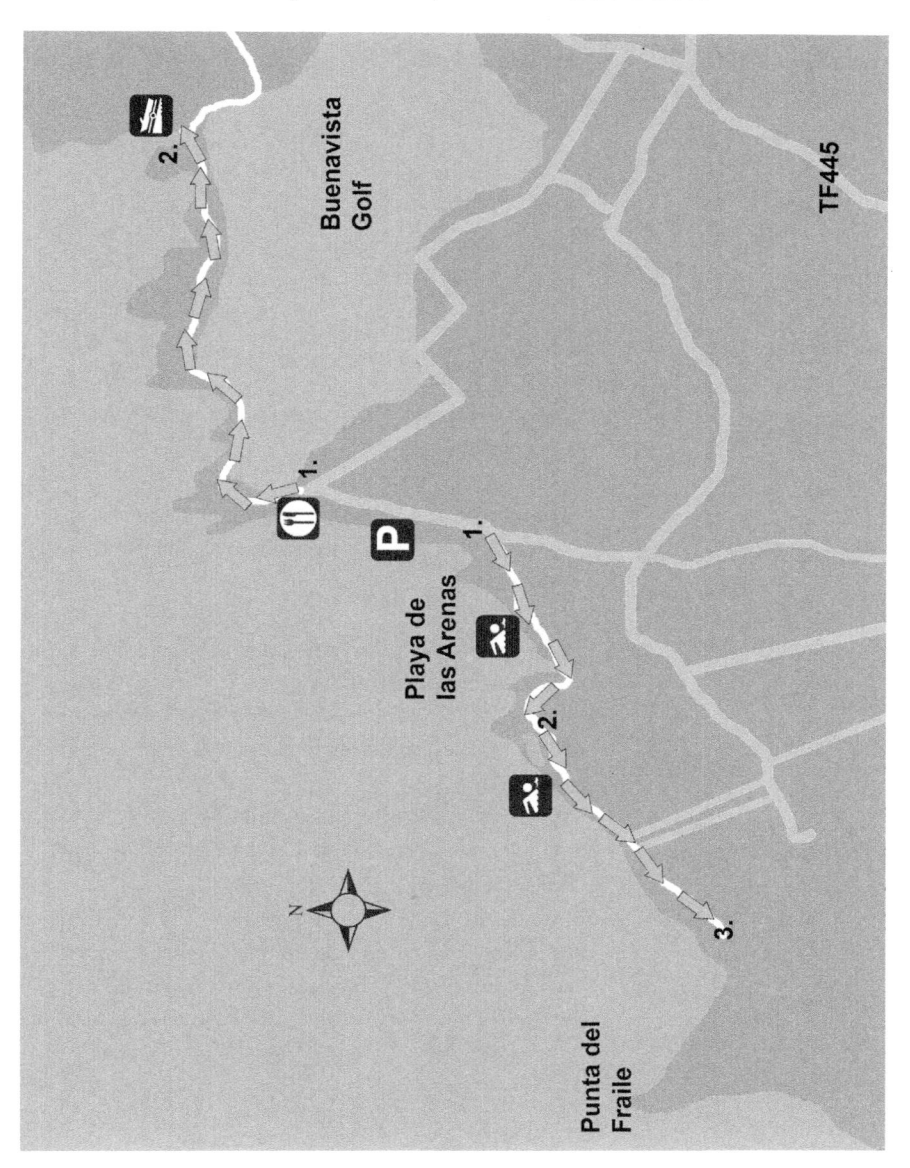

Way Out West, Buenavista del Norte

Location	North west Tenerife.
Circular Route?	No.
How Long?	Approx 50mins
How Far?	5.6 kilometres.
Vertiginous?	No.
Route Difficulty	Level 2 – An easy coastal stroll mostly on the level with a few undulations.
Wow Scenery	Wonderful views of the Teno Massif plunging into the Atlantic as well as a rocky coastline peppered with large rock pools.
Underfoot	A well made and clear coastal path gently meanders along the coast at times dissecting the rocky coastline from the wild mountainous interior and at others from the immaculate greens of Buenavista Golf Course.
Watering Holes	Apart from a little kiosk beside the beach there is the most wonderful restaurant with a terrace draped with fishing nets.
Downside	There aren't any downsides to this walk apart from it being a 'there and back again' route. A downside could be getting hit by a wayward golf ball on one section. But you'd have to be really unlucky for that to happen.

A charming coastal walk that is far from the madding crowd as it's situated in Isla Baja where North Tenerife meets West Tenerife.

The route starts at Playa de las Arenas (the beach beside the Buenavista del Norte golf course; not to be confused with the resort of the similar name on the south west coast). There's plenty of parking behind the beach.

From the beach there are two paths to follow; neither is very long so it doesn't take long to complete both.

How to Get There

By Car
Take the TF445 through Buenavista del Norte and follow the turn off for the golf course. At the roundabout you have two choices. Either take the road toward the golf course, passing the entrance and following it all the way to the coast where there's parking beside the beach of Playa de las Arenas. Alternatively, after the roundabout stay on the Camino el Rincón heading west and after another kilometre take the road heading right to reach Playa de las Arenas and the start of the routes.

Parking
There's plenty of free parking at Playa de las Arenas. The only time it is likely to be busy is during the summer months.

By Public Transport
No matter which route you take, it will involve a walk from Buenavista del Norte to Playa de las Arenas.

Puerto de la Cruz
Take the 363 to Buenavista del Norte.

Playa de las Américas/Los Cristianos
Take the 460 to Icod de los Vinos where you can catch the 363/107 to Buenavista del Norte

Los Gigantes
There's no easy way, but the best route is to take the 325 to Icod de los Vinos and change to the 107 or 363 to Buenavista del Norte.

The Route

1. Stepping Out
The first section starts at the small wooden bridge on the west side of the beach and leads away from the beach along a coastal path toward the Teno Massif, rising dramatically above Isla Baja. The narrow pinnacle on the cliffs ahead is the Mirador de la Monja (the nun's lookout) overlooking, appropriately enough, Playa de El Fraile (the monk's beach) at the end of the path.

The path is broken up by secret paths leading to hidden coves, viewing platforms and rock pools bigger than the famed ones at Garachico. It's a smart move to take a swimming costume on this walk. On blistering hot days, the cool calm waters of these beautiful pools are too inviting to resist.

2. First leg return (1.5km/25mins)
The path comes to a dead end at the Monk's beach where there are convenient benches to sit and enjoy the spectacular cliffs and the Atlantic rollers pounding the beach. In winter, the very last section can be blocked off due to the danger from rockfalls.

Simply turn around and retrace your steps back to the car parking spaces alongside the beach. Follow the pavement along behind the car park spaces all the way to its end at the small roundabout with the El Burgado restaurant on the left. To the right you will see the Municipal Swimming Pool and in between it and El Burgado, a path running towards the coast. This is the start of the easterly section.

3. Heading east (3.3km/55mins)

The path east towards Buenavista del Norte is, if anything, even better. The rocky coastline is characterised by volcanic rock formations on one side and the perfectly manicured greens of the golf course on the other. The man and nature combination compliment each other perfectly along this route. The sea in many places is an artist's palette of azure, cyan and turquoise at the same time. A short distance along the route is an infinity pool built into the cliffs, now sadly empty and unused.

4. The fishermen's beach & homeward bound (3.1km/1hr 20mins)

Continue onwards to the end of the path and down the steep ramp that leads to sea level where, concealed in the cliffs below a small ermita (chapel), you'll discover a fishermen's cove which conjures up romantic notions of a smuggler's den – it's a tranquil spot for a bit of al fresco lunch. From here, simply retrace your steps back to the car parking spaces behind the beach.
6km/1hr 45min

Places to Unlace the Boots

El Burgado (open daily) beside Playa de las Arenas is a castaway's dream of a restaurant as far as looks and location goes. Prices are a bit higher than in traditional towns, but it does look special.

Taste of the Caribbean, Rambla Del Castro

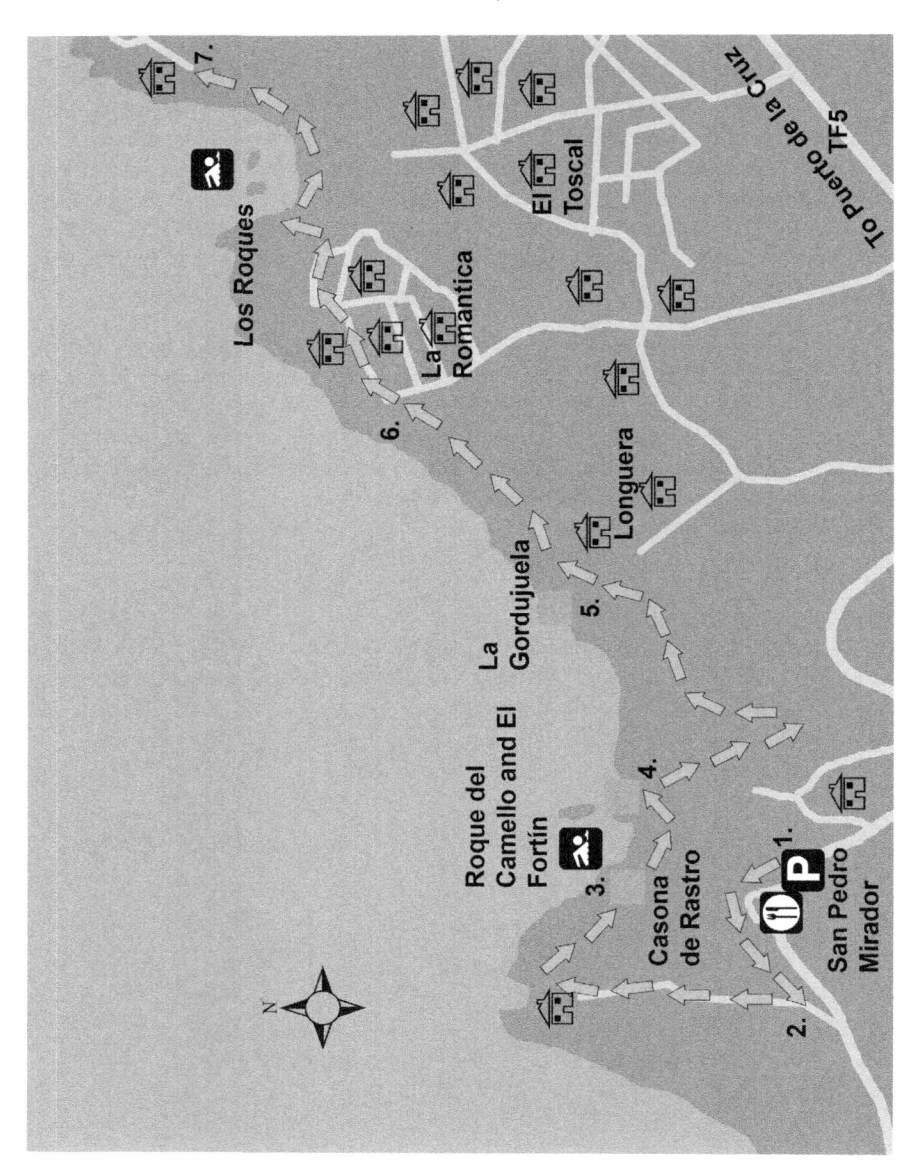

Taste of the Caribbean, Rambla Del Castro

Location	North west Tenerife.
Circular Route?	No.
How Long?	Approx 1 hour (one way).
How Far?	5 kilometres (one way).
Vertiginous?	No.
Route Difficulty	Level 2 – A relatively easy coastal stroll mostly on the level but with a few undulations and a quite steep ascent.
Wow Scenery	This part of Tenerife's coastline is probably as about as good as it gets; dramatic and mostly unspoilt.
Underfoot	Cobbled paths, cliff top dirt trails and rural roads through banana plantations. Variety is the name of the game with palm groves to ravines to paths behind hidden bays and a section through a housing development.
Watering Holes	There's a restaurant and a kiosk at San Pedro. Both boast some of the best views in the area.
Downside	The housing development at Romántica is a bit of a blot on what would otherwise be the perfect coastal walk.

Miradors; banana plantations; palm groves; a rock which looks like an animal; a tiny fort; hidden coves and rickety haciendas oozing history and character. The Rambla del Castro is a coastal path into Tenerife's past.

How to Get There

By Car
The route starts at the San Pedro Mirador which is right beside the TF5 just outside Puerto de la Cruz in the direction of Icod de los Vinos.

Parking
There's a small car park and also parking along the lay by that passes the San Pedro restaurant.

By Public Transport
If based in Puerto de la Cruz, the easiest way to access the route is to simply walk from the town to the Hotel Maritimo beyond Punta Brava. The route can start, or end at the point.

Puerto de la Cruz
Take the 363 to Buenavista del Norte and get off at the San Agustin stop near the San Pedro Mirador.

Playa de las Américas/Los Cristianos
The quickest route is take the 343 to Puerto de la Cruz and change to the 363 for Buenavista del Norte, getting off at the San Agustin stop near the San Pedro Mirador.

Los Gigantes
Take the 325 and get off at the San Agustin stop near the San Pedro Mirador (just before you reach the outskirts of Puerto de la Cruz).

There are a couple of ways to begin this route. One is from a path behind the Hotel Marítimo in Punta Brava, Puerto de la Cruz, but in our view the better option is to begin at the San Pedro Mirador on the road between Puerto de la Cruz and Icod de los Vinos.

The Route

If you want to start the route in Punta Brava, follow the coastal road to the end of the bay where you'll see the unmissable blue towers of the Hotel Marítimo where the road swings left around the mouth of the bay. Turn right along Camino Burgado that runs along the right side of the Hotel, passing the reception and then the residencia on the right and continue all the way to the end of the road (300 metres and around 5mins walking) at the bottom of the car park. In the right hand corner of the cul de sac you'll see the path dropping down towards the distinctive rocks of Los Roques. Follow the route in reverse from there.

1. Stepping out from Mirador de San Pedro

There are two cobbled paths that descend from below the mirador; take the one which passes the small chapel and follow it to the left above the banana plantations, ignoring the turn off to the right after 130 metres, for 600 metres until it emerges at a tarmac road. Head downwards in the direction of the coast. The road meanders for 370 metres, passing a run down hacienda, banana plantations and a quiet housing estate, to arrive at the coast.

At the coast, follow the path to the right, through the mini tunnel, as it winds above coves before heading slightly inland. This area acts as an 'unofficial' launch point for paragliders and occasionally walkers can experience a 'James Bond' moment as a paraglider suspended below a brightly coloured canopy appears directly in front of them as if from nowhere.

2. To the hacienda and beyond (1.4km/25mins)
Shortly before a series of white buildings, a barely discernible path leads off to the left and crosses a rickety plank to emerge in front of the ochre coloured Casona de Rastro. If you miss the turn you'll find yourself at an old stone communal washing area where the path heads up the hill back to the San Pedro Mirador. Back track to find the path you should have taken.

From La Casona, follow signs to Los Roques (you'll follow these the whole way to Punta Brava). The path crosses a wooden bridge and then paths veer off in a number of directions through a palm grove. It's worth taking time out to explore. Follow signs to El Fortín for good views of Roque de Camello (shouldn't take a genius to figure out what sort of animal it looks like) and the path to the little fort of San Fernando whose cannon still point to the horizon in case any scurrilous sea dogs attempt a surprise attack. Sometimes the fort is off bounds due to rock fall.

Rejoin the main path and continue following signs to Los Roques. A path to the left descends to La Fajana beach where low tunnels (with a reputation for gashing heads open) lead through the rocks to other coves. Another path in the direction of San Pedro Mirador, leads you back through Indian bay trees to your starting point – take this route on your return if you're doing the path both ways.

The main path descends into the barranco and up again before emerging onto a wide concrete path where you turn left and follow the path as it sweeps down, passing a small Ermita, with views to the modern housing development of La Romántica. Look down over the cliff to an old ruin whose interior has been turned into a graffiti artist's gallery. It's an odd looking curio and is in fact the building which housed 'La Gordejuela Water Elevator' the first steam engine on Tenerife.

3. Bridge and barranco (3km/1hr)
The path crosses a new wooden bridge and climbs out the other side to emerge into the bland streets of La Romántica. At the road, turn left and follow the road as it runs parallel to the coastline, continuing straight ahead all the way until you reach the white walls of Casa Jngs Martina on the right and you'll see where the path drops down to the left opposite, following in the direction of Los Roques.

4. Los Roques beach(4.5km/1hr 20mins)
　　The final leg takes you to a charming bay in the centre of which two distinctive rocks of Los Roques jut out from the sea. A path leads down to the beach of Los Roques if you feel like getting some swimming or sunbathing in before continuing out the other side on the path which arrives at the Hotel Marítimo and the end of the road.
5km/1hr 30mins

Places to Unlace the Boots
　　The Restaurant Mirador de San Pedro (open daily) sits in a peach of a position overlooking the north west coast. It's ideal for a drink, snack or full blown hearty Canarian meal. Even the Tenerife version of a truckers' stop, a burger van in the car park, is a pleasant spot to sit and have a drink.

A Merchant's Highway, Las Aguas

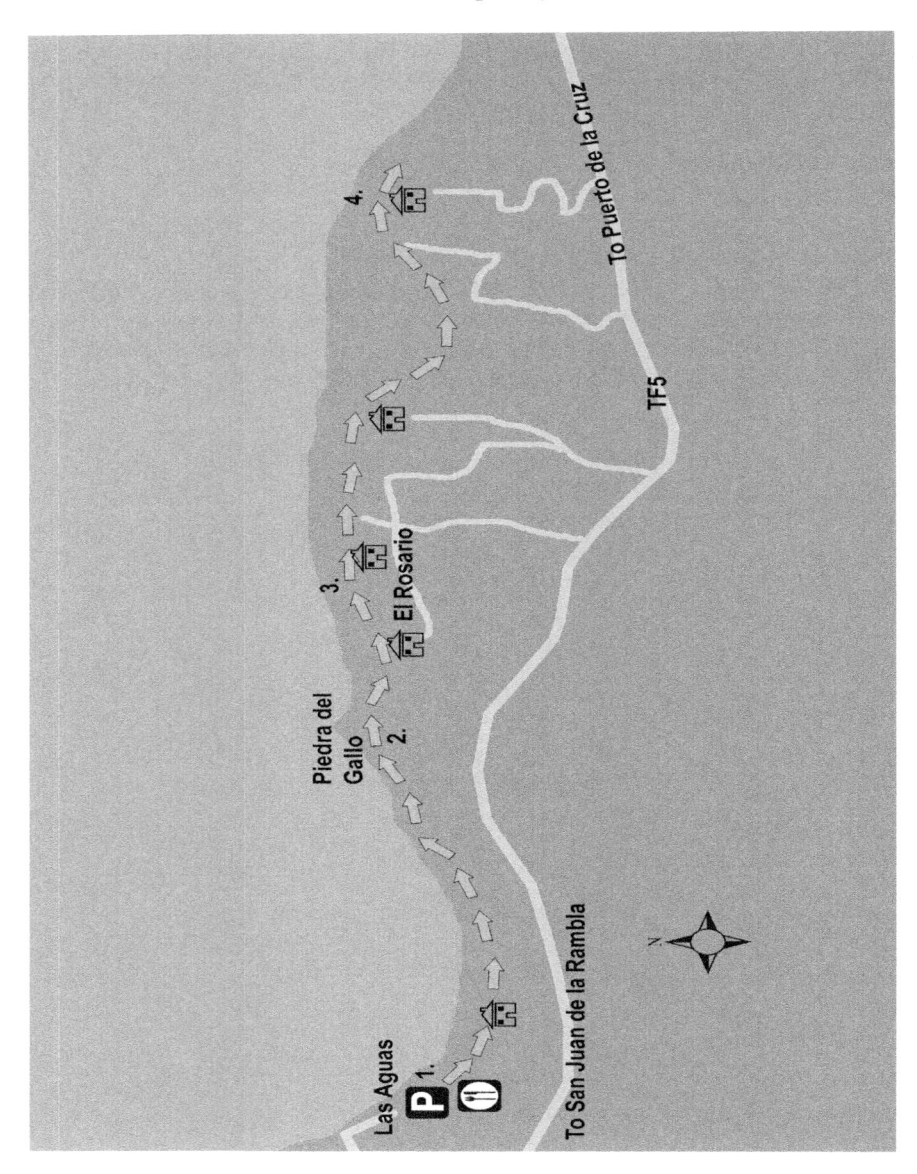

A Merchant's Highway, Las Aguas

Location	North west Tenerife.
Circular Route?	No.
How Long?	Approx 1 hour 30mins (one way).
How Far?	5 kilometres (one way).
Vertiginous?	Although the path winds along the coast above the sea, it isn't vertiginous.
Route Difficulty	Level 2 – A relatively flat path with a few ups and downs but within most people's ability.
Wow Scenery	Great views of the North West coast are a constant companion.
Underfoot	Mostly a dirt track and cobbled merchant trail across the cliff tops. The coastal path winds above the cliffs as it meanders past old mansions and a 'hidden' hamlet along an old trading route.
Watering Holes	Restaurants at Las Aguas are excellent and draw locals from miles around to try their speciality dishes.
Downside	The merchants' trail is slightly eroded at the northern end, but this is only a minor point.

This is another coastal, old merchants' trail which is still relatively unknown, especially as there aren't any signposts pointing the way.

How to Get There

By Car
Take the San Juan de la Rambla exit from the TF5 between Puerto de la Cruz and Icod de los Vinos and then the Las Aguas road to reach the coast and the start of the route.

Parking
There are plenty of parking spaces near the start of the route at Las Aguas

By Public Transport

Puerto de la Cruz
Take the 363 to Buenavista del Norte and get off at the San Juan de la Rambla stop.

Playa de las Américas/Los Cristianos
The quickest route is take the 343 to Puerto de la Cruz and change to the 363 for Buenavista del Norte, getting off at the San Juan de la Rambla stop.

Los Gigantes
The 325 to Puerto de la Cruz passes San Juan de la Rambla but officially doesn't stop there. The nearest stop is at El Cubo, about 400m outside of the town.

The Route

1. Stepping out
From the swimming pool at Las Aguas, below San Juan de la Rambla, the route leads past the left of La Escuela restaurant (the former schoolhouse) and follows the cobbled path along the cliff top where there are commanding views back over Las Aguas and the small bay where in summer months, local kids frolic in the azure waters and divers in wetsuits emerge from the sea with harpoons and strings of fish.

All along the way are the most delightful old houses with lopsided doors and windows and enticing alleys leading to open courtyards whilst nature provides an explosion of colour in the shape of vivid strelitzias and profusions of angels trumpets (datura). It looks like the most perfect place to live...until you realise that, without any road access, even getting the shopping home involves a bit of a trek.

Buildings along the trail are unique and built to accommodate the landscape. One old house is triangular in shape while another, the 'Piedra del Gallo' (Cock's Rock – nothing to do with Priscilla, Queen of the Desert) is built into the rock face.

2. El Rosario (1km/20mins)
Just when you think you've overdosed on quaint charm, you arrive at the hamlet of El Rosario. To say this place has been lost in the mists of time is a bit of an understatement. The main (only) street is a narrow cobbled affair which slopes toward the centre between immaculate, whitewashed buildings. It feels as though it belongs in an old literary classic; Jamaica Inn perhaps.

Unfortunately there isn't actually an inn which is a bit of a shame; the place is crying out for a creaky wooden sign swaying in the breeze. There's a pleasant little square beside the quaint church where you can sit under the shade of the pepper trees.

The path continues beyond the hamlet (look out for the old wooden gate which has an entrance for both cats and mice carved at the bottom) before descending to a pebbly bay and a valley floor full of terraces.

3. The beach (2km/40mins)

From the beach, the path continues quite steeply up the other side of the barranco, passing more old houses as it levels out before descending once again to a pebble beach with a volcanic rock with unusual, organ-like columns. From here, turn around and retrace your steps back to Las Aguas.
5km/1hr 30mins

Places to Unlace the Boots

Las Aguas has a reputation for good seafood and *arroces* (rice dishes not to be confused with paella). Two crackers right at the start of the route are La Escuela (a good place to try parrot fish) and Restaurant Las Aguas whose *arroces* attract people from all over. Las Aguas is open for lunch every day but closes Sunday-Tuesday evenings.

Walking in the Guimar Valley

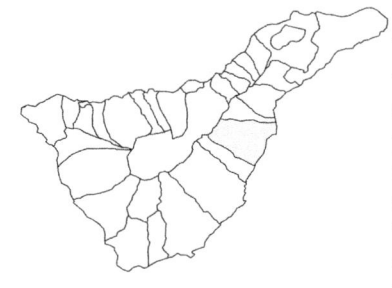

The east coast is still probably one of the least explored by visitors to Tenerife and yet the Malpaís, or badlands, around Güímar is a sacred place to islanders, as this was the place where the Virgin of Candelaria, first made her appearance. The Atlantic currents sweep down Tenerife's eastern coast and wash onto the shores around Guimar, depositing much of the Ocean's flotsam in their wake. One such piece of early wreckage must have been the masthead off a ship or a statue and from this discovery, the islanders began their worship of the Black Madonna who has remained the Patron Saint of the Canary Islands to this day.

Created by the same humongous landslip from the island's spine that created the mirror La Orotava Valley on the north west face, Güímar Valley is La Orotava's antithesis in terms of landscape, weather and flora. The Guimar Valley terrain morphs from alpine pine forests that fall away from the spine of the island, to malpaís, or badlands created by some of Tenerife's most recent volcanic activity which has left the east coast covered in black, solidified lava.

Weather

Nestling in the eastern slopes, dry and breezy is the default setting for Guimar. Walking on the coast here affords little shelter from the sun's rays which, coupled with sea breezes, can create the ideal conditions for getting sunburnt without realising it. Plenty of sunscreen and a hat, preferable one that can be secured in a strong breeze, are the order of the day. As the terrain is mostly rocky and volcanic, thick, sturdy soles are also recommended.

Flora

This may look like a barren land but in fact the Güímar malpaís has 150 species of flora which support 100 types of insect and 60 types of butterfly. Hugging the shoreline alongside a rocky shore are endless clumps of sea heath and intense green sea lettuce. Moving further inland, the terrain is home to spectacular clumps of cardón and tabaibas (euphorbias), some of the best examples on the island, whose branches accommodate endless lizards darting around in the dust. In spring and summer they are joined by hosts of golden hair grass and common Canary grass.

Where To Stay When Walking in the Guimar Valley

Hotel Rural Finca Salamanca

Sugar cane, cotton, coffee, tobacco and bananas have all played a key part in the 150 year life of the Finca Salamanca that nestles in its own botanical gardens in the Guimar Valley. Today, it's avocado trees that dominate the estate surrounding this Mexican hacienda style hotel. Sun dappled trails meander through endless gardens of endemic plants and sub tropical foliage beneath the gaze of the Izaña Mountains. Chunky, Mexican furniture, oodles of floor space, a lovely restaurant in the former tobacco drying shed and more personality than a chat show host, Finca Salamanca has guests returning year after year. [Budget] *Carretera Guimar-Puertito 2, Güímar; (+34) 922 51 45 30;* www.hotel-fincasalamanca.com

The Virgin's Badlands – The Güímar Malpaís

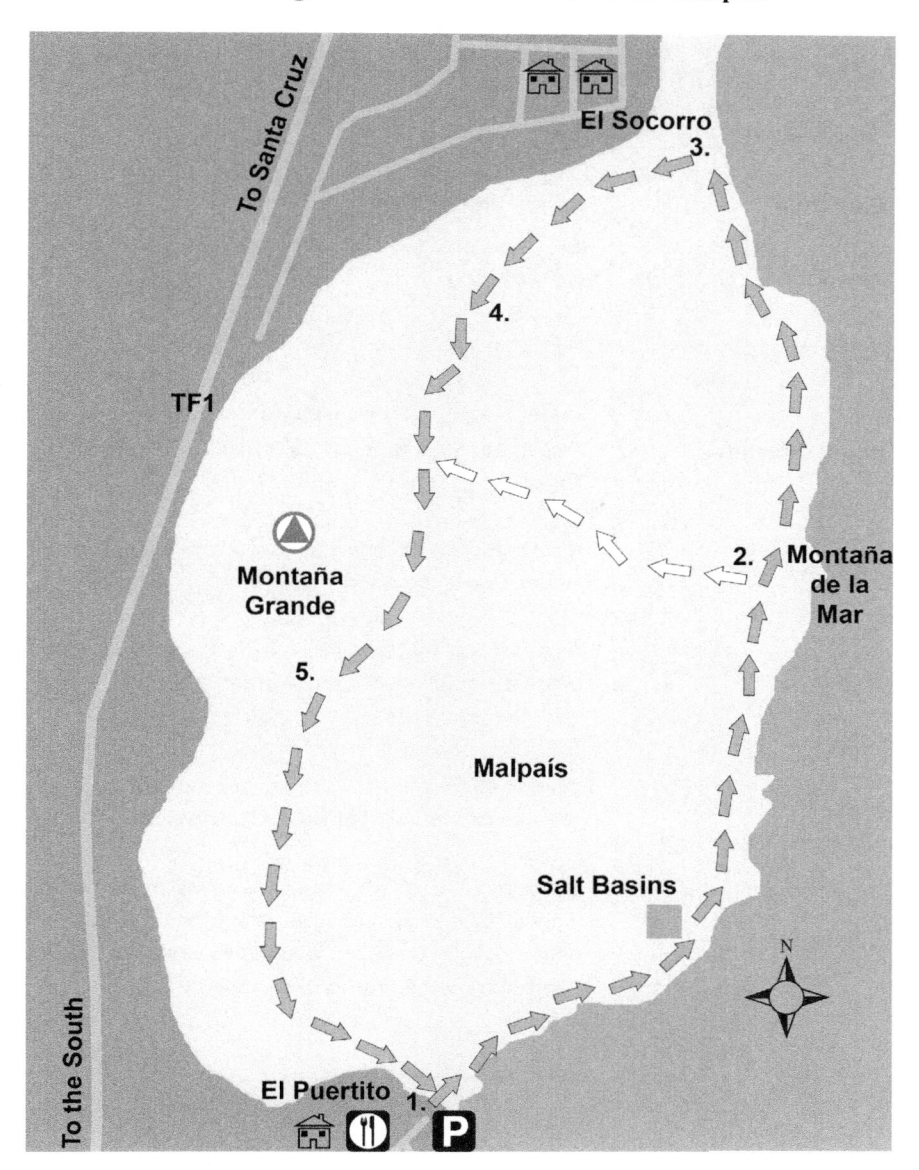

The Virgin's Badlands – The Güímar Malpaís

Location	East Tenerife.
Circular Route?	Yes.
How Long?	Approx 1 hour 50mins.
How Far?	6.2 kilometres.
Vertiginous?	No.
Route Difficulty	Level 2 – A relatively flat path with a couple of steepish ascents but nothing beyond any relatively fit person's ability.
Wow Scenery	No standout WOW moments, just a fascinating landscape and lots of interesting curios.
Underfoot	A coastal path that traverses lava fields, pebble beaches, volcanic cones and a cardón forest. Sections on volcanic rock can be hard underfoot.
Watering Holes	Puertito de Güímar has a handful of great little restaurants overlooking the harbour area.
Downside	This part of the coast is a magnet for flotsam and jetsam dumped by the sea. It can give parts of the shoreline an untidy look. On the other hand there can be some really interesting objects littering the Malpaís.

How to Get There

By Car
From the TF1 take salida 11, signposted Puertito de Güímar to reach the centre of the town.

Parking
It's not a big town, so nowhere is too far from the start of the route. There is a small car park right beside the entrance to the malpaís but we tend to park in the quiet residential streets immediately to the south west of the harbour.

By Public Transport

Puerto de la Cruz
Take the 102/103 to Santa Cruz where you can catch the 120 which will take you to Puertito de Güímar.

Playa de las Américas/Los Cristianos
Take the 111 Santa Cruz bus to the Güímar stop on the TF1 and then either catch the 120 or walk to El Puertito.

Los Gigantes
It's another awkward one by public transport involving the 477 to Los Cristianos, changing to the 111 and then, as above, either catch the 120 or walk to El Puertito.

The Route

1. Stepping out
Puertito de Güímar is the best place to start any walks in the Malpaís. Head east past the harbour to the edge of the town and down Calle Marques de Santa Cruz to find the clearly marked path and an information board which is where the route begins. There is parking next to the start of the path which meanders through a harsh volcanic landscape.

It might not be the prettiest of walks on Tenerife, but it is full of curios. Almost the first sight which greets walkers is a small fishermen's shanty town built into an old military emplacement. Fishing nets and geraniums in painted tin pots have replaced soldiers and guns.

The path clings to the coastline, crossing volcanic fields where the coiled rope appearance of pahoehoe lava is commonplace and the sight of small patches of gold sand amongst the basaltic black is unexpected. Almost a kilometre and 15mins into the route, rectangular salt flats show that humans also found that these badlands had their uses.

At places the shoreline looks positively scruffy; the sea's currents have conspired to make this stretch of the coast a dumping point. But even this is of interest; every bleached oar, mast, coconut shell littering the shoreline has a story and provides a clue, if you were being scientific about this, as to why the image of the Virgen de Candelaria made her appearance here.

A poignant white monument acts as reminder that it isn't just inanimate objects which end up as victims of the sea's fury.

Stay left at the small fork as the path ascends to its highest point at Montaña de la Mar, a slightly grand title given that it is only twenty seven metres high.

2. Montaña de la Mar (2km/40mins)

As you level out after descending from Montaña de la Mar, a path cuts back into the volcanic cones known as the 'Morras del Corcho'. The path straight ahead continues along the coast to El Socorro an unremarkable hamlet aside from the fact that this is the spot where the Virgin de Candelaria appeared to Guanche shepherds and where a re-enactment of the event is held each year in September.

Turn left following the direction of Montaña Grande and follow the path as it weaves through the Morras del Corcho. After 1km and 15mins, turn left with the main path as it turns sharply at an indistinct T junction, now walking with the coat at your back for another 300 metres and 5 minutes to arrive at a clear TJ with another directional post.

3. Homeward bound (3.3km/1hr)

Turn left following the direction back to El Puertito. In 5mins and 200metres you'll reach a further post, continue straight ahead in the direction of El Puertito. The path is now traversing great swathes of euphorbias, including some of the finest examples to be found on the island. Information boards along the path explain how the spurges and their communities survive.

In another 20mins and 1.3km stay left at the small fork. You can see that the path to the right takes you back into El Puertito but keep left to finish back at the information board where you started 5mins later.
5.85km/1hr 40mins

Places to Unlace the Boots

El Puertito is good for trying some local fish dishes. Even if you don't eat, Chibusque (closed Tuesday) and La Charcada at the harbour are good for sitting with a drink enjoying the sea air and life in a small coastal town.

Walks in The South of Tenerife
Adeje

"... At each turn we could see a few fig trees, their spreading branches, of bright green foliage, affording a welcome relief to the eye..." **Olivia M. Stone 1887**

Walking in Adeje

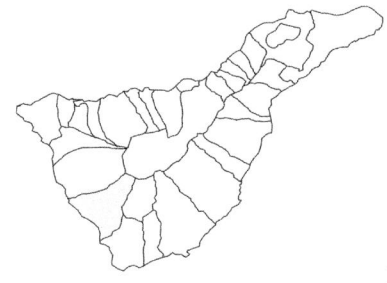

Away from the irrigated hotel gardens and golf courses of Adeje's busy tourist developments that line its vast coastline all the way from Playa de Las Americas in the south to Playa San Juan in the west, Adeje's landscape is arid and dusty, carved by deep barrancos and pockmarked by volcanic cones. But its proximity to Tenerife's main resorts make it a popular choice for walkers who don't want to rent a car. To escape the crowds, head into the hills to the little hamlet of Ifonche and you'll find a world a million miles away from the one you left on the coast. It's a devil of a place to get to by public transport and a car is definitely recommended.

Weather

Hot and dry is the default setting for the south of Tenerife but because of the mountainous interior, clouds quickly bank up as soon as you move away from the coastline and you're just as likely to find yourself walking in warm and cloudy weather than hot and sunny. In the many years we have been visiting the town of Adeje itself, we can probably count on the fingers of one hand the number of times we've seen it not cloudy. Rainfall tends to be infrequent but it's not unknown, especially in winter, and when the cloud descends it can feel quite cool and damp.

Flora

Although the region is predominantly arid, there is a surprising amount of flora to be found. The slopes of the Adeje Mountains are carpeted predominantly in spurges, heather, broom and cistus. Fed by a stream, the Barranco del Infierno becomes quite lush the further into it you progress, with chestnut trees, wild juniper and Canarian palm trees joining the profusion of euphorbias and aeoniums thriving along the banks. In the upper reaches of the barrancos, abandoned agricultural terraces give way to laurel, wax myrtle, tree heath and, from 700 metres above sea level, to pine forests where the air is scented by curry plants.

Call of Nature

I'm afraid it's down to Restaurant Dornejo in Ifonche; Restaurant Otelo in Adeje and the great outdoors for everything in between on these routes.

Eat me

Crispy *pollo al ajillo* (garlic chicken) is the finger licking speciality of the Adeje area. Opinion is split between the best restaurant to try some – Otelo or Oasis – it's no hardship trying both places to decide for yourself.

Where To Stay When Walking in Adeje

The Barranco del Infierno, reopened after many years of closure while politicians argued about collective liability in the event of accidents to walkers using it, is the most popular walk on the island due to its proximity to the resorts of Costa Adeje and Playa de Las Américas. For that reason, when it comes to where to base yourself if you plan to walk it, the brochure's your oyster.

But for walking Above Barranco del Infierno and Ifonche to the Deserted Village, Vilaflor is just a 15 minute drive and a 20 minute bus ride away. See Where To Stay When Walking in Teide National Park and Vilaflor (page 218).

Avoiding Hell's Crowds, Above Barranco Del Infierno

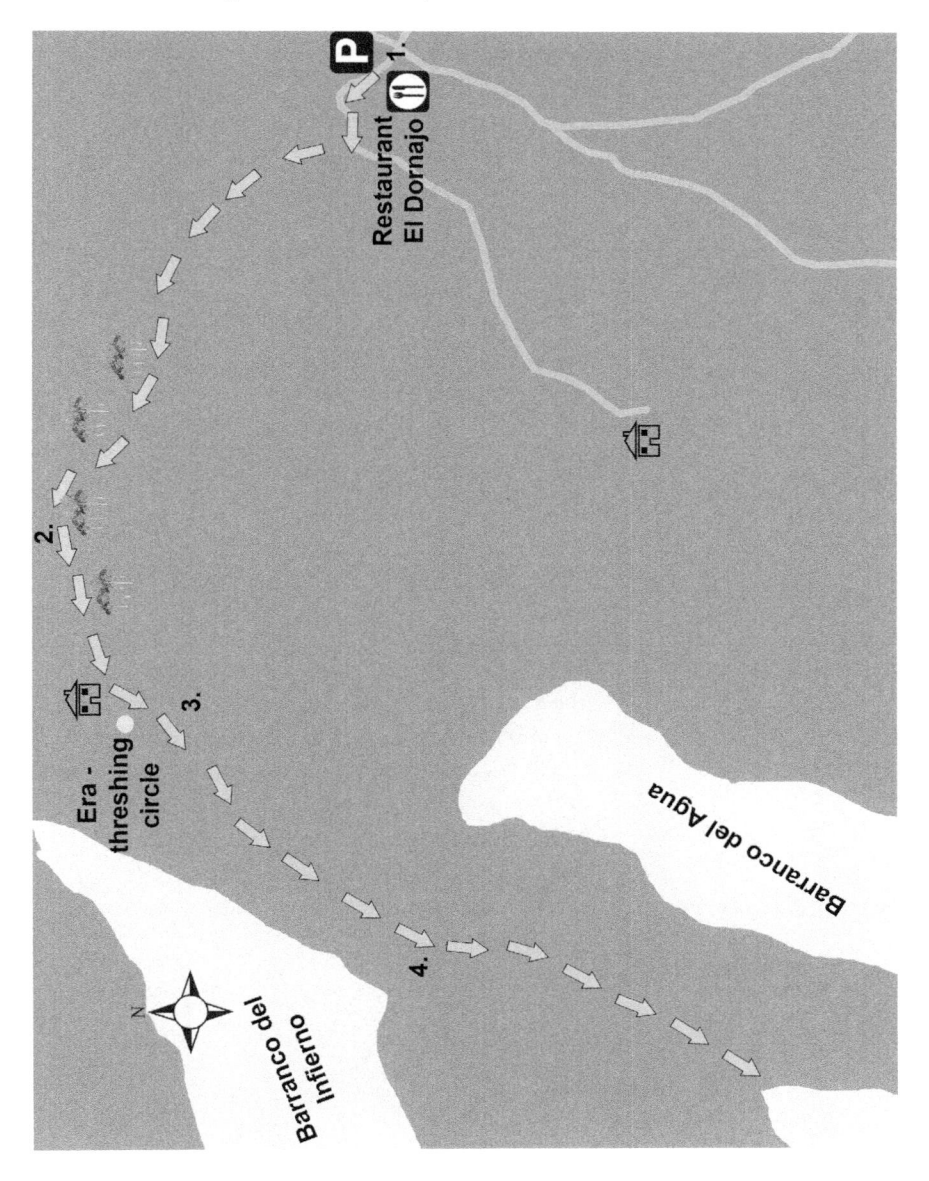

Avoiding Hell's Crowds, Above Barranco Del Infierno

Location	South Tenerife.
Circular Route?	No. But as this is a short route doing it both ways doesn't feel overly repetitive.
How Long?	Approx 2 hours (return).
How Far?	4.5 kilometres (return).
Vertiginous	Yes. The path runs along the side of deep ravines and is narrow in places.
Route Difficulty	Level 2 – There are ascents and descents but this is a short route.
Wow Scenery	Incredible contrasts from the vantage point of one of the island's oldest landscapes to its newest at the southern resorts.
Underfoot	The route begins amongst agricultural land and pine forest becoming more arid as the route progresses. The path is relatively clear most of the way, but it is narrow in parts. Okay for goats, but size twelves need to be a bit more careful.
Watering Holes	There are some great little rural bars around Ifonche.
Downside	Parts of the path have eroded over time which stops the route prematurely.

Barranco del Infierno may be Tenerife's most popular walk, but as it's so close to the popular southern resorts, it's something of a hiker's motorway. It's a very different scene high above the Adeje coast where the upper reaches of the barranco are virtually bereft of walkers and chock-full of scenic views. An ancient camino real once joined the farming community of Ifonche with Adeje. Today sadly much of that path is eroded and progress is halted when precipitous gives way to non-existent. A new trail has taken its place but a short section of the old one still provides you with stunning scenery.

How to Get There

By Car
From the south take the TF51 Mount Teide road to La Escalona. The turn off for Ifonche is immediately before the small town. From the north, the scenic route through Teide National Park to join the TF51 heading south is probably as good as any, following the Ifonche turn off immediately after La Escalona

Parking
There are a few spaces opposite Restaurant El Dornajo and more rough, off road spaces near the start of the route.

By Public Transport

Puerto de la Cruz
Seriously, hire a car. Otherwise take the 343 to Los Cristianos and then as below. But it would require a lot of planning and luck as the services between Los Cristianos are so infrequent.

Playa de las Américas/Los Cristianos
The 342 (Mount Teide bus) and 474/482 to Vilaflor both pass La Escalona (the closest bus stop). They aren't frequent and it's still a bit of a trek to Ifonche.

Los Gigantes
From the Los Gigantes area take the 477 to Los Cristianos and then catch the 342 or 474/482 (see above).

Places to Unlace the Boots
Restaurant El Dornajo (closed Thursday) at the Ifonche crossroads is well placed for refreshments. Tasca Taguara (open daily) further along the road as it's got such a laid back feel that you don't feel as though you're making the place untidy when you slip off the hiking boots.

The Route

1. Stepping Out

Follow the road that drops down the hill from the Restaurant El Dornajo, directly opposite the road coming from the TF51, and in 100 metres, turn right onto the red path following the sign for Adeje 9.8km and the yellow & white striped waymark. In 80 metres, at the small fork, bear left across the rocks following the yellow & white waymarks for 300 metres to reach a wider pista, cross straight over and continue along the path marked with a yellow & white waymark, heading towards the white house in the distance. In another 300 metres, stay right at the small junction, following yellow & white waymarks. Walking past abandoned terraces and sparse pine forest, the scenery is almost heath-like and moody with yellow broom adding a spasmodic splash to the brown earth and green pines while the outline of La Gomera shimmers on the horizon.

2. To the Viewpoint (800 metres /25mins)

The path reaches a crossroads where a flat stone points left to 'La Vista'. Follow the sign and turn left, ignoring the yellow & white X, and follow the path for 150 metres until it reaches a small T junction with a private house on the right hand side. Turn left along the ridge and breathe in the intoxicating aroma of curry plants as you pass by an old threshing circle. On the coast below you can see the hotels of Playa Paraíso while inland, the winding path of Barranco del Infierno disappears between the steep walls of the cliffs, its hikers the size of ants. Continue past a small concrete marker towards the pine trees until you reach a small fork where you stay right following the white directional arrows and a small rock cairn.

3. Cliff Top Trail (1.3km /30mins)

Take the path which drops down to the right and take care with your footing, particularly if it's wet. The path is very narrow in places and crumbly at the edges so don't get too caught up in the views to watch where you're going. 60 metres onto this path you pass through the remains of a gate and brush past spurges and tabaibas. To the right the barranco plunges down the ravine while to your left the cliffs tower above, scarred by erosion and marbled with ruddy seams. Finally you emerge at some wonderful wind–eroded pumice rock formations where you might spot a Troll's face or a skull in the rock shapes (easier to see on the return).

4. As Far as You Can Get (1.8km /45mins)

The path takes you to a clearing on a spur between two barrancos and the path bears slightly left. Stay right and straight ahead across the pumice rocks to where a narrow path runs along the face of the ravine towards the coast. Just 40 metres further the path forks almost imperceptibly and you can miss it if you're not careful.

A green and white cross on a rock shows the path which climbs to the right to be the wrong way. Take the lower path to the left and carefully continue around the cliff face, climbing along a section of fat, old water pipe after 190 metres, until you reach a rocky spur which leads to a pointing pinnacle and expansive views over the south coast. Spread out below you are the five star developments of Costa Adeje all the way round to Puerto Colón. Standing here gives you a God's eye view of the volcanic, arid landscape that has been punctuated by expansive development and the occasional green rug of a golf course here and a banana plantation there. You're standing in the old south, surveying the new south which has taken less than 40 years to change from the landscape you see around you to what you see below.

The path continues to skirt the barranco somewhat precariously until even Lara Croft would be foolish to go further. 120 metres after the rocky spur, at an outcrop with a round boulder that looks as if it's waiting for some giant Ronaldo to boot it down to the coast, the path has finally eroded entirely and it's time to turn around and re-trace steps back to Ifonche.
4.5km /2hrs

Lift Off to the Deserted Valley, Ifonche

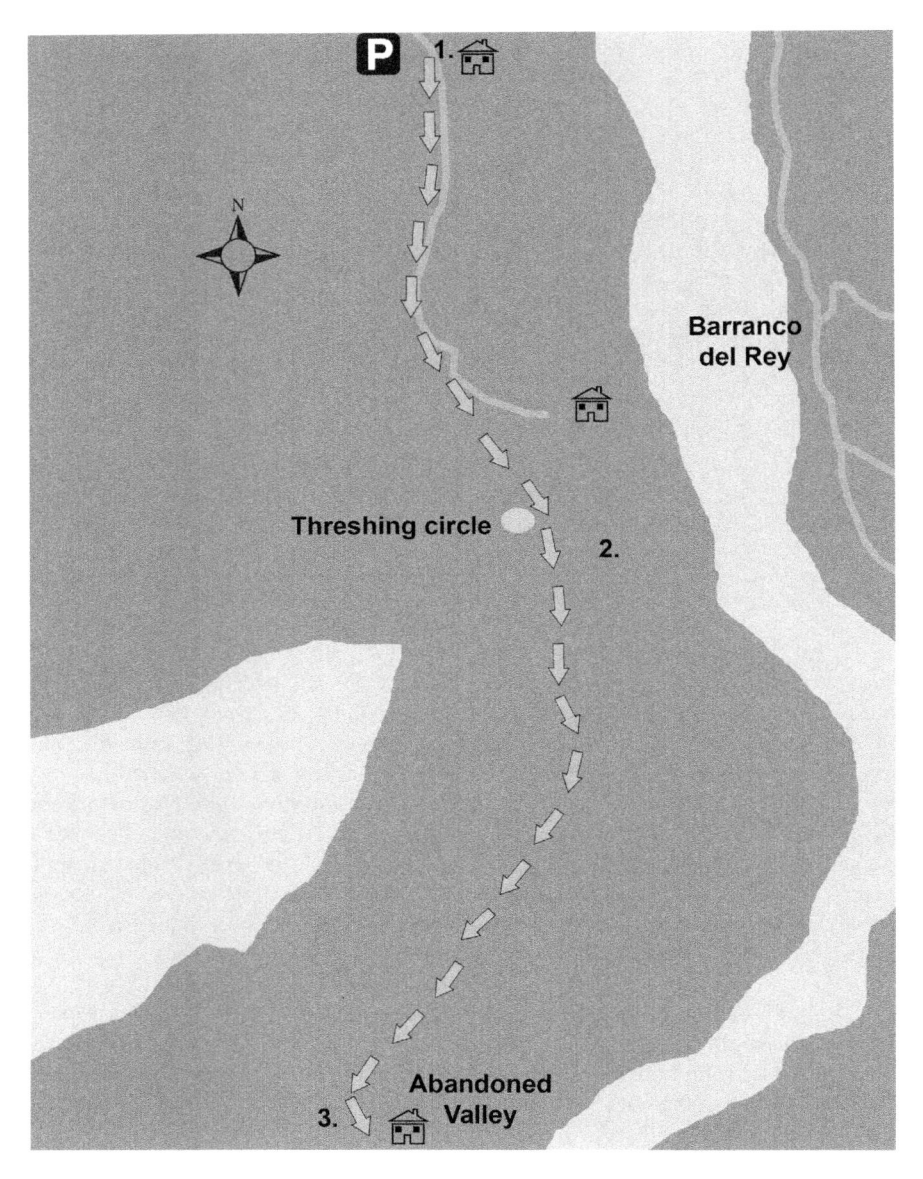

Lift Off to the Deserted Valley, Ifonche

Location	South Tenerife.
Circular Route?	No. But this is a short route so no long slog back over familiar ground.
How Long?	Approx 1 hour (return).
How Far?	3 kilometres (return).
Vertiginous?	The route runs along the side of a ravine so some may find parts vertiginous.
Route Difficulty	Level 2 – There is some ascending and descending but this is an easy route.
Wow Scenery	The sight of an old deserted valley nestling high above the modern southern resorts is quite something.
Underfoot	A solid narrow trail along the hillside. There's a good clear path over mostly arid terrain. Mostly downhill, but that means an ascent on the return journey.
Watering Holes	There are a couple of welcoming rural restaurant bars in the Ifonche area.
Downside	Getting there by public transport isn't easy.

Continuing the theme of views over the south coast, Ifonche serves as the starting point for a second, shorter walk which takes you further along the ridge that skirts Barranco Del Rey and then drops down the cliffside to a deserted valley completely hidden between the folds of the barrancos. You can add this walk onto your 'Above Barranco del Infierno' itinerary to both in the same day.

How to Get There
Follow directions as in page 155 to reach Restaurant El Dornajo. From the Restaurant, drive (3mins) or walk (15/20mins) along the road that runs in front of the restaurant, staying on the lower road as it forks and up past the characterful cottage. Keep straight ahead at the small crossroads with the wooden cross, passing the rock promontory of García's nose on the right. When you see a large farmhouse ahead on the left, watch for a patch of pale pumice on the right with a water pipe running above ground which is where the path begins. Opposite is a small level patch of ground which is a good place to park.)

The Route

1. Stepping Out (5 mins)
Step over the pipe and follow the path across stones and uneven land until you arrive at a large circle laid out on the top of the cliff. This is the take-off point for paragliders who float down between the barrancos and glide above the resorts of the south coast. If you're lucky enough to be up there as some are taking off, it's a chance to get some really stunning photos of them at eye level.

2. Into the Valley (25 mins)
Towards the left hand side of the cliff you will see the start of the path that leads down the barranco. Take this path. Try not to lose your footing as you gawp at the views down over Costa Adeje, the greens of the golf course clearly visible as they break the barren landscape.

The path finally emerges onto a ridge from which you can look down onto the valley below with its amphitheatre neglected terraces and caves dotted around the landscape. Continue on the path until you reach the broken water channel and the derelict house. The caves here would have been used to store the produce from the farm, keeping it at a constant temperature throughout the seasons.

It's a nice place to take a rest, enjoy the solitude and reflect on how it would have looked before the tourism developments of the coast below offered a far less back-breaking way to earn a living. Where once these terraces would have been brimming with produce, today only dried weeds and the lethal spikes of

Agave plants survive until the spring rains revive some colour.

From the hidden valley re-trace your steps back to the start of the walk.
3km/1hr 5mins

Places to Unlace the Boots
See Above the Barranco del Infierno on page 155.

Entering Hell's Ravine at Barranco Del Infierno

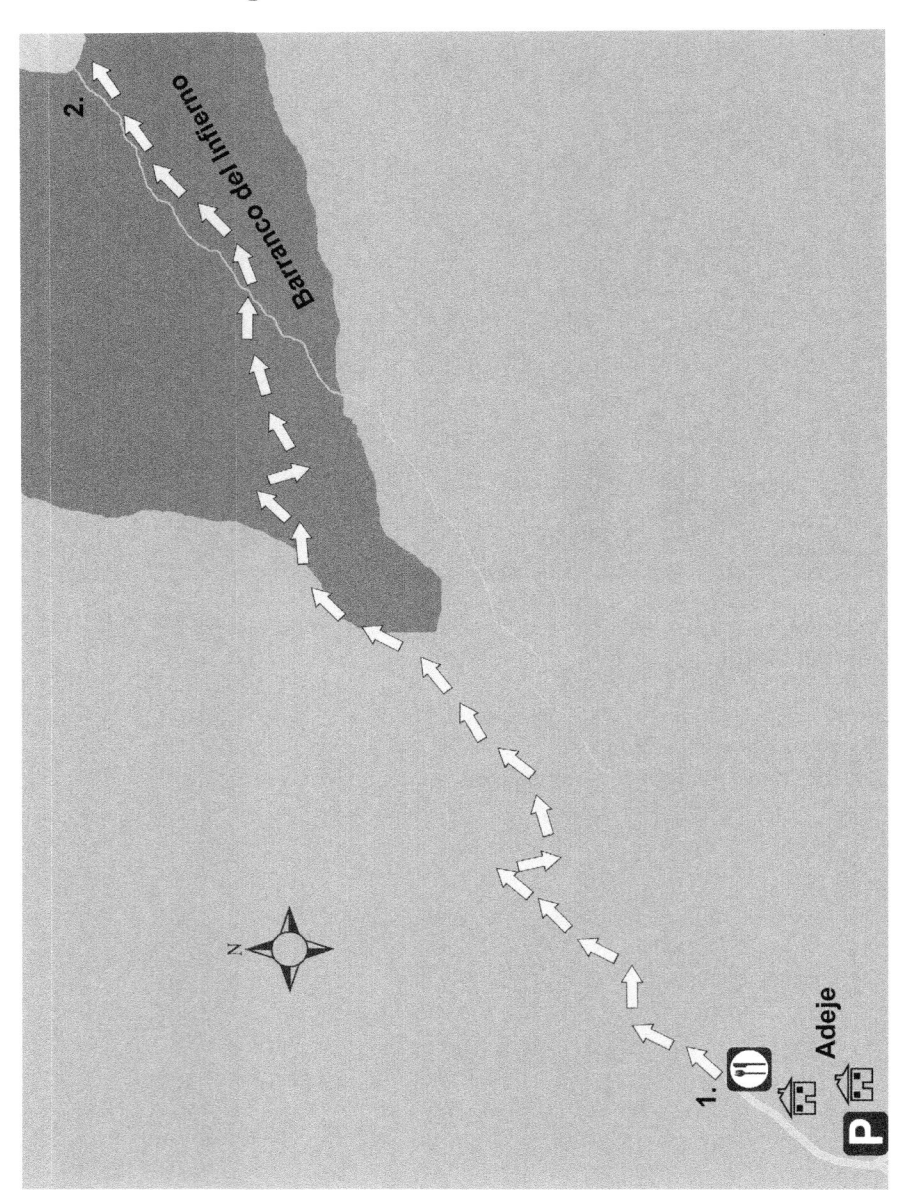

Entering Hell's Ravine at Barranco Del Infierno

Location	South Tenerife.
Circular Route?	No.
How Long?	Approx 3 hours (return).
How Far?	6.5 kilometres (return).
Vertiginous?	No.
Route Difficulty	Level 2 – Maybe not as easy as many people who turn up to do it think, but it's no real challenge for experienced walkers.
Wow Scenery	Walking through an old ravine is interesting but it's the fairy grotto waterfall at the end that is the pay off.
Underfoot	An undulating clear path through a barranco (ravine).
Watering Holes	Restaurant Otelo, the garlic chicken specialists, is right at the start (end) of the route.
Downside	Because it's so close to the main southern resorts, it's a popular walk, even with people who don't normally walk.

Barranco Del Infierno is one of the most popular walks on Tenerife, but that has a lot to do with its location, lying a short distance from the main southern tourist resorts. However, it's a pleasant walk in its own right and directions are not necessary as there is only one way in and one way out, but there are things worth knowing about the route.

How to Get There

By Car

Adeje town lies behind the main southern resort area of Costa Adeje and is easily reached from the main southern resorts. From Los Gigantes, take the TF47 to reach the TF1 and the turn off for Adeje. From the north, the quickest route is to follow the TF5 and then the TF1 to reach the Costa Adeje area.

Parking

It's a steep and narrow road to the start of the route. There is a customers' car park at Restaurant Otelo. We prefer to park in the large car park beside the start of the road leading to the Barranco del Infierno.

By Public Transport

Puerto de la Cruz

Catch the 343 to Los Cristianos and then change to the 417 or 473 service which stops in Adeje town.

Playa de las Américas/Los Cristianos

Simply take the 417/473 to Adeje.

Los Gigantes

From the Los Gigantes area take the 473 to Adeje.

The Route

The entrance to the Barranco del Infierno is found at the very top of the old town of Adeje, just beyond the Otelo Restaurant.

The route is very clear and well maintained unless nature has decided to throw some rocks along it after heavy rainfall. It simply winds its way along the ravine, crossing water channels and sometimes passing above beehives. It's a straightforward path with no real need for specific directions. The path is generally even and suitable for anyone who is reasonably fit, although there is some rock scrabbling towards the end of the route.

As you progress further into the ravine, the path runs alongside trickling streams which is a bit of a novelty in Tenerife, especially in arid southern parts, before ending at an enchanting little grotto and waterfall in the depths of the ravine.

There's an entrance fee (€8 non-residents, €4.50 residents) and visitors might find themselves undergoing a rigorous kit inspection so make sure you have plenty of water, some sun screen and the right footwear. Don't turn up in sandals or they might not let you in. Due to concerns for protection of the environment, there are only 300 visitors allowed into the barranco so it's wise to book a place in advance. This can be done via www.barrancodelinfierno.es which has more information about the park and prices. Some information changed in the first three months after the barranco re-opened in May 2015, so they are clearly subject to change.
6.5km/3hrs

Places to unlace the boots:
Take the opportunity to try some of the local speciality, garlic chicken (*pollo al ajillo*) at the Otelo Restaurant (closed Tuesday) next to the start of the walk. It's cheap and delicious and easy to order – just say for how many people.

Walks in The South of Tenerife
Arona

"The cling-clang from the bells around the necks of a handful of goats pulling at wild herbs take on the intensity of the pealing inside a church tower..."

Walking in Arona

Arona's meteoric growth from simple fishing village where the locals lived in caves to its current position as the most popular resort area on the island is largely down to its climate. The dry air and year round warmth was found to alleviate the symptoms of multiple sclerosis, leading Swedish Health Authorities to send patients here to improve as it was cheaper than treating them at home. Despite being built up, you can easily escape the crowds by heading to protected nature areas like Montaña Guaza and better still, to Roque del Condé where you'll see a very different face to Arona.

Weather

Arona's climate varies from winter to summer in so far as it goes from warm and sunny to hot and sunny. Virtually desert conditions mean that rainfall is scarce except for the occasional winter showers. More of a concern for anyone taking to its walking trails is the heat which can rise to low 40s in summer if a heat wave strikes. Most of the time the presence of trade winds keeps temperatures the right side of bearable. Away from the coast clouds can bank up over high ground from late morning so you may find yourself going from full sun, to cloud, to full sun.

Flora

You have to travel some way back from coastal developments to find the best of Arona's flora where many of the species that have learned to adapt to the soil and weather conditions are now protected. Climbing Montaña Guaza you'll predominantly see spurges, cactus, echiums and aoniums. Traversing the Barranco del Rey en route to Roque del Conde you'll encounter juniper and wild olive trees amongst the palms, cactus, laburnum, broom and grasses.

Call of Nature

There are toilets in the Ayuntamiento (Town Hall) on the plaza in Arona which it's wise to avail yourself of before you set out. No need to sneak in, it's absolutely fine to use them, they're there for the public. With Montaña Guaza you're right at the edge of the main resort so there's no shortage of bars or nip into the Arona Gran Hotel.

Where To Stay When Walking in Arona

For the Holiday Mountain route which is located in Los Cristianos, the resort provides endless accommodation options. Getting to Arona town and the start of the King of the South, Roque de Conde walk (opposite) is quickest and easiest from San Miguel de Abona, just a 20 minute drive away. See Where To Stay When Walking in San Miguel de Abona (page 198).

King of the South – Roque del Conde

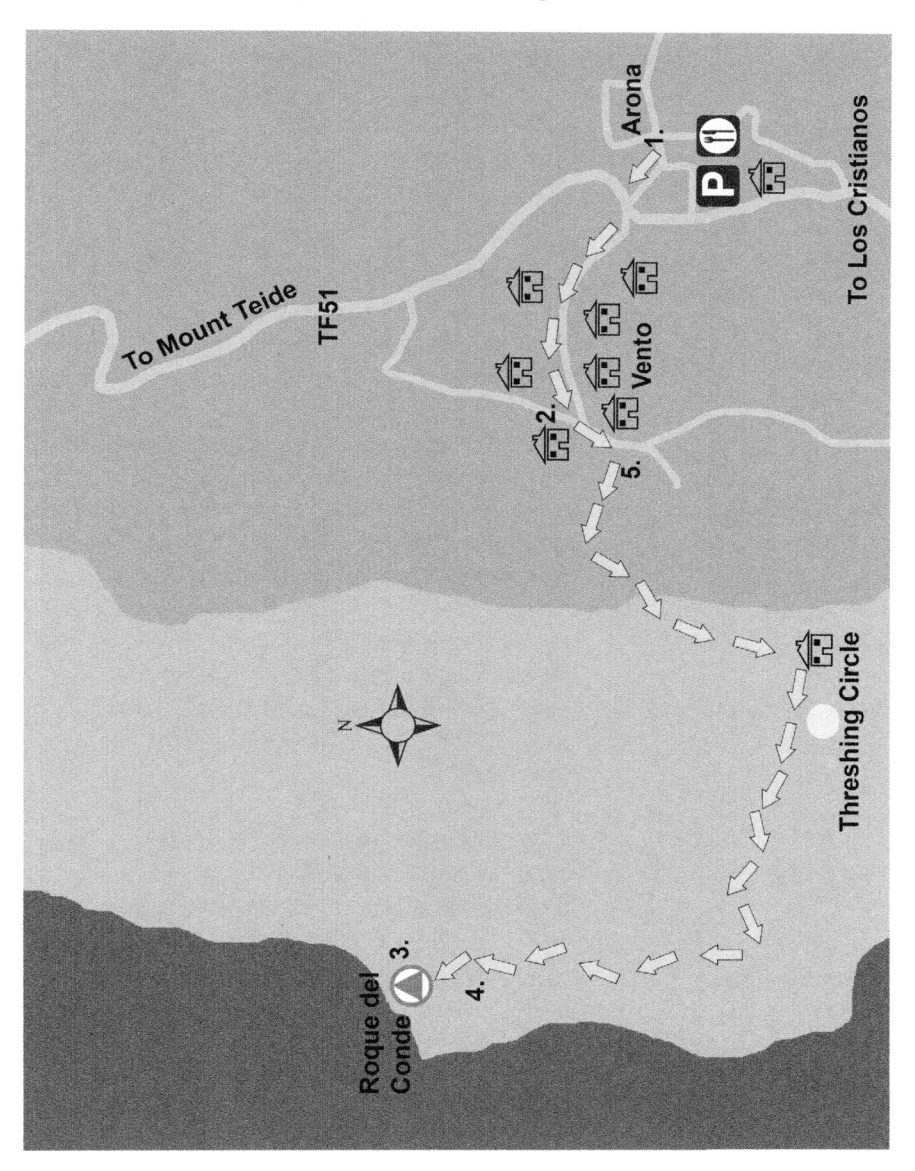

King of the South – Roque del Conde

Location	South Tenerife.
Circular Route?	No.
How Long?	Approx 3 hours (return).
How Far?	7.4 kilometres (return).
Vertiginous?	The final ascent probably won't be suitable for anyone with vertigo.
Route Difficulty	Level 3 – Length keeps this route a level 3; however, the ascent to the plateau at Roque del Condé is narrow and quite steep. It isn't an easy ascent by any stretch, but anyone who is reasonably fit and used to hill walking shouldn't have any problems.
Wow Scenery	The 360 degree views of the south of Tenerife are quite spectacular and take in the modern resorts that dominate the south coast, a landscape of volcanic cones, La Gomera and, if it's clear, even the Los Gigantes cliffs.
Underfoot	A relatively short walk but with a steep ascent on clear but hard paths. It's a good path for most of the way with long, rocky sections that can be hard on the soles.
Watering Holes	There's a choice of bars and restaurants in Arona town.
Downside	It's one of the most popular walks in the south so can be quite a busy one.

The flat-topped Roque del Condé dominates the south landscape, its head often in afternoon clouds. One of the toughest walks in the region, the steep and rocky ascent is not for the nervous or the novice walker and is best tackled early morning to avoid the heat, the crowds and the chance of cloud at the top. This is a demanding trail on uneven surfaces and often loose scree which makes the descent even more testing than the ascent. But the views from the top where, on a clear morning you can see four islands, is ample reward for the effort of conquering the King of the South.

How to Get There

By Car
From Los Cristianos take the TF28 (Mount Teide road) to Arona. From Los Gigantes, take the TF47 and then the TF1, exiting the autopista to join the TF28 to Arona. From the north, the quickest route is to follow the TF5, then the TF1 and finally, like everyone else, the TF28.

Parking
There's street parking in Arona. The further from the town centre you drive, the more likely you are to find empty spaces.

By Public Transport

Puerto de la Cruz
Catch the 343 to Los Cristianos and then change to the 480 for Arona.

Playa de las Américas/Los Cristianos
Simply take the 480 to Arona.

Los Gigantes
From the Los Gigantes area take the 473 to Los Cristianos and change to the 480 to Arona.

The Route

1. Stepping Out

We begin this route from the plaza in Arona and parking can be difficult on the town's narrow streets. If you're struggling, drive to the TF51 road to Vilaflor and park at the turn off to Vento, just above the Arona plaza, where you'll find plenty of spaces and you can join the route from there.

From Arona Plaza and church (Cristo de la Salud), walk to the junction of Calle Domingo Alfonso and Calle San Carlos Borromeo and turn right onto Calle San Carlos Borromeo following the signpost direction to Roque del Condé. In 190 metres you'll reach the junction with the TF51 and the turn off to Vento. Cross over the TF51 and turn left following the signpost direction Roque del Conde, Ifonche 6.2km and La Esperanza 85.2km. In 200 metres ignore the turn off to the right and continue straight ahead to arrive in the small village of Vento.

2. Rocks and ravines (800m/12mins)

At the junction with the statue of Christ in the village of Vento, turn left along Calle Vento in the signpost direction of Roque del Condé and walk along the street for 60 metres until you see the sign pointing right (at house number 78) to Roque del Condé, Ifonche and La Esperanza. Drop down the steep path and steps into Barranco de Las Casas. There is a green/red/white waymark on the right hand side. After climbing back out of the barranco (ravine), you reach a junction where the path to Ifonche separates from the Roque del Condé route. Stay left at the junction following the signpost direction to Roque del Condé. The waymark is now green/white.

Stay on the clear path as it descends into the impressive Barranco del Rey where you may see goats grazing its sides and pools of water in its depths if there has been recent rain. The climb out of the barranco is a tough one with steep steps and a loose surface of slate so worth taking your time over. As you climb out of the barranco, an information board tells you a little of the history of Roque del Condé.

The relentless, 180 metre ascent continues for a kilometre and half an hour, passing two 'eras' or threshing circles where the wheat was separated from the chaff in days when cereal was grown here, before you emerge onto a ridge where the whole of the south coast opens up at your feet and on the horizon, if it's clear, you may be able to see the neighbouring islands of La Gomera and El Hierro. The path levels out for an all-too-short section before it then takes a turn to begin the final, tough ascent of 172 metres over 1km which will take you, in half an hour, to the summit.

3. On top of the world (3.3km/1hr 30mins)

Once you reach the summit, views open up even more with the possibility that you could now also see the island of La Palma (to the right of La Gomera) and across the other side, the island of Gran Canaria, as well as the entire south and south west coast. If you want to ensure that you've been right to the very top of Roque del Condé, take any of the trails that traverse the almost 500 metre width of the top to the graffiti'd post at the far side which marks the highest point.

4. A skittery descent (3.8km/1hr 40mins)

Once you've had your fill of views and selfies at the summit post, begin your descent by making your way back to the path you arrived on. Take care on the descent as the surface can be loose and skittery. The toughest section is the 500m stretch from the summit to where the path levels out on the way back to the ridge so once you're past that, you've done the worst of it.

An hour and 2.5 kilometres of steady descent later, you'll find yourself back at the junction where the Ifonche path split from the Roque del Condé path. This is where you head right, back down the Barranco de Las Casas and up the cobbled path to arrive back in the village of Vento.

5. Homeward bound (6.5km/2hrs 48mins)

Turn left alongside house number 78 and then right at the junction with the statue of Christ to retrace your steps back to the junction with the TF51 Vilaflor road and drop down the road opposite to arrive in the plaza and time to *Unlace the Boots* at one of the cafés in Arona and reward yourself for conquering the King of the South.

7.4km/3hrs

Discover More: The Story Behind the Roque del Condé

Like quite a few other places in the Canary Islands, Roque del Condé is known by more than one name - Roque de Ahiyo and Roque de Ichasagua. Ichasagua was one of the last Guanche Menceys (kings) on Tenerife.

After most of his compatriots had signed the treaty of Realejos, bringing an end to war between the Guanches and Spanish conquistadors, Ichisagua continued to resist the conquest of his island.

Using his knowledge of Spanish fighting tactics, he continually outwitted the invaders by launching a series of guerrilla raids from the maze of ravines in the Tenerife hills.

Ichasagua's resistance came to an end when, at a meeting near Roque del Condé, he learned some of his freedom fighting colleagues had signed an agreement with the Spanish, he plunged a dagger into his chest rather than sign allegiance to the enemy.

Holiday Mountain, Montaña Guaza

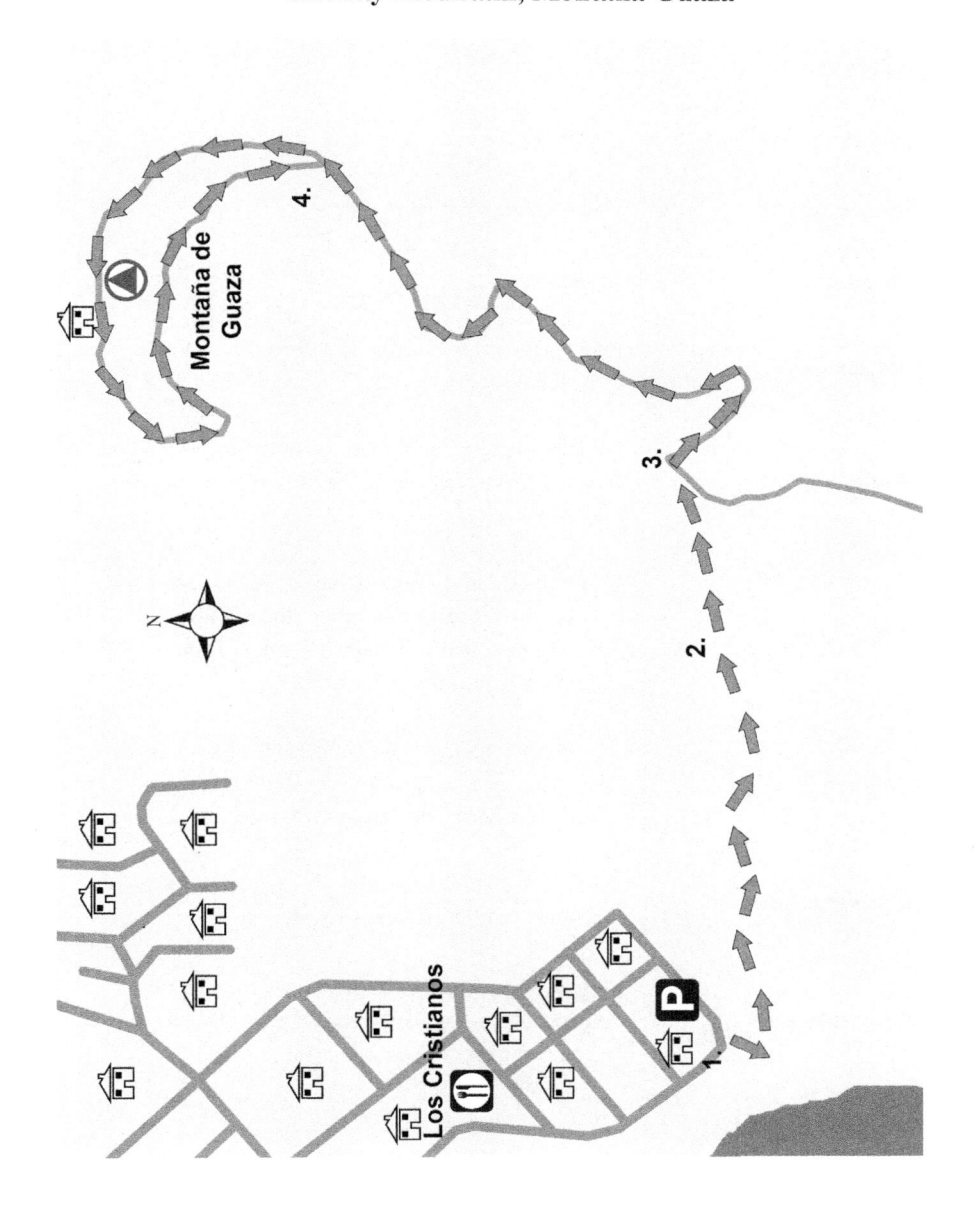

Holiday Mountain, Montaña Guaza

Location	South Tenerife.
Circular Route?	Partially.
How Long?	Approx 2 hours 40mins.
How Far?	8 kilometres.
Vertiginous?	No - despite the route ascending to the summit of Montaña Guaza.
Route Difficulty	Level 3 – It's a climb all the way to the top of the volcanic cone that towers over the eastern end of Los Cristianos.
Wow Scenery	From the summit, views stretch south west across the main tourist resorts; east where there is less development and inland to a volcano riddled landscape... plus there's La Gomera.
Underfoot	The initial section can be quite eroded but after that paths are solid, wide and easy to walk on. It's mostly a good even track which makes the ascent easier.
Watering Holes	The route starts and ends in Los Cristianos. Plenty of choice for a post-walk beer overlooking the ocean.
Downside	The lower section can be quite busy thanks to its proximity to a popular tourist resort. The higher you climb, the fewer people you meet.

It's impossible to miss Montaña Guaza dominating the skyline at the southern end of Los Cristianos and a walk to its volcanic cauldron of a summit rewards with views all along the southern coast. This isn't a difficult route to follow and it's hugely popular with holidaymakers, but the surface is loose and rocky and completely unfit for flip flops, and the ascent is testing in hot weather. Sunscreen, a hat and plenty of water is essential. The route starts beside Playa Callao, beyond the Arona Gran Hotel and Paloma Beach Apartments, and there are parking spaces along the street.

How to Get There

By Car
From Los Gigantes, take the TF47 and then the TF1 to Los Cristianos. From the north, the quickest route is the TF5 and the TF1 to Los Cristianos.

Parking
There's plenty of street parking in the streets near the start of the route.

By Public Transport

Puerto de la Cruz
Catch the 343 to Los Cristianos.

Playa de las Américas/Los Cristianos
No need. Walk to the start of the route.

Los Gigantes
From the Los Gigantes area catch the 473 to Los Cristianos.

The Route

1. Stepping Out
Follow the footpath of Calle La Marea to its end and swing right alongside the green railings that edge the small ravine. The path is quite clear to see and snakes up the hill at the side of the beach. Follow the path upwards for 200 metres to reach a small T junction and go right, passing the Espacio Natural de Protegido sign, to continue zigzagging up for another 600 metres (20 minutes into the route) until you come to an indistinct T junction where a stone cairn (small pile of rocks) marks the path. Turn left here and follow the path which runs upwards along the side of the ravine. Don't miss this point or you'll end up in a spaghetti junction network of trails and struggle to reach the summit.

2. Onwards and upwards (800 metres/20mins)

200 metres and 5mins later, the path once again divides but a barrier of small stones across the path on the left helps to ensure you stay to the right. In just a few steps (20 metres), go left at the next small T junction and then left again in another 50 metres, up the steps and follow the path left as it heads towards a dry stone wall before continuing on its upward journey.

Keep the ravine sweeping down to Los Cristianos on your left hand side. The path is clear and runs parallel to the ravine, skirting rows of abandoned terraces. Don't be tempted to follow any of the little deviations that present themselves, just stick to the main path until you spot a gap in the dry stone wall onto a dirt path, directly opposite a green dot daubed on the wall. Turn left along the dirt path and follow it for 300 metres and 6 minutes until you reach a wide, winding path.

3. Final ascent (1.6km/42mins)

Turn left onto the wide track and stay on it as it winds its way steeply towards the satellite masts that festoon the summit.

1.5km and almost half an hour later, just below the summit, the path forks with one way leading up to the upper level of masts and the other running off below them, around the edge of the crater, towards a lower set of masts. We're going to do a summit circle. Stay right and climb the final 300 metres to reach the very summit of Montaña Guaza. Enjoy the views over Montaña Roja, El

Médano, Los Cristianos, Playa de Las Americas and Costa Adeje on the coast and to the flat topped summit of Roque Condé inland before continuing straight ahead on the path as it now descends towards the lower set of satellite masts.

Beyond the lower masts, the path descends to the left and then turns sharp left to skirt the volcano crater and return to the point where you began your summit circle.

4. All downhill from here (4.9km/1hr 50mins)
Stay right at the fork and retrace your steps back down the winding, wide path for 1.5km and 25mins until you reach the point at which you turn off to the right, marked with small cairns. Continue back the way you came, dropping right through the gap in the stone wall at the green dot 400m and 5mins later and keeping to the right, hugging the ravine and following the obvious path until you finally arrive back, footsore from that terrible surface, at the end of Calle La Marea having climbed a mountain – well, a little one anyway. There are any number of seafront bars in Los Cristianos for that end of walk drink.
8km/2hrs 40mins

Walks in The South of Tenerife
Guia de Isora

"The path is lined by a string of derelict brick kilns, overgrown threshing circles and abandoned terraces filled with the swaying and bowing heads of wild wheat..."

Walking in Guia de Isora

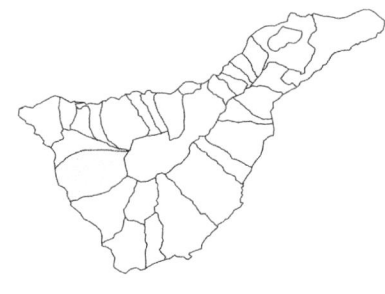

Administrative centre for the popular coastal resorts of Alcalá and Playa San Juan, the town of Guia de Isora has little charm to offer the visitor. But climb up into the hills above the town and you'll find the ghosts of an agricultural and manufacturing past in the abandoned terraces and threshing circles of the area's prolific cereal production and the derelict ovens of its valuable tile manufacture. Tucked deep into the folds of its hills you'll discover a picturesque village that has changed little over the centuries and one that was abandoned as people moved to the coast for work but that is now finding new life. With most visitors reluctant to leave their sun loungers, walking in Guia de Isora can be a satisfyingly solo experience.

Weather

Guia de Isora's climate is predominantly warm and dry. Cooled by sea breezes, the coast has an average temperature that fluctuates between 20 and 22 degrees, winter to summer. The coldest months are December, January and February and the hottest are July, August and September when, if the wind blows in from Africa, temperatures can soar to the high 30 degrees. Inland and above 500 metres the temperatures are generally lower and a sea of clouds can settle in the barrancos and on top of the highest ground bringing moisture to the vegetation and joy to the farmers.

Flora

The arid conditions favour the typical Canary Islands malpaís flora of spurges, echiums, euphorbias and broom along the lower slopes between the coast and around 500 metres above sea level. Where once cereals thrived, now dry grasses and wild olive trees take their place. At higher levels willow and the occasional juniper trees give way to pine forest at whose feet, white broom, brambles and heather grow.

Call of Nature

After you've left Vera de Erques, it's the great outdoors only for the Lost World route. On the Guia to Chirche route you'll have to hold out until you reach the Mirador de Chirche or until you return to Guia de Isora where you'll find toilets in the bus station.

Where To Stay When Walking in Guia de Isora

Accessing the start of the Guia de Isora routes involves a half hour drive regardless of whether you choose to stay on the coast or in the hills. For the authentic life, see Where To Stay When Walking in Santiago del Teide (page 70).

Hotel Gran Melia Palacio de Isora, Alcalá

A pretty beach, inviting rock pools and the largest seawater, infinity pool in Europe occupy the headland alongside the fishing village of Alcalá and are just the tip of the luxury iceberg at Hotel Palacio de Isora. Tenerife's most stylish hotel which combines opulent tones of the Far East with classic colonialism. From sexy, contemporary room décor and capacious patios of dancing fountains and light shows, to seven on-site restaurants and seven swimming pools, you'll need a week to try it all. And then there's that spa... [Expensive]
Avenida Los Océanos s/n, Alcalá; (+34)922 86 90 00; www.melia.com

Hotel Rural El Navio, Alcalá

The 11 rooms of this little finca are set in a banana plantation a kilometre stroll from the sea. Tranquillity, tradition and nature's beauty are the key here. Every room is traditionally furnished and has a private terrace with views over the bananas to the sea and sunsets over La Gomera. Breakfasts set you up for the day and there's a restaurant serving good home cooking. Alcalá has good dining options and is a rustic, torch lit walk away. [Mid-range]
Avda Los Pescadores; Finca El Navío, Alcalá; (+34) 653 23 90 03; www.elnavio.es

Cereal Killers – Guia de Isora to Chirche

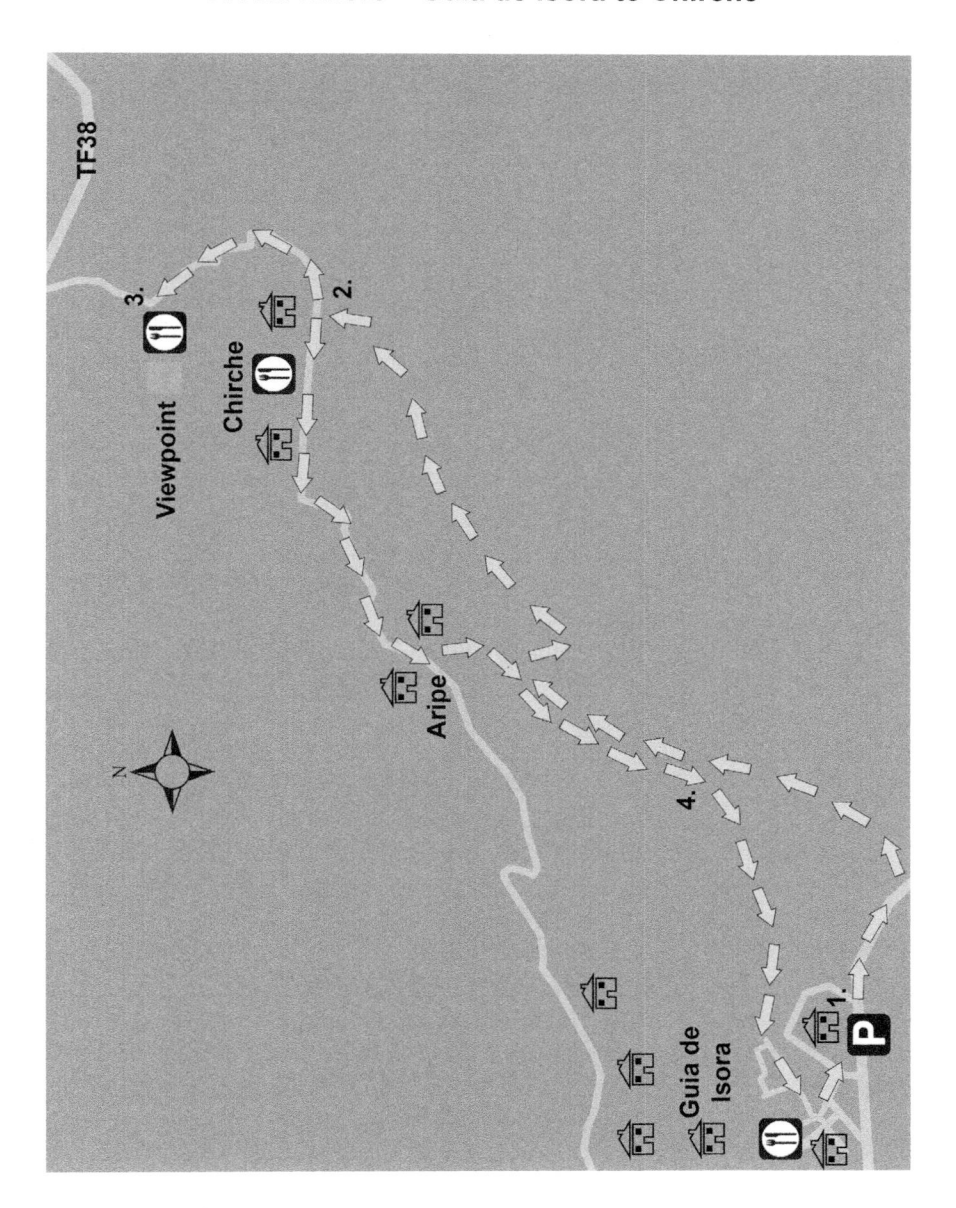

Cereal Killers – Guia de Isora to Chirche

Location	South Tenerife.
Circular Route?	Yes.
How Long?	Approx 2 hours 30mins.
How Far?	7.2 kilometres.
Vertiginous?	No.
Route Difficulty	Level 3 – The route to Chirche is all uphill which is why it earns a three rating. From Chirche it's downhill all the way home.
Wow Scenery	There are great views along the south coast especially from the Chirche Mirador. The wow factor here is more about discovering quaint villages which bear no relation to the Tenerife at the coast below.
Underfoot	Begins amongst agricultural land and pine forest becoming more arid as the route progresses. A partly cobbled merchant trail covers much of the route whilst a quiet country road links the two villages en route.
Watering Holes	There are a number of options in Gua de Isora, but a more quaint option is to enjoy some of Chirche's hospitality in a traditional tasca.
Downside	The start of the route involves walking a short distance along a busy road and it ends amongst rather bland houses in Guia de Isora.

Beginning at the small car park outside the cemetery which is on the TF82 main road at the southern end of the town of Guía de Isora, administrative capital for Playa San Juan, Alcalá and Playa de la Arena, and winding its way across abandoned terraces and through pretty rural hamlets, this walk takes in the remnants of an agricultural past. Once a major producer of cereals and centre of tile and brick production, changes in world production sources brought the cultivation of fruit crops and a move to the coastal areas. Consigning cereal production to the past alongside dried up water canals, weed-filled threshing circles and a string of old tile kilns; this route is like the ghost of farming past.

How to Get There

By Car
From Los Gigantes, take the TF47 and head uphill toward Tejina at Aguadulce outside of Playa San Juan. From Tejina take the TF82 heading north west to Guia de Isora. From the south follow the TF1 till it changes to the TF82 towards Guia de Isora. From the north, drive to Santiago del Teide and take the Guia de Isora road (TF375 becoming the TF82).

Parking
There are parking spaces at the cemetery at the start of the route.

By Public Transport

Puerto de la Cruz
Catch the 325/354/363 to Icod de los Vinos and change to the 460 Guia de Isora service.

Playa de las Américas/Los Cristianos
The 417 route goes from the resorts to Guia de Isora.

Los Gigantes
From the Los Gigantes area catch the 493 to Guia de Isora.

The Route

From the cemetery, walk to the right along the TF82 Guía to Costa Adeje road, staying on the right hand side as there's more room. After 300 metres you'll see a water tank set back from the road on the left hand side. Cross over and take the concrete path climbing up to the right just past the water tank. The path climbs steadily, past dried up water tanks, levelling out at a chain barrier. Ignore paths running off to the left and continue along the path flanked by old water channels and keep left at the chained off fork, until you reach the signpost.

1. The Kiln Trail (735m/15mins)

At the signpost stay straight ahead on the path, following the direction for Aripe and Boca Tauce. A fork to the right hand side is chained off, stay left alongside the vineyard where the route is clearly marked by yellow and white stripes.

After 655m and 15mins you'll reach a signpost below a stone cottage. Follow the 'Chirche/Boca Tauce' direction which runs to the right side of the cottage. On your left you'll see the tranquil hamlet of Aripe through which the return route will take you. Behind you, the outline of La Gomera sits on the horizon, crystal clear if you're in cloud and shrouded by cloud if you're in full sun.

Steadily climbing, in 150m you arrive at the first of the old tile/brick kilns beside a large 'era' or threshing circle. Ignore the turn off to the left (white and yellow X on the rock) and continue straight ahead, over the water channel, passing more eras and kilns as you progress.

Another 630m and 20mins and the path swerves to the right, crossing the water channel and continues along the embankment, flanked by deserted terraces. Kestrels nest in the pine trees to the right, hovering on the hot up-draughts on the look out for lizards.

Continue on the path until you arrive at a large water tank beside a vineyard and orange grove just above the village of Chirche. Stay on the path to the signpost and then continue in the direction of Boca Tauce to arrive at the old drinking fountain in Chirche.

2. Climb to a View (2.7k/1hr)

Turn right in the village, past the former drinking fountain (now sealed) and begin the STEEP uphill slog towards Boca Tauce. Your thighs and calves will protest but ignore them – it's not far, it's well worth it and then you get to come back down! Stay straight ahead on the cobbled path until, 300 thigh screaming metres later, you reach the road.

Turn left and walk along the road for 5mins and another 300m until you reach the Mirador de Chirche.

3. Mirador de Chirche (3.3k/1hr 20mins)

Time for a sit down to drink in the views over the south west coast. The temptation is to kick back, order lunch and enjoy the vista and you can do exactly that but it'll cost you more than the equivalent which you can get in Chirche – your call.

Retrace your steps from Mirador de Chirche, back down the path and into the village, passing the water fountain and continuing downhill to arrive, 700m and around 15mins after you left the Mirador, at Chirche plaza. There are benches in the plaza on which to enjoy the solitude of the village and watch the comings and goings of its few residents and the struggles of cars to make the steep climb in anything other than first gear.

Leaving the plaza, continue along the road downhill, passing the infant school on the right hand side, to the T junction at the end of Camino Viejo. Turn left, following the road downhill into the little hamlet of Aripe until, 1km after you left the Plaza, you arrive at a signpost on the left hand side. Turn left off the road at the sign, following the path in the 'Guía de Isora/Chirche' direction for 300 metres.

The way is marked by yellow and white painted stripes and curves round to the right towards a large, red house at the end of the path. Passing the quaint Cabaña de Galipana on your right, follow the path as it runs alongside the red house, climbing a small embankment over a water channel and dropping down the other side to the lower path signposted for Guía. You're now back on the original path which in 740m and 15 or so minutes will bring you back to the first signpost you encountered.

4. Cross the Lava Fields (6k/2hrs 15mins)

At the signpost, instead of going straight ahead to retrace your steps to your starting point, turn right following the direction towards Guía and traverse the lava fields that back the town until you emerge, 620m and 10mins later, at the side of a house in Guía.

Follow the road to the left and keep going straight and down, ignoring the SP trying to send you to the right along Calle Don Manuel Gorillo to Guia de isora (you're parked at the south end of town) and continuing straight ahead down Calle Las Britas which is so steep it needs a handrail. At the bottom of Las Britas, turn left onto Calle Guarpia and continue straight ahead, passing the Town Hall buildings on the right hand side, until you emerge opposite the cemetery.

7.2k/2hrs 30mins

Places to unlace the boots
The restaurant at the Mirador de Chirche (closed Monday) is a spectacular spot for a mid walk refreshment, but it can be a stop-off for excursions and subsequently prices can be higher than restaurants aimed at locals. A more authentic lunch venue is the Brasas de Chirche (also closed Monday) in the village. It's a typical Canarian bar/restaurant with an extensive menu of traditional dishes. Don't expect anything fancy.

Discover More: Chirche – A Village of Cultural Interest
Perched on the edge of a lava field, Chirche was declared to be a place of cultural interest in 2008. It's one of the most charming villages in the south of Tenerife and standing at 800 metres above sea level, feels like time as much as distance separates it from the coast.

Its higgledy piggledy streets deserve exploration by foot and the jeep safaris that occasionally shatter the peace on their way down to the coast from the Teide National Park don't sit easily with the gentle and olde worlde atmosphere.

A stroll around the village unearths traditional handicrafts, rooms for rent in quaint cottages and signs on houses informing that the owner sells their own honey or wine.

One of the best times to visit Chirche is El Día de las Tradiciónes around mid July, when the townsfolk make candles, grind cereals and prepare cheese using traditional methods from a century ago.

The Lost World, Las Fuentes

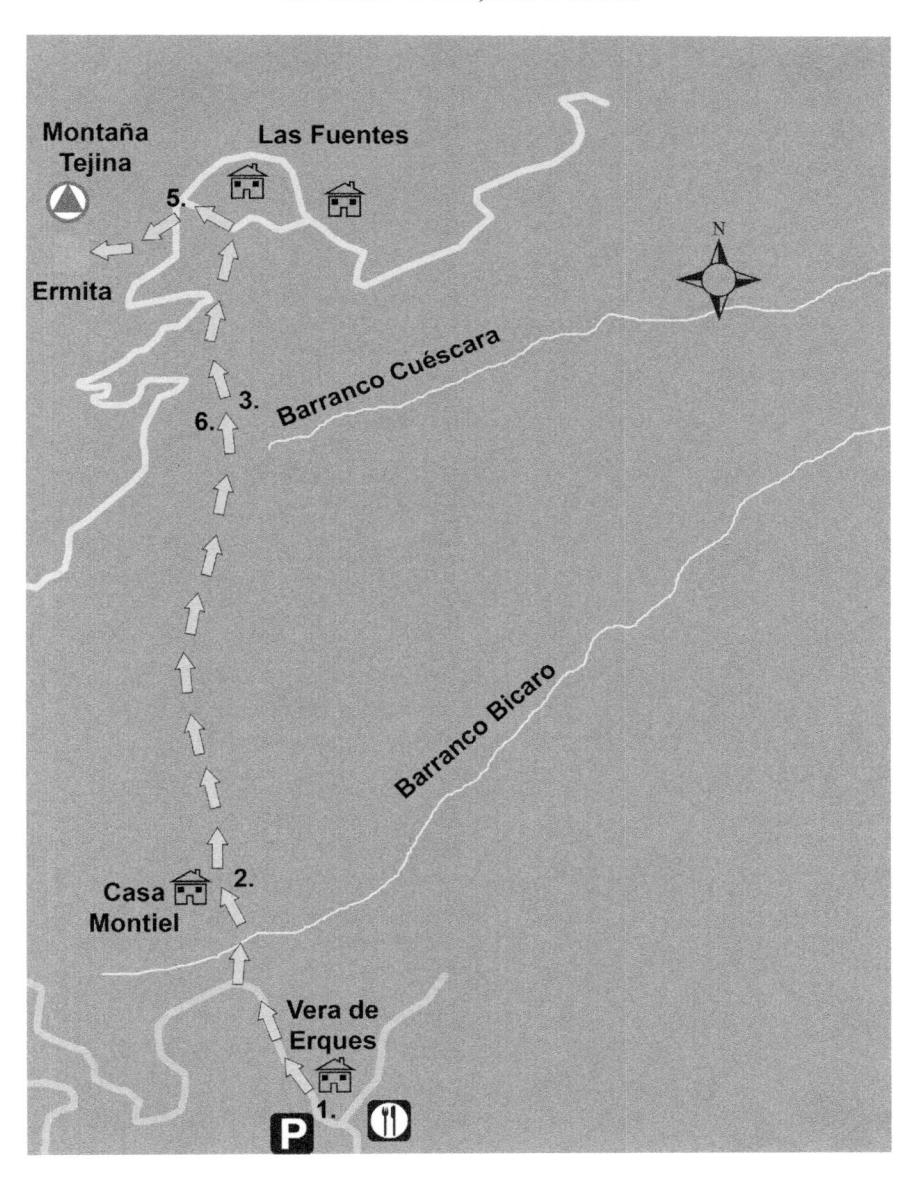

The Lost World, Las Fuentes

Location	South Tenerife.
Circular Route?	No.
How Long?	2 hrs 10mins (return - not including detour to ermita on Montaña Tejina).
How Far?	5.5 kilometres.
Vertiginous?	No.
Route Difficulty	Level 3 – There's some ascending and descending smallish inclines, but nothing that should trouble any reasonably fit walkers. Hiking to the summit of Montaña Tejina is more or less a straight ascent up without a discernible path.
Wow Scenery	The first sight of Las Fuentes is guaranteed to WOW, but even better awaits at the summit of Montaña Tejina.
Underfoot	A fascinating route over an undulating landscape that was once prime agricultural land in the south west of Tenerife. There's an old merchant path for a lot of the route, which can mean some uneven cobbles.
Watering Holes	Vera de Erques has a very relaxing hostelry for some post walk refreshments.
Downside	Apart from the fact that this isn't a circular walk, there isn't really a downside. This is a lovely walk with a real surprise waiting at Las Fuentes.

The pot of gold at the end of this rainbow walk is the hamlet of Las Fuentes. Completely hidden from view in a fertile valley watched over by Montaña Tejina, lies an abandoned village of some thirty or more houses. In the 1930s when the area was an important cereal production region, 150 people lived here. Then irrigation systems brought water to the coast shifting production and labour with it. One by one, families were forced to leave until in the 1970s Las Fuentes was abandoned. Today life is returning to this enchanting valley.

Although this is unfortunately a linear walk, the views on the return journey are so different that it feels like a circular one. At the moment the only way to make this route circular includes a very boring descent with a long stretch of the return journey by road – yuk.

How to Get There

By Car

From Los Gigantes, take the TF47 and head uphill toward Tejina at Aguadulce outside of Playa San Juan. From Tejina take the TF82 heading south and then the TF465 to reach Vera de Erques. From the south follow the TF1 till it changes to the TF82 towards Guia de Isora and take the TF465 to Vera de Erques. From the north, drive to Santiago del Teide and take the Guia de Isora road (TF375 becoming the TF82) and then the TF465.

Parking

There are some parking spaces in the centre of Vera de Erques.

By Public Transport

Puerto de la Cruz

Catch the 325/354/363 to Icod de los Vinos and change to the 460 Guia de Isora service. Change again in Guia de Isora to the 490 to Vera de Erques (working days only).

Playa de las Américas/Los Cristianos

The 417 route goes from the resorts to Guia de Isora. Change in Guia de Isora to the 490 to Vera de Erques (working days only).

Los Gigantes

From the Los Gigantes area catch the 493 to Guia de Isora and change to the 490 for Vera de Erques (working days only).

The Route

1. Stepping Out (400 metres/5mins)

The path begins just outside the village of Vera de Erques, on a right hand bend in the road just before the school, and is clearly signposted 'Camino Montiel'.

As you go up the brow, a cement path veers off to the left which you follow for a couple of metres until it drops down to the left to a green gate which is the entrance to a private finca. You leave the concrete path and continue straight ahead on the cobbled path as it skirts the barranco (ravine).

The path continues to a large pine tree from where you can see the remains of a brick tile kiln on a mound to the right. Stay on the path heading downwards and across another small barranco. After 130m you reach a water pipe crossing the path. Don't cross the pipe, take the right fork keeping the water pipe on your immediate left. After 30m, on the right hand side you'll find three old stone basins alongside a disused water tank; one was used for laundry and the other two held water for livestock.

Opposite, you can see the abandoned Casa Montiel; an idyllic little place with views over the south west coast and now in need of a lick of paint.

2. Casa Montial (389 metres/10mins)

The path slogs upwards from Casa Montiel for 300 metres with the horizon stretching further as you climb until eventually you can see all the way from Playa Paraiso in the south to Varadero in the west. The path levels out and begins to undulate and 13 mins or so after leaving Casa Montiel you reach a disused tank on the right side of the path, alongside a dried up fountain. The water pipe is now running along your right hand side. Shortly you will see your destination; Montaña Tejina with its small white shrine atop. The land here was formerly used for growing cereals; wheat, barley, lentils and chickpeas were all grown here and the landscape is riddled with circular stone 'eras' or threshing circles, now half hidden by overgrown weeds and grasses.

190m beyond the water tank, the water pipe crosses the path and, stepping over it, you leave it to go its own way as you continue ahead on the clearly defined path.

After 340m you reach a fork in the path. Stay left (boulders across the entrance to the right denote that you stay on the path you're on) on the path which drops down to finally reach the bottom of the ravine where the silence is broken only by the birdsong. In another 200m you reach the small blue 'Espacio Natural Protegido' (ENP) sign on your left side and the path faintly forks again.

3. Hidden Paths (2km/47mins)

Stay right at the 'Espacio Natural Protegido' (ENP) sign and carefully climb the overgrown path up the hill, looping back on yourself and winding your way upwards for a short but intense 190m slog. At the top the path levels out and bends to the right.

In another 60m you find yourself standing on an old water channel above the Tejina road. Turn right, walking along a small section of the channel before the path re-emerges. After 110m the path reaches a T junction, stay on the right hand side past the ENP sign as the path traverses the rich barranco floor alongside a cactus grove, vines and fig trees. Walk through the ravine with the mountain on your left hand side, passing more ENP signs en route. An indistinct path joins from the right hand side, ignore it and continue straight ahead.

The path widens out alongside a fat water pipe and you climb steadily up through tall grasses which cover the path until you emerge below pale, jablé (pumice) terrace walls, alongside a neat allotment at the start of the abandoned village of Las Fuentes.

4. Las Fuentes (2.7km/1hr 10mins)

Turn left along the path which skirts the terraces and passes a group of caves which are used for storing produce because they maintain a cool, even temperature inside regardless of external conditions.

In 130m, at the brow of the hill you reach a T junction with a wonderful cave house straight in front of you and a signpost showing El Jaral 3.4k and El Choro 1.3k to the right. The path straight ahead and to the side of the cave house leads to views over Guaria ravine.

Take time out to explore the largely abandoned Las Fuentes by following the path to the right. One or two houses have been renovated and life is creeping back into the village. To the left just beyond the Yanes well is the path to Acojeja which traverses the Guaria ravine to the neighbouring hamlet of El Choro before continuing to Acojeja. Beyond that, the fountain on the right contains fresh spring water and is a good place to refill water bottles.

Turning left at the cave house, almost immediately you can see a dry stone wall running up Montaña Tejina and some flat rocks and a small crucifix at the foot of the wall. Follow the path that hugs the wall for an 8 minute sweat and gasp climb to the summit and some of the best views in the south west. Before you, the 'hidden' valley of Las Fuentes lies with its neatly carved terraces; beyond and to the left is the hamlet of El Choro; on the skyline to the right is the flat top of Roque de Conde; ahead and to the left is the peak of Mount Teide, flanked to its right by Mount Guajara. Behind you lies the settlement of Tejina and beyond, the shimmering south west coast with La Gomera above the horizon. The descent of the mountain takes almost as long as the ascent did, taking care on the loose stones.

5. About turn…

With the biggest exertion now behind you it's time to retrace the route back to Vera de Erques.

Head back along the ridge to the cave house and drop down to the right opposite it, retracing your steps past the cave store-rooms to the tall grasses and fat water pipe of the almost invisible path on which you arrived in Las Fuentes. Drop down through the grasses to the ravine floor and head back along the path to the left, keeping Montaña Tejina on your right hand side. Keep left at the fork, passing the cactus grove which is now on your right hand side, until, 500m after you left Las Fuentes, you reach an inverted Y junction with a purple X on the rock ahead. Turn left and climb back up to the old water channel where you emerged above the ravine floor.

From the water channel, turn left on the ledge at the two water pipes where you emerged on the outward journey and retrace your path up the hill and along the ridge as it bends to the left, dropping carefully back down the serpentine descent to the top of the barranco at the 'Espacio Natural Protegido' sign.

6. Barranco Cuéscara (3.8km/1hr 40mins)

Go left and continue around Barranco Cuescara and across the ravine floor, climbing up the path flanked by small stone walls until the path levels out. Continue straight ahead with Montaña Tejina at your back, ignoring the fork to the left and skirting the former cereal fields that lie on a lower level on the left. Crossing the water pipe which now rejoins you, keeping it on your left hand side as you retrace the agricultural past of the area alongside abandoned terraces and threshing circles. As you continue past the old water tank to the brow, views over the whole of the south west coast open out in front of you. Drop down the path for 300 metres, passing Casa Montiel on your right and the old stone basins on your left, until you reach the water pipe and the T junction at the edge of the ridge where the path turns sharply to the left.

Follow the path to the left, crossing the barranco and climbing up to the large pine tree with the old brick kiln off to your left hand side. With Vera de Erques on the horizon, the path continues through the scrubland and skirts Barranco Bicacaro before the cobbles turn into concrete to take you up the small brow where you turn right onto the wide concrete path that leads back to the start of the route.
2hrs 10mins/5.5km

Places to unlace the boots

The leafy, shady terrace at Casa Juan Luis (closed Monday) in Vera de Erques is perfectly located for falling into a chair at the end of a hike to the hidden valley. The owner might not look the friendliest of people, but that's just the way some older Canarios can appear at first.

Try a friendly buenos dias, or buenas tardes if it's the afternoon, and his demeanour will change...but only a little.

Walks in The South of Tenerife
San Miguel de Abona

"Sin agua no hay vida - without water there is no life."
A reference to the La Hoya spring.

Walking in San Miguel De Abona

You don't have to move far from the tourist developments of the south coast to discover the 'real' Tenerife. One of the oldest towns in the South, San Miguel's history dates back to the island's original inhabitants, the guanche. In the hills surrounding the town, caves, mummified remains and important rock carvings have all been found that throw light on the origins and beliefs of these primitive people. Lying 600 metres above sea level, the terrain once produced high yields of cereals and was farmed with camels who took easily to the arid conditions. Livestock rearing and agriculture were the mainstay of the area and even today, potatoes, tomatoes and vines are important contributors to the economy.

Weather
With an average annual temperature of 19°C with an annual rainfall of less than 130mm (the UK average is 1091mm), the climate is near desert. Having said that, due to its height winters can be chilly, particularly on cloudy days, so dressing in layers is best. Light showers between December and March are not unheard of but you'll be very unlucky to encounter heavy rain.

Flora

Once you leave the town and start to traverse the barrancos, your route will be lined with neat terraces of potatoes and unruly fields of prickly pear cactus. Once clear of the smallholdings, sweet spurges and the cactus raised arms of cardón will dominate the landscape along with the occasional hairy football-shaped clumps of 'balo', wild olive trees and junipers. You may even catch sight of an occasional coffee plant or a wolfsbane.

Call of Nature

The Mirador de Centinela and the great outdoors are your only choices once you've left the convenience (ouch!) of your hotel or apartment.

Where To Stay When Walking in San Miguel de Abona

The wonderful thing about San Miguel de Abona is that you can access multiple walking routes straight from the door of your hotel. Throw in its proliferation of good restaurants and you've got the ideal base for a walking break.

Hotel Rural San Miguel de Abona

A sequestered, manor house and farm which has been in the hands of the Feo family since the 17th century, Hotel Rural San Miguel has been beautifully converted into a unique place to stay. Every room is different and each has its own personality but they all have lots of floor space, lovely bathrooms and an inviting outside space on which to chill. There's a thermal bath permanently heated to 33°C in a cave beneath the pretty, courtyard garden; a rooftop sauna and solarium; and a cosy honesty bar packed with local information. [Budget]
Calle de las Morales, 2, San Miguel de Abona; (+34) 922 16 79 22; www.hotelruralsanmiguel.com

Hotel Quatro Esquinas

200 Years of history sit within the stone walls, pretty courtyards and excellent restaurant of the Hotel 4 Esquinas (four corners). Just 7 rooms, named after the seven volcanoes that feature in the area, are located around a proliferation of pretty terraces and picturesque patios. Each is individually styled and combines the best of tradition and modern convenience with period furniture, power showers and free, fast broadband connection. A wine cellar, a bar and a small store of local produce as well as the popular restaurant, provide a real taste of rural Tenerife, while Agustín and Rosaria provide a genuinely warm welcome. [Mid-range]
Calle Obispo Perez Caceres, 19, San Miguel de Abona; (+34) 922 70 11 87; www.hotel4esquinas.com

Road To A View, San Miguel to the Centinela Mirador

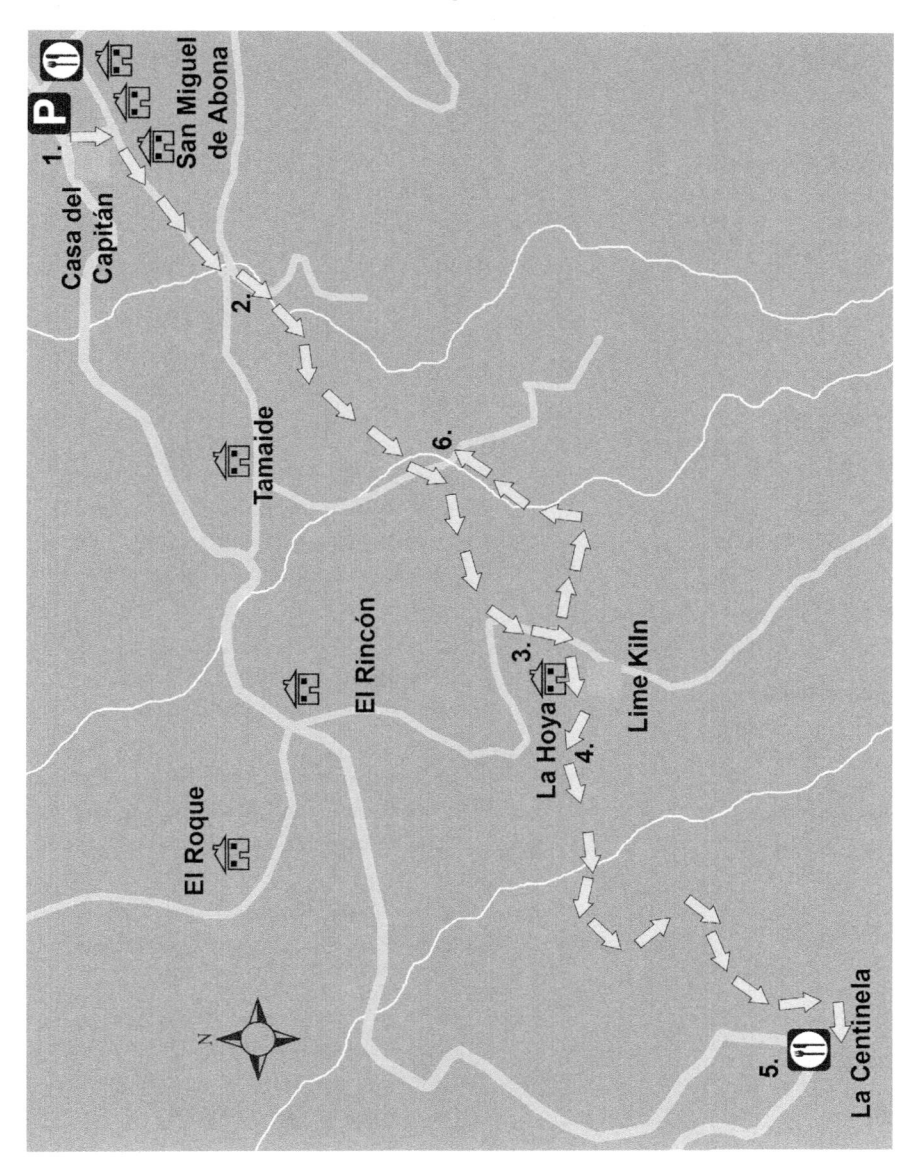

Road To A View, San Miguel to the Centinela Mirador

Location	South Tenerife.
Circular Route?	Partial. The route is mostly linear but there is one section which adds a slightly circular element to it.
How Long?	2hrs 55mins.
How Far?	9.2 kilometres.
Vertiginous?	No.
Route Difficulty	Level 3 – Much of the route is on quite level ground but there are a couple of quite steep descents/ascents in and out of ravines. There's also a decent ascent to the Centinela Mirador.
Wow Scenery	Surprising vistas of the volcanic cones which pockmark the south coast.
Underfoot	Charming partly cobbled merchant trail leading from a typical historic southern hill town through forgotten hamlets.
Watering Holes	There's a choice at either end of the route. San Miguel has some great restaurants.
Downside	There isn't really one with this walk, it's simply a very pleasant stroll through a part of the south of Tenerife which feels relatively unchanged by time.

This lovely walk follows the old 'camino real' (Royal road) which was formerly a trading route and which climbs from the pretty hamlet of San Miguel, into the Barranco del Drago, and up to the Mirador restaurant of La Centinela (closed Mondays) with its views over the volcanic landscape of the south. The landscape is characterised by white, jablé lined terraces that take any precious moisture from the air and trap it for the potatoes that are grown here.

How to Get There

By Car
From Los Gigantes, take the TF47 and then the TF1. Exit the TF1 at Las Chafiras to head up the hill to San Miguel de Abona. From the south take the TF1 to Las Chafiras and then follow signs for San Miguel de Abona. From the north, take the TF5 and TF1 south, exiting at Las Chafiras like everyone else.

Parking
There is plenty of free parking on the main road through San Miguel de Abona. The area above the Casa del Capitán on the southern side of the town is usually less busy.

By Public Transport

Puerto de la Cruz
Catch the 343 to Los Cristianos and change to the 416 for San Miguel de Abona.

Playa de las Américas/Los Cristianos
The 416 route runs to San Miguel de Abona from the main southern resorts area.

Los Gigantes
From the Los Gigantes area catch the 473 or 477 to Los Cristianos and change to the 416 for San Miguel de Abona.

The Route

1. Stepping Out
Driving along the TF28 main road that links San Miguel and Granadilla above the south east coast, park in one of the many spaces on the main road, near the southern San Miguel town boundary sign where a brown tourist attraction sign indicates the turn off to Casa de El Capitán Museo. Walk down Calle El Calvario following the direction of that sign, passing the small museum

(see Discover More), to a T junction with a small shrine in front of you.

Turn right at the shrine and walk along the road until you reach a bright, mustard yellow house where Calle de la Iglesia becomes Calle Tamaide. Turn left onto Calle de la Cruz and then right at the stop sign, with the mosaic windows on the right hand side and continue past the reservoir tank to a signpost showing the start of the route to Aldea Blanca (6.5km). There may be a car parked at the entrance here so be careful not to miss it. Turn right following the signpost direction onto the path.

2. Outskirts of San Miguel (1km/20mins)
The old path descends, then climbs, before zigzagging along through pleasant farmland past prickly pears and tabaiba, passing a lovely finca where purple clematis climbs the side of the building and vines creep along the top of the wall. After 10 minutes and 700 metres you reach a tarmac road, turn left and walk along the road for 60 metres before leaving it again as it bends to the left and you continue straight ahead along the path with a green and white waymark. In another 100 metres you reach a fork and take the right hand fork, ignoring the green and white X and dropping into Barranco del Drago (the left fork will be your return route).

3. To the Abandoned Village (1.8km/35mins)
The path zigzags down for 10 minutes and 440 metres until it reaches another tarmac road. Turn left and walk along the road with white jablé lined terraces to the left and a menagerie of turkeys, goats and chickens behind the wall on the right. Continue past the green fencing until you reach a turning to the right where some derelict houses mark the once abandoned settlement of La Hoya where now some renovation is taking place and people are moving back.

Turn right at the old well on the corner, following the signpost direction to Aldea Blanca but just further along the road is an old tile oven which you might want to look at before you continue.

4. Climb to a View (2.8km/1hr)
Follow the path down the hill with the reservoir tank on the left hand side until you reach the beautiful, stone, casa rural with its enclosed gardens and crimson bougainvillea. The path continues in front of the house (ignore the yapping dogs, they're all talk!) and then drops down a slope on the left at the end of the driveway to the start of the climb to the Centinela. There are shallow pools in the rocks and natural caves along the way and neat, combed jablé terraces all around as you thread your way up to the viewpoint.

After 1km and 20 minutes of gradual ascent, ignore the Aldea Blanca turn off to the left marked with a small cairn, and continue on the path as it winds up to La Centinela. Once you reach Centinela, you get 360 degree views down over the volcanic landscape. To the south lies Los Cristianos; to the east is Golf Del Sur, the busy south airport and the iconic red mountain of El Médano, while peeking above the ridge of the Cañadas is the peak of Teide. There's a nice little restaurant here (closed Mondays) and some benches placed around the gardens from which to enjoy the views before heading back down to re-trace your steps towards San Miguel.

5. A Rocky Return via Lomo del Medio (4.6km/1hr 30mins)

Retrace your steps down to the bottom of the valley, climb out at the casa rural and continue back through the abandoned village of La Hoya to the road where you turn left. But instead of retracing your steps back beyond the green fencing, turn right at the walking information board set back slightly from the road, along the path marked with a green and white waymark. After 100 metres the wide path bends left, continue straight ahead on the narrow path with the low dry stone wall on the right and the prickly pear cacti lining it.

In 150 metres you reach an information board where the path turns sharp left to descend into Lomo del Medio where the path seems to come to an end in the valley floor but scrabbling between the rocks takes you to a small wooden bridge and across to the Fuente de Tamaide natural spring which used to be used as a laundry area. Notice the caves in the valley walls which were dwellings of the Guanche, original inhabitants of the island. Climbing out of the Lomo you arrive at a noticeboard where you go left, following the green and white striped waymark (there's an X on the path to the right).

6. Homeward Bound (7.6km/2hrs 30mins)

After 200 metres, the path from Barranco del Drago which you took on the way out, joins from the left and you continue straight ahead to emerge at the outskirts of San Miguel almost 1km later. Turn left to retrace steps back through the village on Calle de la Iglesia to your starting point.
9km/2hrs 55mins

Note: If you stay on Calle de la Iglesia rather than turning left at the small shrine, it will take you past the La Vieja Bodega restaurant and along a pretty, cobbled street to the lovely 19th century Baroque church of St Michael Archangel in its leafy plaza and the 18th century library which used to be the prison.

Places to unlace the boots

There's the Mirador Centinela restaurant (open daily) at one end and a selection of good eateries at the other. Time your walk to end with a tapas lunch at the delightful former tobacco storehouse and post office, La Tasquita de Nino in San Miguel (closed Tuesday).

Discover More: The Captain's House in San Miguel de Abona

This old traditional building is now a museum of local crafts and traditions. There are exhibits based on the history of the house and the way of life in the hills, including a room dedicated to how camels were used as agricultural beasts in the area. There are also examples of traditional local products and a wine shop.
(Calle El Calvario, 1; open 8am-2.30pm & 4pm-7pm Monday to Friday)

Walks in The South of Tenerife
Coastal Routes

"The yellow-tinged terrain is broken by splashes of pink-red orchilla and bulbous prickly pair balanced on the edge of cactus paddles like tin ducks in a shooting gallery...."

Exploring the Red Mountain, El Médano

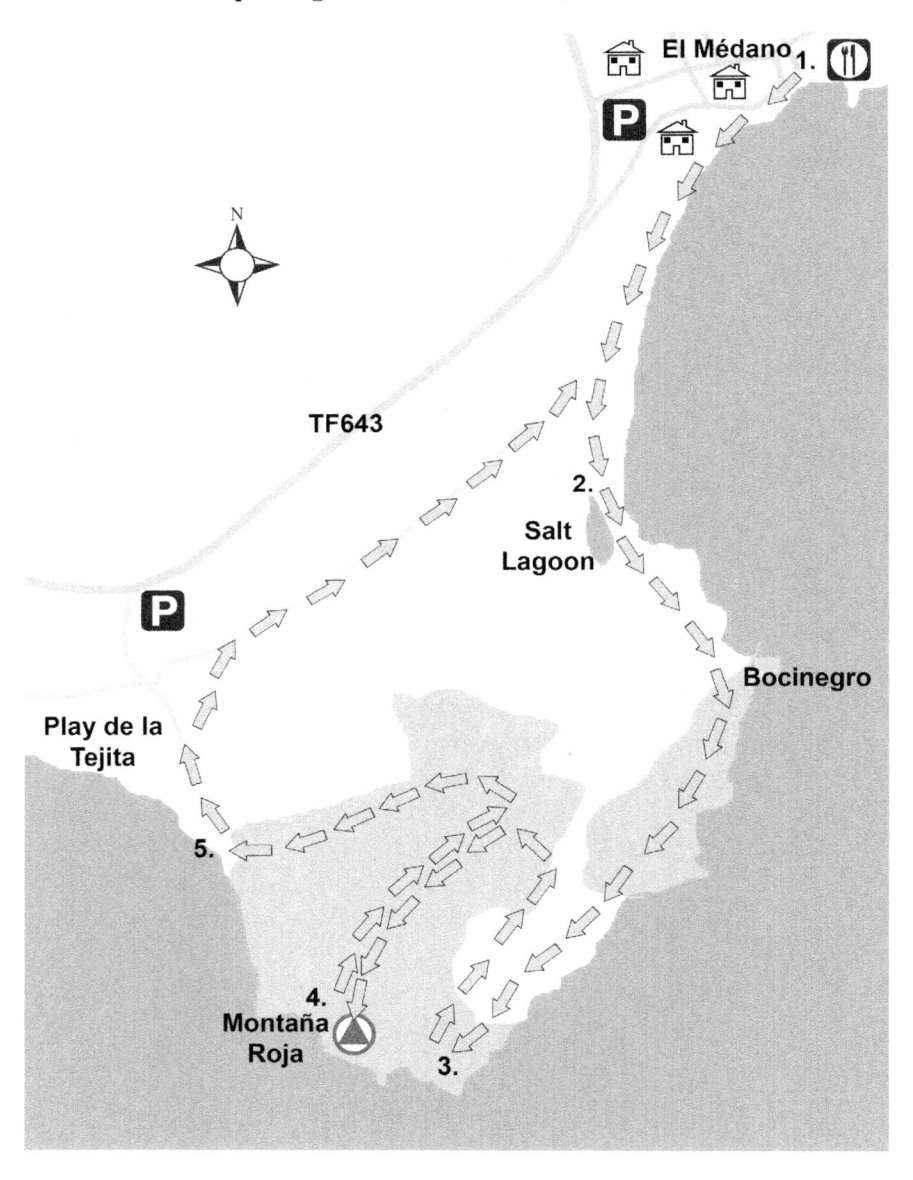

El Médano 1.
TF643
2.
Salt Lagoon
Bocinegro
Play de la Tejita
5.
4.
Montaña Roja
3.

Exploring the Red Mountain, El Médano

Location	South Tenerife.
Circular Route?	Yes.
How Long?	2hrs.
How Far?	7 kilometres.
Vertiginous?	The climb up the side of Montaña Roja is a bit of a ridge and could be difficult for vertigo sufferers.
Route Difficulty	Level 2 – Apart from the ascent of Montaña roja, this is an easy route to walk.
Wow Scenery	The coast is full of unusual rock formations but the pay off is the view from Montaña Roja.
Underfoot	Mostly sandy underfoot with some rocky sections. But generally it's soft to the point of sometimes being too soft.
Watering Holes	There are lots of great boardwalk cafes in El Médano. The only problem is choosing one.
Downside	When you spot the army of brightly coloured kites and sails it soon becomes clear what the downside to walking in El Médano is – the wind. It is nearly always breezy, even when a few kilometres along the coast is completely calm.

El Médano is one of our favourite towns on the south coast; it has a unique charm and character and is a great place to start one of the most interesting coastal walks in the south.

How to Get There

By Car
Unless you arrived on Tenerife by ferry or via the north airport, you'll have already been close to El Médano as it lies on the coast just beyond the end of Tenerife Sur Airport's runway. Access the town from the San Isidro exit of the TF1.

Parking
El Médano isn't the easiest town to find parking. There is parking around the main plaza and you might get lucky, but we tend to stay in the streets behind the beach on the southern edge of town, reached from the road leading to Los Abrigos.

By Public Transport

Puerto de la Cruz
Getting to east coast towns is a slow and complicated business from the north. The quickest way is to catch the 102/103 to Santa Cruz, change to the 111/112 to the San Isidro and then pick up the 116/470 to reach El Médano. There are ways to do it catching only two buses, but it will probably take longer as the El Médano bus from Santa Cruz stops everywhere along the route.

Playa de las Américas/Los Cristianos
It takes a while, but the 470 travels from Los Cristianos to El Médano every hour.

Los Gigantes
From the Los Gigantes area catch the 473 or 477 to Los Cristianos and change to the 342.

The Route

1. Stepping Out
Follow the wooden boardwalk out of town towards the distinctive Montaña Roja. Even at the start of the route, the jagged pumice rock formations and coloured sails of kite-boarders and windsurfers provide plenty of interest for the eyes. At the Hotel Playa Sur Tenerife (after pausing to have a look at the

frivolous stone and driftwood sculptures) head across the dunes, still in the direction of the 'red mountain', staying parallel to a low rope fence.

2. The Salty Lagoon (1.2k/20mins)
Just behind the dunes is an inland salt lagoon which is now out of bounds to the public due to it being a bit of a bird sanctuary. There are boards skirting the small lake's length which provide snippets of information about the history of the area and its geological features.

400m after reaching the salt lagoon is a series of paths (1.6k) which lead around and up Montaña Roja. We'd recommend following the path to the left of Montaña Roja toward Bocinegro.

The trail skirts a machine gun post from WWII before descending to a coastline whose surreal rock formations look as though they belong on another planet.

2. Martian Beach (2.8k/50mins)
The path ends at a striking red beach. This area is a popular area with naturists so be careful where you point the camera or you might find more than you bargained for in the frame.

From the red beach, the path doubles back and after 200m a path on the left is the start of the ascent to the top of Montaña Roja. It's not a particularly steep or strenuous climb if you're reasonably fit and will reward with views of Tenerife's southern coastline and the naturally pale gold beach of Playa de la Tejita way below.

4. On Top of the Red Mountain (3.8k/1hr 15mins)
After taking time to enjoy the 360 degree views, take the path back down the mountain and, after 700m take the path at the base to the left.

The landscape might look arid nowadays, but in the not so distant past there were agricultural plots and tomato plantations in the area. However, there was a clue why this was never going to be good agricultural land…they had to use camels to plough the terrain instead of oxen.

The path ends above the sweeping bay at Playa de la Tejita. There are a number of trails. Stay on the one traversing the mountain until you reach a delightful and sheltered cove where you can literally let it all hang out.

5. Playa de la Tejita (5.3k/1hr 35mins)
After you've spent time at Playa de la Tejita, take the path leading away from the coast to the right of a small square building then take the right turn a few metres after the hut to reach a T junction after another 250m.

This path continues in a straightish line, crossing a few other paths all the way back to El Médano.
7k/2hrs

Places to unlace the boots
The boardwalk at El Médano has loads of suitably laid-back inviting cafés. Our favorites are surf dude hangout Flashpoint (open daily) near the Montaña Roja end of the resort and Veinte 04 (closed Monday) in the main plaza.

Exploring the Yellow Mountain, Costa del Silencio

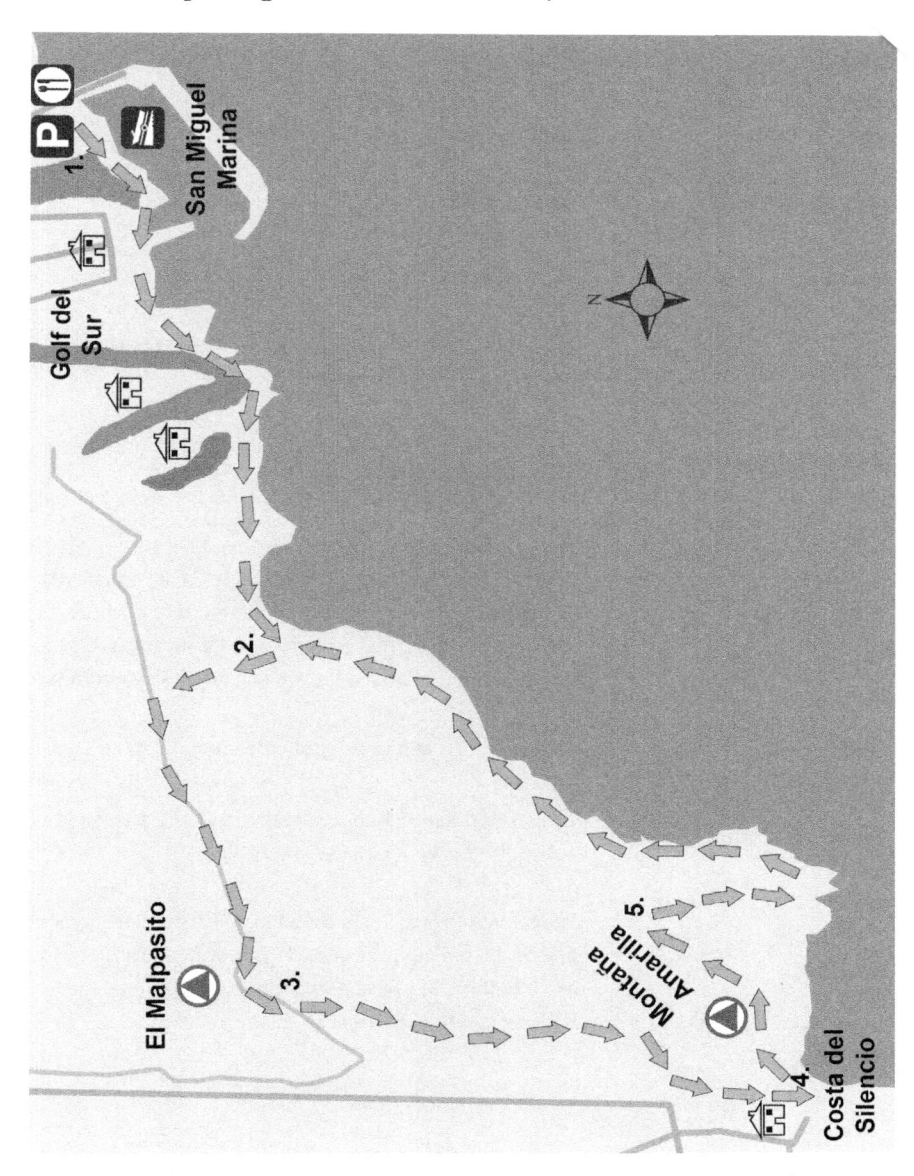

Exploring the Yellow Mountain, Costa del Silencio

Location	South Tenerife.
Circular Route?	Mostly.
How Long?	2hrs 40mins.
How Far?	9 kilometres.
Vertiginous?	Only if you climb Montaña Amarilla where the route runs along the crater ridge.
Route Difficulty	Level 2 – Apart from the ascent of Montaña Amarilla, this is an easy route to walk.
Wow Scenery	Views from the top of Montaña Amarilla are impressive, but the highlight of this route is descending to the small cove at the base of the mountain where the view of the surreal rock formations jutting over the sea is one of the most eye-catching views on Tenerife.
Underfoot	Mostly soft terrain underfoot with some rocky sections.
Watering Holes	The café on the rocks has superb views and a magnetic atmosphere – you won't want to leave.
Downside	The approach into Costa del Silencio isn't pretty. In fact one of the buildings beside the yellow mountain looks like it belongs in a seriously deprived 1980s inner city housing estate in Britain.

Bookended by two purpose built resorts (Golf del Sur and Costa del Silencio), this route reveals a quite surprising face to this part of the south of Tenerife. The landscape is typical malpaís, but there are a few surprises along the way. It's a great little coastal walk which includes one of the most unusual coastal views on Tenerife.

How to Get There

By Car
From the TF1 take the Chafiras exit and follow signs for Golf del Sur and then for the marina.

Parking
The route begins at the San Miguel Marina on the southern end of Golf del Sur. As well as a rough car park beside the marina, there are plenty of spaces on the road leading to it.

By Public Transport

Puerto de la Cruz
Getting to east coast towns is a slow and complicated business from the north. Probably the quickest way is to catch the 102/103 to Santa Cruz, change to the 111/112 to Las Chafiras and pick up the 483/470 to reach Golf del Sur.

Playa de las Américas/Los Cristianos
Both the 483 and 470 run between Los Cristianos and Golf del Sur.

Los Gigantes
From the Los Gigantes area catch the 473 or 477 to Los Cristianos and change to the 470 or 483.

The Route

1: Stepping Out
From the rough car park overlooking the marina, follow the path south that runs between the golf course and the coast. In the marina you might spot the little yellow submarine, promptly filling your head with a certain song.

The path continues to run between a mix of golf greens and apartments on one side and rocky coves on the other till you reach the end of the development and the first surprise; a small jade lagoon behind a pebble beach.

Follow the path along the curve of the beach to reach a second pebbly beach which has a couple of resident 'happy campers'.

2: Head Inland (1.9k/35mins)

The path splits at another ramshackle abode at the other end of the beach (if the wind or the authorities haven't removed it). Turn inland at this point, with your back to a Prohibido Tirar Basura sign, and follow the path in the general direction of a small volcanic cone, El Malpasito.

Leave the coast with its splashes of orchilla, sea heath and sea lavender for a more desert like landscape whose arid terrain is decorated with euphorbias and prickly pear. In the distance, Mount Teide peeks above the crater rim of Teide National Park.

After 400m the path reaches a T junction. Turn left along it, now heading towards the cone of El Malpasito.

3: El Malpasito to the Coast (3.2k/55mins)

After you pass the small volcanic cone, and before reaching the road straight ahead, take the path on the left, heading towards Montaña Amarilla at the coast. It should be marked by a small cairn but it doesn't really matter if you don't follow the correct path. The area is full of criss-crossing trails. All that matters is that you're heading towards Montaña Amarilla.

After 700m you should reach a small wall circling the base of the small mountain. Step over it and turn right along the path, skirting Montaña Amarilla and heading towards the edge of the resort of Costa del Silencio.

Stay on this path as it continues around the mountain, trying to ignore the dilapidated apartment block ruining the scenery, until the path crosses another path which heads up to the summit of the volcanic cone. Turn right and down towards the coast and the small café on the rocks.

4: From the Café to the Summit (4.6k/1hr 15mins)

The views from the rocks at the café are what makes this route quite special. The surreal formations are the result of a magmatic chamber coming into contact with water following an eruption. It's a magnificent scene and the addition of the small chillout café just finishes it off perfectly. It's not a spot that's easy to drag yourself away from.

Retrace your steps to the path and this time follow it straight up the slope to the rim of Montaña Amarilla. It's only 300m to the top, so not as bad as it looks. Once at the top, the path levels out, skirting the rim of a crater.

Follow it right as it runs along the wide ledge before it gently descends in the direction of Golf del Sur.

5: Back to Golf del Sur (5.4k/1hr 40mins)

As the path reaches the base of Montaña Amarilla you arrive at a crossroads with a large cairn in the centre. Veer right on the path heading to the sea to follow the coastal path as it passes rocky coves, dark volcanic formations and the occasional fisherman before arriving back at the pebble beach where you headed inland.

From there rejoin the path leading back to Golf del Sur and the start of the route. **9K/2hrs 40mins**

Places to unlace the boots

The kiosk on the rocks below Montaña Amarillo is a joy to sit at, or lounge in as the seating is on the eclectic side. It's only a wooden hut the size of a garden shed but it's got a magnetic personality.

Walks in Central Tenerife
Teide National Park

"The horizon gradually became like a rainbow, with that peculiar effect it always has of being on a level with one, and the world beneath curved like a bowl..."

Lady Isabel Burton 1897

Walking in Teide National Park

A volcanic crater measuring 17km (10 miles) in circumference and rising over 2000 metres at Mount Teide, this landscape is like nowhere else in the Canarian Archipelago and indeed, like few places on the planet. A UNESCO World Heritage Site, the park is Tenerife's most popular day trip destination and yet, you don't have to stray far from the tourist coaches and car parks to leave the crowds behind and find yourself virtually alone in this extraordinary landscape. An arid, alpine zone, lips and throats quickly parch and the sun's rays can be fiercely penetrating. Lip salve, water, a hat and strong sunscreen are essential, regardless of the time of year. Cold in winter and hot in summer, layers are the dress order of the day.

Weather

Climatic conditions in the crater are unlike anywhere else on the island. In winter the daytime air temperature is low enough to maintain snow and ice at ground level while at night it can plummet to - 7° at the summit and – °4 in the crater floor. Very low humidity all year round and scarce rainfall make it an extremely arid zone where little cloud cover is experienced. Summers can be unbearably hot, particularly on days when there is no breeze.

Flora

A subtropical alpine zone, there is a surprising variety of flora to be found in the park and including some that are found only here. The most common ground cover comes from the Teide white broom and the yellow sticky broom, joined by the pretty little Teide violets which you'll find on higher ground. A spectacular sight in late spring are the 3 metre high, spikes of crimson tajinaste or Teide bugloss.

Call of Nature

There are toilets in the Portillo Visitor centre towards the north edge of the crater; in the Teide Parador café at the southern edge and in the cable car station at the base of Mount Teide. There is very little cover for al fresco emergencies in between.

Where To Stay When Walking in Teide National Park and Vilaflor

Parador de Cañadas del Teide

Stretch the credit card for a night in the most most amazing landscape you're ever likely to stay in. The hotel itself doesn't particularly impress with its décor and furnishings but it's warm, comfortable and cosy and anyway, that's more than compensated for by the wow factor outside the window. These are starry nights Vincent Van Gogh would be blown away by and a landscape that, incredible by day, morphs into surreal by night. The food's excellent too but expect to spend most of your evening in the dining room as woefully inadequate staffing leads to service the slow side of leisurely. [Expensive]

Teide National Park, La Orotava; (+34) 922 386 415; www.parador.es

Hotel Villalba, Vilaflor

Alpine lodge meets country chic in the pine forests of Spain's highest municipality, and it comes with a spa and feng shui comfort that brings audible sighs of pleasure after a long day's walking. One of our favourite hotels on the island, the Villalba has it all - the looks, the facilities, the food and the location. Access to the basement spa is included in room rates, and the elegant dining room provides traditional dishes prepared with organic vegetables and herbs from the garden and served with the family's own wine label. It's a 20 minute drive from Vilaflor into Teide National Park. [Mid-range]

Camino San Roque s/n, Vilaflor; (+34) 922 70 99 30; www.hotelvillalba.com

Hotel Alta Montaña, Vilaflor

A friendly, funky and relaxed little hotel set above the vineyards of the village of Vilaflor, with views down to the south east coast. Rooms are chalet style with good heating and lashings of hot water for that essential post-walk shower, and have small terraces on which to leave muddy boots and to relax. Quirky corners abound, and a large terrace is the perfect place from which to enjoy those views accompanied by a sundowner. Eco-friendly and convenient for village restaurants. The hotel offers home cooking in its panoramic dining room. [Budget]

Camino Morro Elcano 1, Vilaflor, (+34) 922 70 99 95; www.hotelaltamontaña.com

Climbing The Wall, Guajara

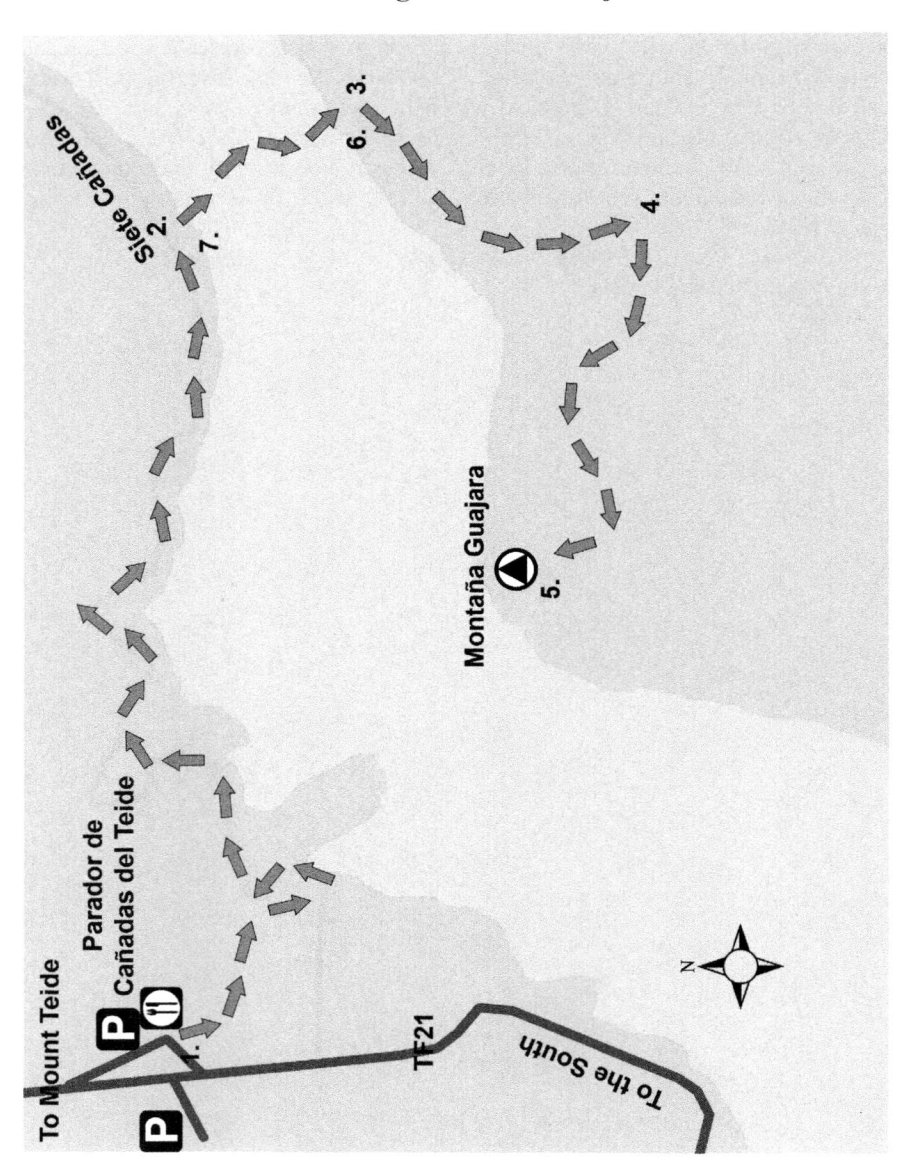

Climbing The Wall, Guajara

Location	Central Tenerife.
Circular Route?	No.
How Long?	5hrs (return).
How Far?	13.3 kilometres.
Vertiginous?	Yes. This isn't seriously vertiginous but there are sections which could be uncomfortable for anyone with vertigo.
Route Difficulty	Level 4 - The first part of this walk is good for acclimatising to walking at altitude as it involves a relatively gentle stroll along a wide path. From stage 2 it's uphill all the way to Guajara's summit.
Wow Scenery	To enter the Mount Teide Crater is to enter another world. It might seem like an over-used term, but this really is unique territory and the views are epic.
Underfoot	An amazing route passing through a unique volcanic landscape. On the flat it is easy walking on good paths. Once you hit the slopes the going can be a bit tricky, especially descending steep inclines on loose volcanic scree.
Watering Holes	There are a few places for refreshments inside the park, most overly expensive, but the location compensates for the feeling you've just been legally mugged.
Downside	Heavy snow and high winds can sometimes put the crater out of bounds in the winter.

Leaving the crowds of coach trippers behind, this walk sets out from behind the Teide Parador to ascend the highest section of the remaining crater wall. Climbing 715 metres above the crater floor, the views from Guajara across the National Park and over Vilaflor to the south are extraordinary. Don't miss the short cut at the start and end of the walk; very few people know about this little trick and it will save you a lot of extra walking. Watch the look on the faces of people who passed you when you re-emerge way ahead of them!

How to Get There

By Car
From Los Gigantes, take the TF82 to Tamaimo and then follow signs for Guia de Isora. At Chio take the TF38 Boca Tauce road all the way to Teide National Park. From the south take the TF21 to reach Teide National Park. From the north, it's also the TF21.

Parking
There are lots of parking spaces around the Parador de Cañadas del Teide and also the Roques de García.

By Public Transport
From both north and south there is only one bus up and down to Teide National Park each day, so it's important to plan accordingly.

Puerto de la Cruz
Catch the 348 direct to Teide National Park.

Playa de las Américas/Los Cristianos
Catch the 342 direct to Teide National Park.

Los Gigantes
From the Los Gigantes area catch the 473 or 477 to Los Cristianos and change to the 342.

The Route

1. Stepping Out
Setting out from the Parador, the trail begins off the little roundabout to the side of the cafeteria and toilets and is clearly signposted as Path Number 4 Siete Cañadas. The cinder and rock path snakes its way clearly through the lava debris towards the crater wall until it meets the wide pista of Siete Cañadas.

Turn left onto the Siete Cañadas path and follow it past the little ranger's office and the traffic barrier.

The Short Cut - Continue along the path for a kilometre until you see some large water pipes emerging from below the left hand side of the path. When you reach the pipes, leave the wide path (which continues around to the left) and follow a narrow path on the right hand side that climbs up the small cone. The path has loose stones so watch your footing. Down the dip on the other side and slightly up again, in 100m you reach a second, smaller ridge. Take the little spur that breaks off to the left and climb up to rejoin the Siete Cañadas path. Continue along it heading to the right.

After another kilometre you pass a turn off to the left which is path number 16 leading to the cable car. Stay on the Siete Cañadas path and continue for another 360m until you see the turn off for path number 5, 'Degallado de Guajara' on the right hand side.

2. First Ascent (3.2km/50mins)
Follow the path that leads from the sign and snakes its way up the first section of crater wall. This is a steady ascent which will make itself known to your thighs and get you used to the extra effort of walking at altitude.

In winter the path can be littered with packed ice and snow which make the going a little harder.

After 1.2km you emerge, breathless, onto the spur with views down over Vilaflor (provided they're not under the sea of clouds) and back behind you to Teide and Pico Viejo. Take a short, well-earned breather.

3. Towards Guajara (4.4km/1hr 25mins)
You're now (temporarily) on path number 8. Follow the path to the right as it traverses the top of this section of the crater wall and continue for 530m until you see a small sign at ground level which shows Sendero 15 and points the way up the mountain.

Don't miss this turn off or you'll find yourself heading towards Vilaflor.

4. Climbing Guajara (4.9km/1hr 50mins)
In winter the path can be difficult to see as rains dislodge small stones and sends them scurrying down the hillside forming lots of small, rock strewn gulleys. It helps to stop and take a look ahead to where a section of path may reveal itself.

There are also a small number of red number 15 signs attached to rocks which reassure you that you're on the right path but to be honest, it's a bit like playing 'spot the path number'.

Your legs will be feeling the effects of the altitude by the time you emerge, 1.7km later, onto the crest of Guajara and the view opens up below you.

Two small stone benches serve as perfect lunch spots and you can peruse the Parador, Roques de Garcia and the Ucanca Plains spread like a vast moonscape at the feet of the volcano. Behind you are the remains of the small hut which housed the world's first high mountain observatory, erected by Scotsman Piazzi Smythe in 1856 and remodelled by the French astronomer Jean Mascart who made camp here in the ice and snow to photograph Halley's Comet as it neared the Earth in 1910.

5. Coming down the mountain (6.7km/2hrs 50mins)
Dragging yourself away from the views, some people return to the crater ridge by a more 'as the crow flies' route that descends to the right. Be prepared to dry ski your way across loose scree all the way and don't be surprised if you lose the seat of your trousers in the process.

Far easier, although not entirely without it's wey-hey moments, is to re-trace your steps back down the way you came to the ridge which will take you 45 minutes.

Turn left on the ridge and head back to the spot where you climbed up from Siete Cañadas.

6. It's all downhill from here (8.9km/3hrs 45mins)

A descent of 25 minutes takes you back down the zigzag path that emerges onto Siete Cañadas.

7. Homeward Bound (10.1km/4hrs 10mins)

Turn left onto the wide path of Siete Cañadas and follow the path.

After 1.4km (approx 25mins), keep an eye out on the left hand side for the short cut. It's marked by a barely discernible little row of stones like a threshold.

Having cut out a huge chunk of the path, re-emerge above the water pipes and continue left, glancing over your shoulder to see people who passed you now a considerable distance behind!

Beyond the traffic barrier and the ranger's stone hut, keep an eye out after the next bend for the signpost which points the way back to the Parador and turn right, following the direction Parador Nacional/Cañada Blanca for the final 700m of lava walk to the Parador to *'Unlace the Boots'*.
13.3km/5hrs

A Place to Unlace the Boots

The terrace of the Café Los Roques (open daily) beside the Parador is a quite special spot to end a walk. The bad news is that it's also a bit of a rip off and takes advantage of its captive audience.

Volcano Surfing, Arenas Negras

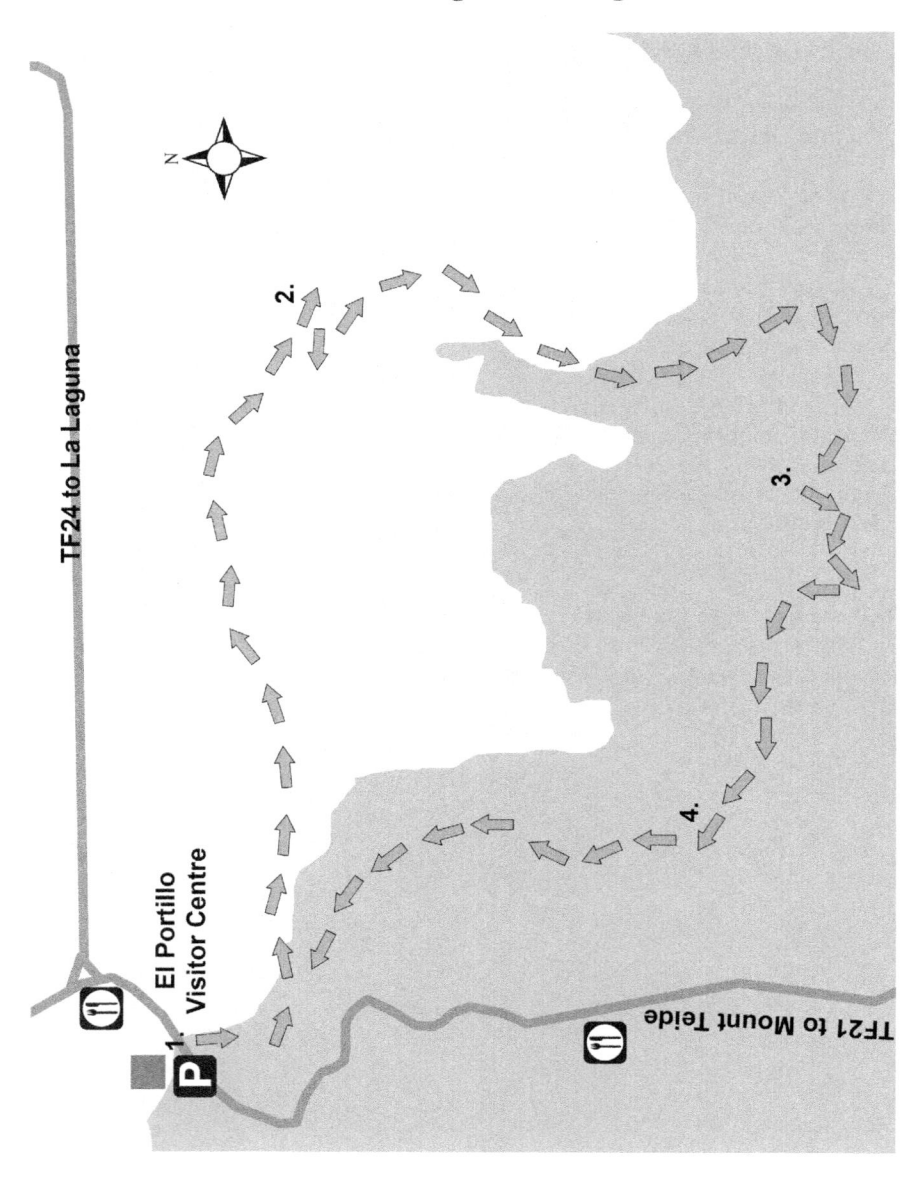

Volcano Surfing, Arenas Negras

Location	Central Tenerife.
Circular Route?	Yes.
How Long?	2hrs 30mins.
How Far?	8.2 kilometres.
Vertiginous?	Not particularly. The only potential problem might be for any vertigo sufferers when they reach the Arenas Negras slopes.
Route Difficulty	Level 3 - There are some ups and downs on this route, but these amount to no more than a pleasant work-out. Walking at altitude may make this route seem more strenuous than it actually is.
Wow Scenery	Like any of the walks in Teide National Park, you're accompanied by volcanic scenery most of the way. But the views into the crater are something else.
Underfoot	On the flat it is easy walking on good paths. Once you hit the slopes the going can be a bit tricky, especially descending steep inclines on loose volcanic scree. A good even path all the way... apart from the Arenas Negras surfing section.
Watering Holes	There is a café/restaurant near the Visitor Centre
Downside	There aren't really any downsides to this walk, apart from maybe getting some grit in your shoes during the downhill section.

This is a great walk for the family as it's a sensible distance; it's not difficult; it starts and ends at the Visitor Centre where there's good parking, toilets and lots of things to see (don't miss the colony of lizards that live on the rock outside the centre – if they get one sniff of a crisp, they'll be out in force!); and you get to part run/part surf down a volcano.

How to Get There

By Car
From Los Gigantes, take the TF82 to Tamaimo and then follow signs for Guia de Isora. At Chio take the TF38 Boca Tauce road all the way to Teide National Park. From the south take the TF21 to reach Teide National Park. From the north, it's also the TF21.

Parking
There are lots of parking spaces at the El Portillo Visitor Centre.

By Public Transport
From both north and south there is only one bus up and down to Teide National Park each day, so it's important to plan accordingly.

Puerto de la Cruz
Catch the 348 direct to Teide National Park.

Playa de las Américas/Los Cristianos
Catch the 342 direct to Teide National Park.

Los Gigantes
From the Los Gigantes area catch the 473 or 477 to Los Cristianos and change to the 342.

The Route

1. Stepping Out
The clearly marked path begins through the barrier opposite the El Portillo Visitor Centre at the sign for "Siete Cañadas route 2". Go around the barrier and follow the wide path down the dip and up the other side for 8 minutes and 370m until you reach a small fork in the path.

Take the left hand fork following the '2' direction.

500m and 6mins later you reach a second fork, stay left and follow the path as it climbs a small spur and then heads off to the left, down the dip and up again. Below you, to your left, the TF24 winds its way into the crater above the northern coastline, running parallel to our path. On the horizon, you should be able to see the twin peaks of the island of La Palma floating above the sea of clouds.

After another 200m and 6mins you reach an information board which tells you about bee-keeping in the Teide National Park. Suitably informed, continue straight ahead at the board and in 1.5km and 25mins, turns sharply to the right.

2. Crater Highs (2.6km/50mins)

You now have a steady 100m ascent as the path climbs in a series of switchbacks which make it an easy ascent. Nevertheless, remember that you're walking at altitude here and attempts to walk at Northern European pace will result in some air-snatching lung moments.

Take your time, admiring the views of the Izaña Observatory, like a Bond villain's lair on the horizon, and of the mountain and the crater floor. From this height, the path which climbs Montaña Blanca to the summit of Mount Teide is very clear and if you're feeling tired, you can console yourself with the fact that you're not half way up that!

After half an hour and 1.4km of ascent, you emerge onto a plain and a number 2 waymarker. The path levels out, curving to the right alongside a small dry-stone wall. 620m and 12mins along this path, you reach another number 2 waymarker at the amazing wind eroded stone gorges with their beautiful layered cake colours. The path skirts these wonderful rock formations until it leads you to the top of Arenas Negras with its vantage point views over the mountain, the crater and the restaurants below.

3. Volcano Surfing (5.2km/1hr 30mins)

The path zig-zags its way steeply down the loose scree face of Arenas Negras. Be careful that you don't pick up too much speed or you might find yourself heading over the edge at the switchback turns! The height that took 40mins to reach, is descended in just 15mins as you discover the new sport of volcano surfing! When you reach the crater floor – hopefully in one piece – continue along the rock and lizard-strewn path until you reach the T-junction with Siete Cañadas.

4. Homeward Bound (6.5km/2hrs)

Turn right along the Siete Cañadas path, following Sendero 4 towards El Portillo and follow it back to the Visitor Centre where you can pick up the car, or turn right and continue on foot, following the road to the Portillo Restaurant to *'Unlace the Boots'*.
8.2km/2hrs 30mins

A Place to Unlace the Boots
The El Portillo Restaurant (open daily) is located where the TF21 meets the TF24, a short stroll from the Visitor Centre. This is where local bikers hang out when they visit the crater and your wallet won't be left gasping for breath after you 'refreshed' yourself here.

Discover More: El Portillo Visitor Centre
The entrance is a mock-up of a volcanic tube, complete with pretend burning river of molten lava beneath your feet.

On the lower level, interactive displays demonstrate how different types of volcanoes erupt. Information shows how Mount Teide was formed, whilst more interaction involves lifting different weights of the various fallout rocks that are typically thrown during an eruption, ranging from the muscle tearing basalt lava to the feather light pumice.

A cinema screens volcanic eruptions in close up while upstairs, walls are covered in amazing photographs of the various elements that make Teide National Park such an incredible environment.

A giant lizard and a three dimensional model of Tenerife dominate the final room which has charts showing the flora and fauna in the park.

Open every day from 9am to 4.15pm; entrance free; displays in English, Spanish and German; there are toilets near the entrance.

Take It To The Wall, La Fortaleza

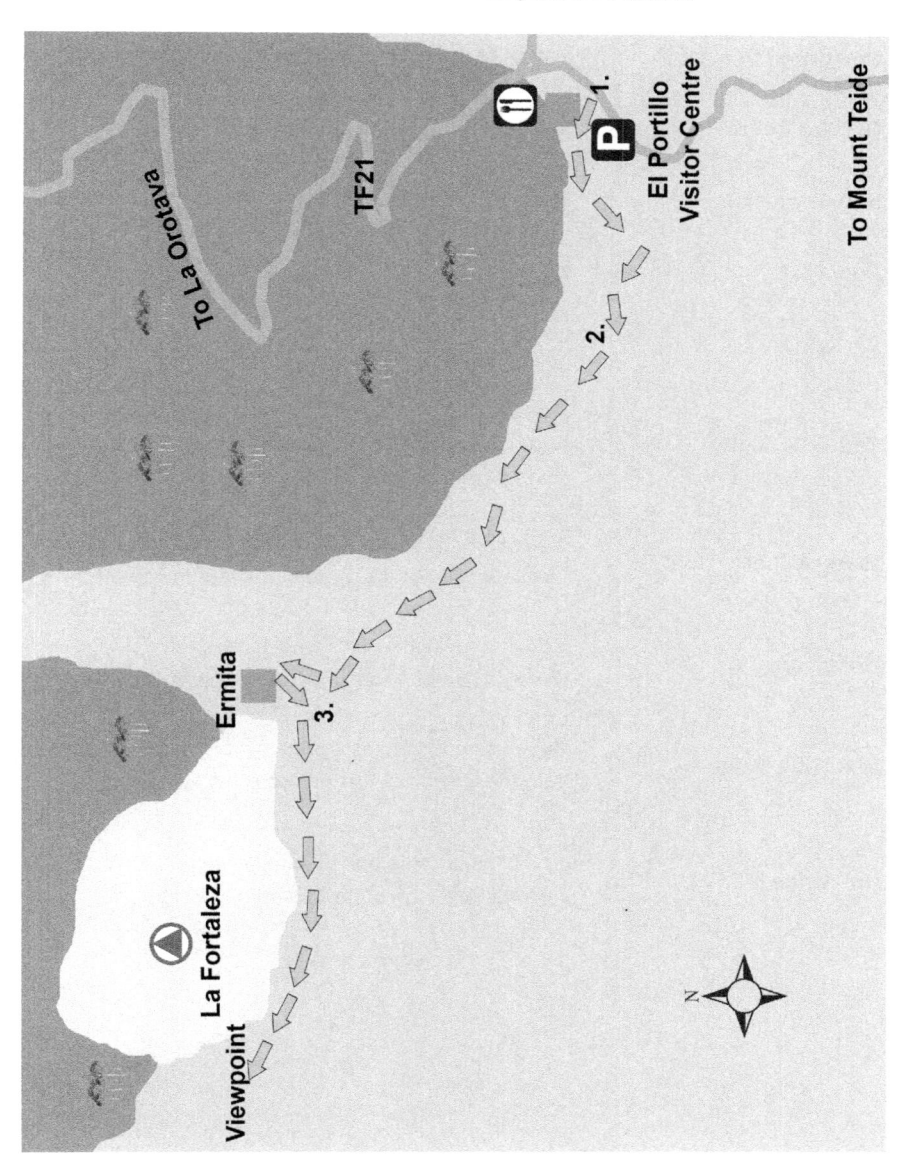

231

Take It To The Wall, La Fortaleza

Location	Central Tenerife.
Circular Route?	No.
How Long?	3hrs.
How Far?	10.6 kilometres.
Vertiginous?	No.
Route Difficulty	Level 3 – It's not a particularly long or difficult walk, but altitude, lack of shade and a climb to the ermita make it more of a challenge.
Wow Scenery	You get a different view of the National Park when La Fortaleza and Mount Teide share the same scene.
Underfoot	A clear path all the way through relatively flat lands. There's a good surface underfoot most of the way.
Watering Holes	There's a good bar/restaurant just around the corner from the El Portillo Visitor Centre.
Downside	It's a popular route and during the winter months can be quite busy with other walkers.

How to Get There
Exactly the same as the Arenas Negras route (see page 228).

The Route

1. Stepping Out
Facing the El Portillo Visitor Centre, the path begins at the left hand side of the centre, beside a walking board showing Sendero 1, La Fortaleza and heads up behind the centre, bearing left at the Y-junction in 140 metres and going through the little turnstile gate. 200 metres and around 8 minutes beyond the gate you reach a fork where you stay right following the Sendero 1 directional signpost. The path is very clearly laid out and a little rocky at first. After walking for just over 1 kilometre and 20 minutes, reach a junction where Sendero 6 goes off to the left. Continue straight ahead on Sendero 1 for another 250 metres to the next junction.

2. In the crater (1.3km/25mins)
At the junction with Sendero 24 at Portillo Alto, take the right hand path and continue for 870 metres where the Sendero 25 comes in from the right and Sendero 22 comes in from the left. Continue straight ahead and in a further 250 metres the landscape opens out into a wide, flat plain. After 150 metres in the basin, a path runs off to the right, signposted Degollada del Cedro and leads to the small Ermita on the hilltop and some wonderful views. It's just a 700 metre

return detour with a bit of a sandy climb on the way up but it's worth it for the views over the plains. Return back down the same path and rejoin the route.

3. The Wall (4km/1hr 15mins)

With the imposing crater wall dominating the right flank and Mount Teide dominating the scene on the left, continue to follow the path for 1.6 kilometres and 25 minutes to arrive at the edge of the crater with views down over the north coast or a sea of clouds depending on the weather. When you've had your fill of the scenery, turn around and retrace your steps back to the Visitor Centre and once through the small turnstile, follow the path that runs through the endemic plant garden before returning to the Centre. After that it's a short journey to Restaurant El Portillo for refreshments (see page 230).
10.6km (incl. detour to ermita and viewpoint)/3hrs

A Rocking Good Walk, Roques de Garcia

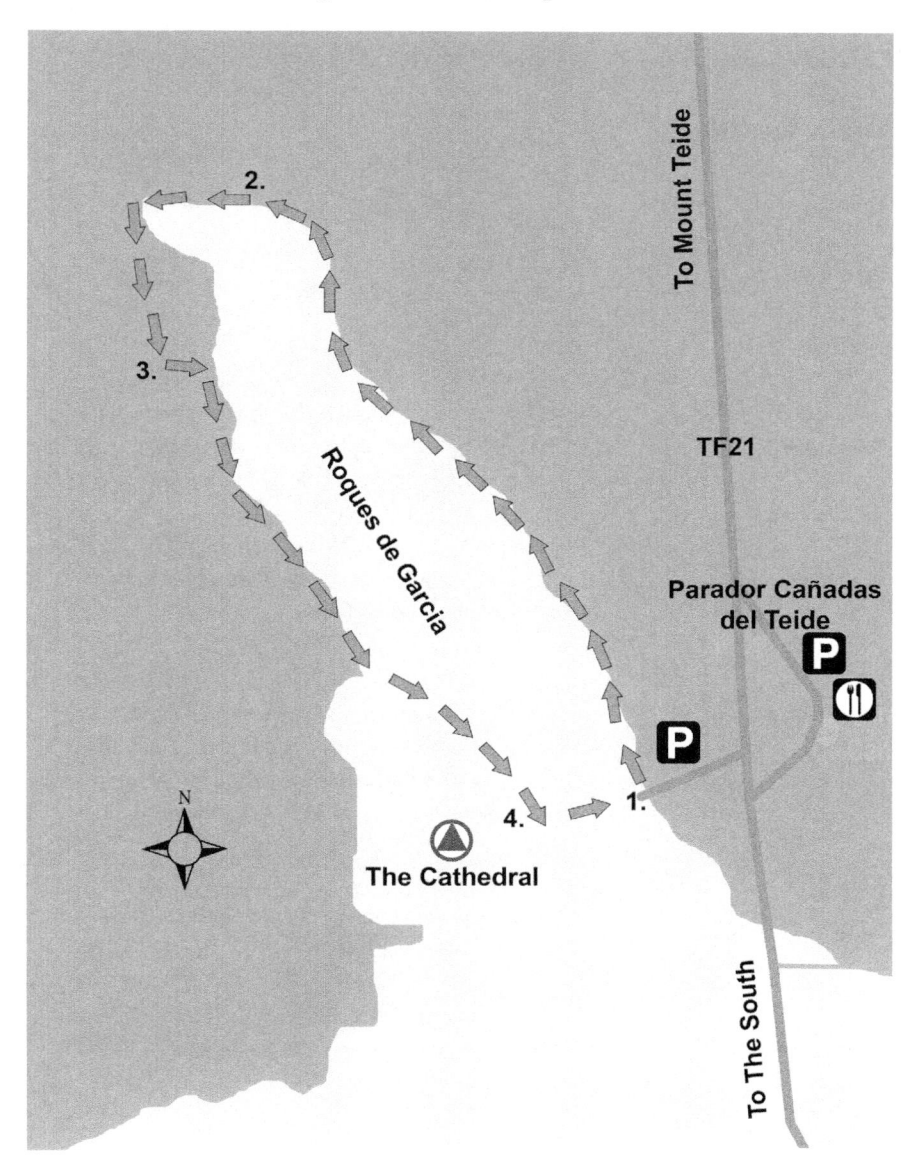

A Rocking Good Walk, Roques de Garcia

Location	Central Tenerife.
Circular Route?	Yes.
How Long?	1 hr 30mins.
How Far?	3.7 kilometres.
Vertiginous?	No.
Route Difficulty	Level 2 – Although there's a bit of a descent and a bit of a lung testing ascent right at the end, this is a short enough route for most relatively fit people to manage.
Wow Scenery	Seeing the Roques from a different angle is quite an eye opener. They look completely different from the 'common' view... even better.
Underfoot	Initially a good path, but it narrows and becomes rockier for the descent to the Ucanca Plains. In some ways slightly different from other crater walks as the Roques create a barrier on one side with the expansive Ucanca plains offering an extreme contrast on the other.
Watering Holes	Café Los Roques beside the Parador is a convenient, if expensive, watering hole.
Downside	Only the fact that the Roques are incredibly busy. But in a way this enhances the route as you know you're seeing something the masses aren't.

If time is short and the idea of viewing the much visited Roques de Garcia from an unusual angle appeals then a short-ish walk of just under 4 kilometres circling some of Tenerife's most photographed landmarks to view them from an unusual angle may just be the ticket.

How to Get There
Exactly the same as the Montaña Guajara route (see page 222). The route starts at Roques de Garcia on the opposite side of the road from the Parador.

The Route

1: Stepping Out
The path (number 3 on the Teide National Park official walking routes) leaves from the car park beside the Roques de Garcia passing the shillelagh shaped Roque Chinchado which looks as though it could topple over at any moment. Keeping the rocks to the left, simply follow the path at the base of the walks in the direction of Mount Teide.

2: The Melted Auditorium (1.4k/25mins)
The path is clear and easy to follow all the way till you see a lone rocky outrcop that looks like a melted rock version of the iconic Tenerife Auditorium building in Santa Cruz. At this point a path veers off to the right towards Pico Viejo. Stay on the path heading straight ahead toward the 'Auditorio'.

Within a few minutes you arrive at a gap in the rock at the top of impressive, solidified lava falls. The lava break in the rocks has created a wonderful, natural viewpoint overlooking the Llano de Ucanca (Ucanca Plains). This is the only point the path ahead is indistinct. Continue straight underneath the base of the rock at the other end of the lava falls and it will soon become clear again.

Almost immediately is another viewpoint which looks back along the Roques de Garcia from an angle not usually seen. The path then descends to the floor of the plains.

3: Toward the Rocks (2.2k/50mins)
The only other uncertain section of the route is after 2.2km when the path turns sharply left in the direction of the rocks whilst another continues straight ahead. Take the left path to reach the clear trail that runs below the rock formations.

Ahead on the plains is the huge rock formation known as the Cathedral. It doesn't require an overactive imagination to see why.

The path runs between the Cathedral and the Roques de Garcia. Occasionally trails split from the main path, but they rejoin it after a short distance.

As the path begins to ascend you might hear disembodied voices. Scan the sheer walls of the Cathedral, it's popular with rock climbers.

4: Homeward Bound (3.4k/1hr 20mins)
The path ascends to a T junction on a small ridge. Right are more views across the plains. Head left to tackle the final climb back to the busy viewpoint overlooking the Llano de Ucanca.
3.7k/1hr 30mins

What goes down must go up again and after a nice easy stroll you face the uphill slog back up to the main mirador (viewpoint) overlooking the plains. After that it's just a short stroll to the Los Roques café for a reward (see page 225).

The Ultimate High, Climbing Mount Teide

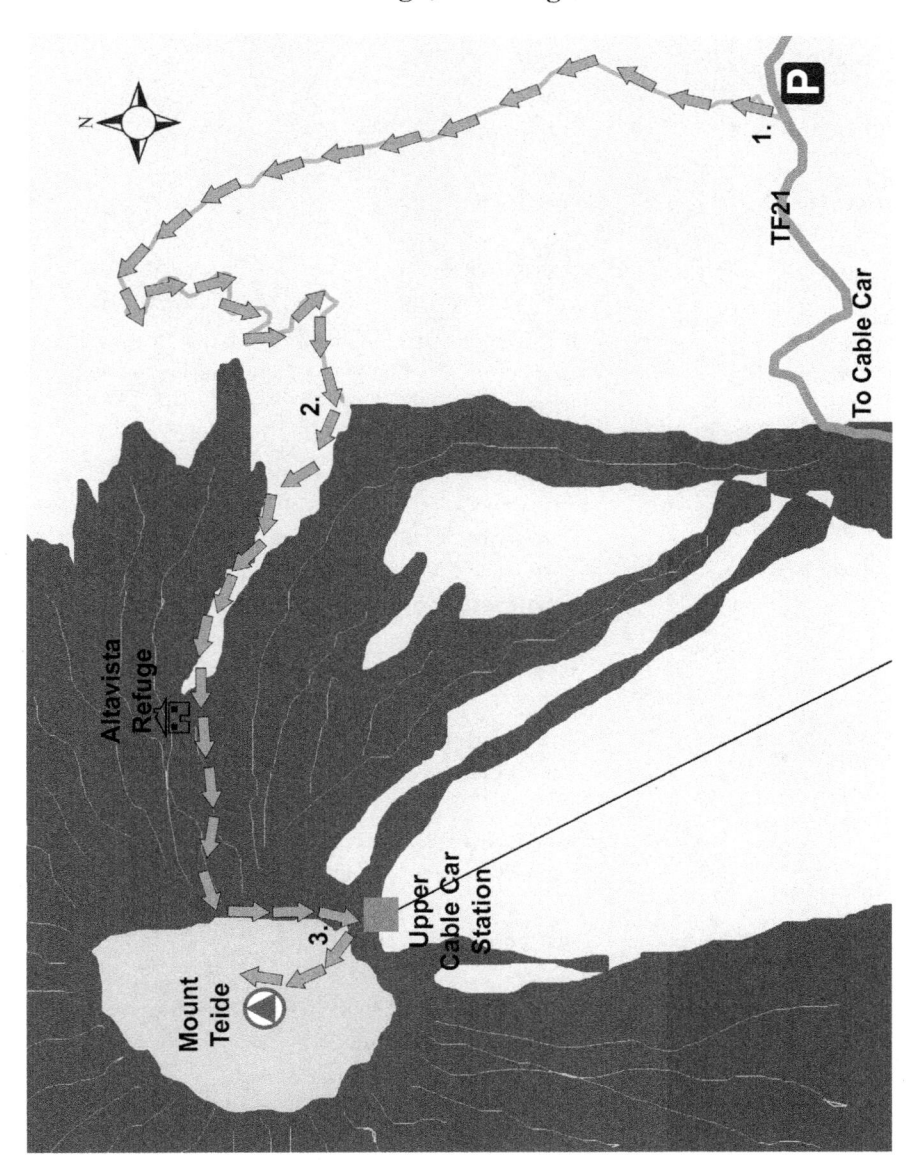

The Ultimate High, Climbing Mount Teide

Location	Central Tenerife.
Circular Route?	No.
How Long?	Approx 6hrs.
How Far?	9.5 kilometres.
Vertiginous?	It's Spain's highest mountain. Saying that, there are no sheer drops. But those views down may be too much for some.
Route Difficulty	Level 5 - We believe that you have to be in very good shape to climb Mount Teide. Not because of distance, or even the difficulty of the route; there's a good path pretty much all of the way. Climbers start this walk at almost the point that altitude sickness can kick in and it doesn't get any easier the higher you climb. Lots of rests along the way are recommended.
Wow Scenery	The top of Spain, a huge volcanic crater and the other Canary Islands – unbelievable.
Underfoot	An ever changing volcanic landscape with lava flows, pyroclastic bombs and an amazing range of colours. The route ranges from a flat path to hard volcanic rock and loose scree in parts.
Watering Holes	Unless stopping at the Altavista Refuge, there are none. If coming back down by cable car, there is the restaurant/café in the lower station.
Downside	The possibility of suffering from altitude sickness.

Tenerife's ultimate walk is to climb to the summit of Teide and stand on the peak of Spain's highest mountain (3718 metres). We don't feel a map is really necessary for this one as your objective is sort of unmistakeable.

How to Get There

By Car
From Los Gigantes, take the TF82 to Tamaimo and then follow signs for Guia de Isora. At Chio take the TF38 Boca Tauce road all the way to Teide National Park. From the south take the TF21 to reach Teide National Park. From the north, it's also the TF21. The start of the route is between the cable car and the Minas de San José. It's signposted and easily spotted from the road

Parking
There are limited spaces right at the start of the route as well as some rough off road areas where people leave their cars. But it fills quickly.

By Public Transport
Getting to the Teide National Park is the same as other routes in the crater. The Montaña Blanca bus stop is right at the start of the route.

The Route

1. A Gentle Start
The route starts on the TF21 at the Montaña Blanca signpost. There's very limited parking, so an early start is recommended. The wide trail from there to the Estancia de los Ingleses near the base of Montaña Blanca takes about an hour and you'll find yourself in the company of plenty of other walkers on this section. It's an easy section for acclimatising to walking at these altitudes.

Towards the end of this stage look out for the pyroclastic bombs known as Teide's eggs. These huge balls were thrown out by the volcano and I swear one looks like Elvis Presley.

2. The Only Way is Up
From the Estancia de los Ingleses the route is quite clear, winding up between the two black, basaltic lava flows which bookend the path. This is the point when you find out how you react to walking at altitude. The views from this part are truly spectacular and a teaser that even better is to follow. Depending on fitness levels and the amount of stops you make to soak up the vistas, approximately 3 hours later the path leads weary legs straight to the door of the Altavista refuge. As this is a refuge, not a hotel, amenities are basic.

3. The Final Push

The path leads from the refuge southward around the mountain to join the main path leading from the cable car to the viewpoint overlooking La Fortaleza and the north. Head left toward the upper cable car station. Just beyond it is the point where the path ascends again and where, when the cable car is running, a guard will check for permits. The route straight ahead leads to views over the south and Pico Viejo. From the cable car station, the route climbs the last few hundred metres to the summit of Mount Teide, an hour to an hour and a half later after leaving the refuge (it can feel an awful lot longer). In daylight it's easy to follow, but if you're doing the climb to reach the summit at dawn, a head torch is essential. As you reach the top be careful of steadying yourself by using rocks beside the path, some are hot, hot, hot to the touch. The sulphurous smell should be a warning when you're in the vicinity of any.

And then that's it; you're on the top of Tenerife's world. Be prepared to be WOWED, especially if you're there to witness the dawn.

A Place to Unlace the Boots

If staying overnight at the Altavista Refuge there are basic amenities – a vending machine. Returning from the summit via the cable car means you can end with a drink/meal in the comfort of the lower cable car station, hypnotised by views over the volcanic landscape.

Permit to Climb Mount Teide
There are two ways to complete the climb to the summit. The first involves applying for a permit online. The easy way to do this is via the routes information in the Teide Cable Car section of the Teleférico website (www.telefericoteide.com). There's lots of additional and useful information on the website even if you don't plan to climb Spain's highest mountain.

The second, and the one we'd recommend as this really is the ultimate high, is to break up the climb with a stay overnight at the Altavista refuge (see website above; 0034 922 010 440; €20) and complete the climb in the early morning just in time to see sunrise from the summit – a true out of this world experience... and no permit is required as long as you're back through the gate behind the upper cable car station before 9am.

Mount Teide's Shadow
One magical sight to look out for at sunrise on Mount Teide is the shadow the volcano casts on either the actual sea or the sea of clouds if the sky isn't clear. Whilst being amazed by the huge shadow, think of this: why is it a triangle when Mount Teide itself doesn't have a pointy tip?
The answer, according to NASA, is because you're basically looking down a long corridor where the sunrise shadow stretches to the horizon, eventually tapering to a point.

Walks in Central Tenerife
Vilaflor

"As we strolled in warm sunshine enjoying the charms of Tenerife's highest town, Vilaflor, we spotted something that just shouldn't have been there – a tajinaste rojo partly in bloom..."

Walking in Vilaflor

Lying at 1400 metres above sea level, Vilaflor is an alpine village sitting high above the south coast, on the edge of the Teide National Park. Backed by pine forests and fronted by neat rows of jablé (pumice) lined terraces that climb the hillside like the layers of a wedding cake, the town is known for its picturesque position; its potatoes, which are the best on the island; and as being the birthplace of Tenerife's only saint, Hermano Pedro, who founded the Order of the Bethlehemites. A Victorian spa centre formerly known as Chasna, and one of the most important municipalities on the island, Vilaflor is blessed with superb hiking trails created by the guanche and sustained over centuries by the feet of merchants, explorers and scientists.

Weather

It doesn't matter what time of the year it is, Vilaflor will be considerably cooler than at the coast and in winter, nights will be cold. Because of its altitude, there will be days when you climb above the sea of clouds to enjoy sunshine and on other days, the cloud will envelope the town bringing moisture and dropping temperatures. Conditions can even change by the hour. Although it's a predominantly arid climate, the low cloud brings moisture in winter. Dress in layers and make sure you have warm clothing for January and February particularly,

Flora
Vilaflor is a town almost perpetually in bloom. From the pots of geraniums, marigolds and roses that line the streets, and the gorgeous displays of almond blossom that burst into life in late January and early February, to the early blooming tajinaste in June, there is often a floral display to be enjoyed. Outside of the town you'll be walking through pine forests with carpets of broom, bright orange California poppies and cistus. Just outside the village you'll find the fattest (pino gordo) pine tree on the island.

Call of Nature
The Fuente de Hermano Pedro café in the plaza has toilets for customers' use, after that, it's just you and the pine forest!

Eat me
Vilaflor is serious potato growing country. You'll find *papas arrugadas* (salty wrinkled potatoes) all over Tenerife but with all those terraces filled with potatoes, they really should be tried in Vilaflor, accompanied by mojo rojo and mojo verde (Canarian sauces made from peppers, garlic, spices, olive oil and or coriander/parsley).

Where To Stay When Walking in Vilaflor
See page 218/219 for recommendations about where to stay for easy access to Vilaflor routes.

Walking To The Moon - Vilaflor to Paisaje Lunar

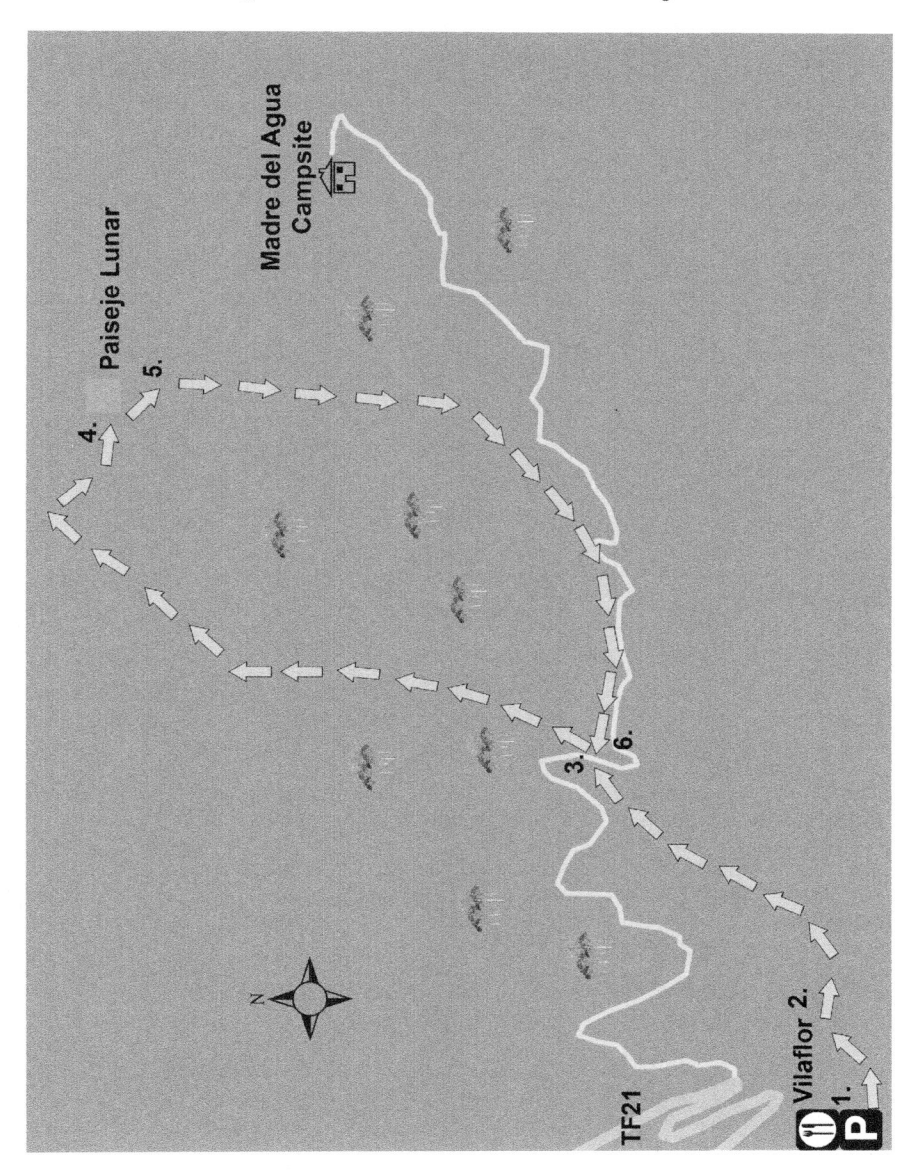

Walking To The Moon - Vilaflor to Paisaje Lunar

Location	Central Tenerife.
Circular Route?	Partially.
How Long?	4hrs 30mins.
How Far?	13.5 kilometres.
Vertiginous?	No.
Route Difficulty	Level 3 – The first half of the route involves a near constant ascent which can take its toll. It's not a steep climb, it just seems to go on for a while. However, the scenery acts as a good distraction.
Wow Scenery	The lunar landscape is one of Tenerife's most unusual attractions.
Underfoot	Mostly pine forest and agricultural terraces. After a rocky path start, a feet friendly forest path for most of the route.
Watering Holes	There's plenty of choice in Vilaflor.
Downside	The path doesn't officially go all the way to the surreal rock formations.

Beginning in the plaza of the picturesque, mountain village of Vilaflor which lies at 1400 metres above sea level in the hills above the south east coast, this excellent walk is Alpine in nature. Ascending the ancient camino real of Camino de Chasna, the route climbs above the village, traversing the bed of a ravine before climbing through red earth pine forest to reach the amazing lunar landscape of Paisaje Lunar. Here, over half a million years, the elements have sculpted fantastical shapes from volcanic fallout to create a unique and fascinating landscape. An almost 600 metre, gradual ascent which is downhill all the way home.

How to Get There

By Car
From the south take the TF21 to reach Vilaflor. From the north, the best way is to take the TF21 through Teide National Park and continue on it to drop down to Vilaflor. From Los Gigantes, drive to Los Cristianos and take the TF21 to Vilaflor.

Parking
There are parking spaces around the plaza in Vilaflor and there is a car park behind the church at the top of the plaza.

By Public Transport

Puerto de la Cruz
This is a really awkward one from the north, involving getting to Los Cristianos (343) in time to catch the 482 or the 342.

Playa de las Américas/Los Cristianos
Catch the 342 Teide National Park bus or the 482 to Vilaflor.

Los Gigantes
From the Los Gigantes area catch the 473 or 477 to Los Cristianos and change to the 342 or 482.

The Route

1. Finding the way
The route begins in the town of Vilaflor and the hardest part is actually finding the start. From the south end of Plaza de Vilaflor, at the Hermano Pedro fountain and bar restaurant, a signpost shows 'PR72 Camino de Chasna Paisaje Lunar 6km' and points the way down from the plaza.

Walk right, down Calle Castaños, in the direction of the signpost, take the immediate first left onto Calle El Canario and follow it for 180 metres, all the way to the T junction at the bottom.

Turn right onto Calle Guatemala and walk down the hill for 2 minutes and 80 metres until you reach a cobbled path leading off to the left, way-marked by red, white and yellow stripes. Turn left onto the cobbled path and follow it over a small barranco (ravine). On the opposite wall is a white arrow and a waymark, go right up the hill, passing a red striped, GR131 marker and turn right immediately after it at the white arrow on the stone and climb steeply following the clearly way-marked path.

2. Following the GR131 (530 metres/10mins)
The route follows the GR 131 path all the way to Paisaje Lunar or Los Escurriales as they're known.

In 800 metres and 25 minutes you reach an indistinct fork in the path and stay left uphill following the waymark stripes. On a clear day, the views down to coast are worth stopping to get your breath back for. In a further 3 minutes and 200 metres you pass a signpost showing Camino de Chasna/ Vilaflor 1.5km back the way you have ascended. Continue ascending straight ahead. Another 10 or so minutes and 650 metres you arrive in a small, circular cul-de-sac where there's a clear waymarked gap in the low wall, and follow the path as it descends to the bottom of the barranco. Cross the floor of the barranco and begin to ascend on the other side through forest, continuing to follow the clear waymarks.

The path reaches the dirt road which links the Madre del Agua campsite to the TF21 Vilaflor to Teide National Park road. Turn right on the road and you will see where the path continues on the other side, 20 metres along. Cross the road and follow the path that ascends to the left. 10 minutes and 130 metres from the road you reach a T junction where the signpost shows Los Escurriales/Paisaje Lunar 3.6km in one direction and 3.7km in the other. This is where you begin the circular route to Paisaje Lunar and where you will return to on the route back to Vilaflor.

3. Onwards and upwards to the moon (2.9km/1hr 10mins)
Take the left path signposted 3.6km and begin the gradual ascent. After 5 minutes and 350 metres of ascent, the stone benches set in the shade of the pine tree make a good spot to sit, catch a breeze and take in the views down to the east coast. Continue to ascend for another 15 minutes and 600 metres to reach a small, indistinct crossroads of paths where you go straight across. There's a clear X on the paths to right and to left denoting that they are not the way to go.

5 minutes and 120 metres later cross a pista (forest path) and go through the barrier, following the path as it continues to ascend and in another 15 minutes and almost 1km you get a taster of the type of surreal rock formations formed by wind erosion of layers of compressed cinders and ashes resulting from volcanic activity in this area around half a million years ago. Continue ascending as the path climbs to the left and in another 20 minutes and 1km you arrive at a signposted crossroads showing Vilaflor 5.8km back the way you came. Go right on the path signposted to Los Escurriales 0.6km and make a rocky and narrow descent to arrive, 5 minutes and 400 metres later, at a small mirador (viewpoint) with a stone seat, overlooking the moon.

4. Gazing at the moon (6.3km/2hr 15mins)
   Around 500,000 years ago a powerful jet of cinders, stones and ash from a volcanic eruption was carried on the wind, and rained down onto the slopes of the barranco, settling in a thick layer and melding the various elements together as they cooled. A further eruption then covered the area with another layer of harder, more erosion resistant materials. Over thousands of years the top layer has been eroded to reveal the cinders and pumice layer beneath which, highly susceptible to erosion by wind and rain, has been sculpted into these fantastical shapes.

   After detouring slightly to the little viewpoint, the path continues to the right (to the left if you have your back to Paisaje Lunar) and in 5 minutes and 300 metres arrives at another pretty mirador and more views. A rough, rocky and indistinct path runs down to the left of the post marked '9' which leads directly to the rock formations but, fearful of their erosion, walking within the sculptures is discouraged by the environmental department. Visitors should respect conservation efforts and simply enjoy gazing upon them.

5. Woodland trails (6.6km/2hrs 20mins)

When you've filled your memory stick with moonscape images, continue along the path from the mirador following the signpost direction of Vilaflor 6.5km, as it descends gently through the woodland. In 35 minutes and 1.8km you reach the junction with the Madre del Agua route and continue to the right, following the Vilaflor 4.7km signpost direction.

In 5 minutes and 300 metres you pass a signpost showing Vilaflor 4.4km and you continue straight ahead along the path for another 10 minutes and 430 metres to reach a wider dirt pista. Go straight across the pista and continue along the clearly marked path the other side as it descends into the barranco and crosses over a dry stream bed before then climbing out the other side.

7 minutes and 390 metres later you cross the pista again and continue descending following the yellow and white striped waymarks. In 420 metres you reach a large sign asking you to 'Respetemos La Naturaleza' (Let's Respect the Countryside) and the path now hangs right alongside some ruined cottages and descends through the forest for 200 metres and 3 minutes to arrive at a broad forest path.

Turn right along the wider path for a small section until you reach the third yellow and white striped post on the right hand side with a sign showing no cyclists or horseback riding. Turn right here and head briefly up into the forest again. Emerge, 5 minutes and 200 metres later at the crossroads where we began our circular route to Los Escurriales, now arriving from the 3.7km direction.

6. Descent to Vilaflor (10.5km/3hrs 30mins)

Turn left and rejoin your original route as it heads down towards the Madre Del Agua road. Cross the road and continue to descend from the other side, following the path you took up from Vilaflor.

In 500 metres and 10 minutes you'll arrive back at the little cul-de-sac and turn left to descend along the Camino de Chasna, back to Vilaflor.

In 35 minutes and 1.7km, don't forget to turn left at the white arrow on the wall and cross back over the small barranco to arrive at the end of the cobbled path in Vilaflor. Ignore the signpost, turn right and slog uphill to take the first turning on the left onto Calle El Canario. Go down the dip and up the other side,

cross over the small side street and hang right along Calle Castaños where a few steps will take you back to Plaza de Vilaflor where you can Unlace The Boots over a deserved cold beer or cup of coffee and a slice of their home-made cake at bar restaurant Fuente Hermano Pedro.
13.5km/4hrs 30mins

A Place to Unlace the Boots

If only after a coffee/cerveza then Restaurante Fuente Hermano Pedro (open daily) in the plaza is perfect. If the cloud descends, it's quite cosy inside where homemade cakes do their best to tempt. It's also good for food but our favourite place in Vilaflor is El Rincón de Roberto (closed Tuesday) on Calle Hermano Pedro. On a cool day the Canarian *degustación* (taster selection) beside the roaring fire goes down a treat.

APPENDICES

A quick guide to choosing the route to suit

APPENDIX 1

Walks Under 10km (6.2 miles)

Route	Area	Length of Walk (km)	Grade	Page Nº
Arenas Negras	Teide National Park	8.2	3	226
The Ultimate High	Teide National Park	9.5	5	239
Roques de Garcia	Teide National Park	3.7	2	235
A Glimpse of Rural Life	La Orotava	7.5	2	56
Pools & Pines	Santiago del Teide	6	3	80
Camino de la Virgen de Lourdes	Santiago del Teide	1	2	85
An Explosive Landscape	Chio	7	2	86
In Ancient Footsteps	Masca	6	4	110
Following the Lava	Garachico	5.6	3	120

Route	Area	Length of Walk (km)	Grade	Page Nº
Taste of the Caribbean	Los Realejos/Puerto de la Cruz	5	1	132
Virgin's Badlands	Guimar	6.2	1	145
A Merchant's Highway	San Juan de la Rambla	5	1	138
Way Out West	Buenavista	5.6	1	127
The Lost World	Vera de Erques	5.5	3	189
Cereal Killers	Guia de isora	7.2	3	183
Above Barranco Del Infierno	Ifonche	5	2	153
The Deserted Valley	Ifonche	3	2	158
Road to a View	San Miguel de Abona	9	3	199
Barranco del Infierno	Adeje	6.5	3	162
Holiday Mountain	Los Cristianos	8	3	175

Route	Area	Length of Walk (km)	Grade	Page Nº
King of the South	Arona	7.4	3	169
Exploring the Red Mountain	El Medano	7	2	206
Yellow Mountain	Costa Del Silencio	9	2	211

APPENDIX 2

Walks 10km – 20km (6.2 miles – 12.4 miles)

Route	Area	Length of Walk (km)	Grade	Page Nº
Climbing the Wall	Teide National Park	10	4	220
Take it to the Wall	Teide National Park	10.6	3	231
Walking to the Moon	Vilaflor	13.5	3	247
Northern Exposure	La Orotava	11.8	4	49
The Guanche Way	La Orotava	15	3	61
Into the Valley	Santiago del Teide	14.2	3	72
Forest to Cave	Anaga Mountains	12.4	3	22
Hamlets & Hillsides	Anaga Mountains	13.3	3	30
To the End of the Island	Anaga Mountains	11.7	4	38
Up Country	El Palmar	10.5	3	95
Black Caves & Broken Cottages	Los Silos	17.5	4	103

APPENDIX 3

Walks 2 Hours and Under

Route	Area	Time	Grade	Page Nº
Roques de Garcia	Teide National Park	1hr 30mins	2	235
Virgen de Lourdes	Santiago del Teide	30mins	2	85
Following the Lava	Garachico	1hr 55mins	3	120
Taste of the Caribbean	Los Realejos/Puerto de la Cruz	1hr	1	132
The Virgin's Badlands	Guimar	1hr 50mins	1	145
A Merchant's Highway	San Juan de la Rambla	1hr 30mins	1	138
Way Out West	Buenavista	50mins	1	127
Above Barranco del Infierno	Ifonche	2hrs	2	153
The Deserted Valley	Ifonche	1hr 5mins	2	158

APPENDIX 4

Walks 2hrs to 4hrs

Route	Area	Time	Grade	Page Nº
Volcano Surfing	Teide National Park	2hrs 30mins	3	226
Take it to the Wall	Teide National Park	3hrs	3	231
A Glimpse of Rural Life	La Orotava	2hrs 20mins	2	56
Into the Valley	Santiago del Teide	3hrs 50mins	3	72
Pools & Pines	Santiago del Teide	2hrs 15mins	3	80
An Explosive Landscape	Chio	2hrs 10mins	2	86
Forest to Cave	Anaga Mountains	3hrs 30mins	3	22
Up Country	El Palmar	4hrs	3	95
In Ancient Footsteps	Masca Barranco	2hrs 40mins	4	110
The Lost World	Vera de Erques	2hrs 10mins	3	189
Cereal Killers	Guia de Isora	2hrs 30mins	3	183
Road to a View	San Miguel de Abona	2hrs 55mins	3	199

Route	Area	Time	Grade	Page Nº
Barranco del Infierno	Adeje	3hrs 30mins	3	162
Holiday Mountain	Los Cristianos	2hrs 20mins	3	175
King of the South	Arona	3hrs	3	169
Yellow Mountain	Costa Del Silencio	2hr 40mins	2	211

APPENDIX 5

Walks Over 4hrs

Route	Area	Time	Grade	Page Nº
Climbing the Wall	Teide National Park	5hrs	4	220
The Ultimate High	Teide National Park	6hrs	5	239
Walking to the Moon	Vilaflor	4hrs 30mins	3	247
Northern Exposure	La Orotava	4hrs 25mins	4	49
The Guanche Way	La Orotava	4hrs 45mins	3	61
Hamlets & Hillsides	Anaga Mountains	4hrs 50mins	3	30
To the End of the Island	Anaga Mountains	4hrs 50mins	4	38
Black Caves & Broken Cottages	Los Silos	6hrs 20mins	4	103

APPENDIX 6

Mountain Walks

Route	Area	Length of Walk (km)	Grade	Page Nº
Climbing the Walls	Teide National Park	10	4	220
The Ultimate High	Teide National Park	9.5	5	239
Northern Exposure	La Orotava	11.8	4	49
Forest to Cave	The Anaga Mountains	12.4	3	22
Hamlets & Hillsides	The Anaga Mountains	13.3	3	30
To the End of the Island	The Anaga Mountains	11.7	4	38
Up Country	Teno Rural Park	10.5	3	95
Holiday Mountain	Los Cristianos	8	3	175
King of the South	Arona	7.4	3	169

Route	Area	Length of Walk (km)	Grade	Page Nº
Red Mountain	El Medano	7	2	206
Yellow Mountain	Costa Del Silencio	9	2	211

APPENDIX 7

Forest Walking (a substantial section of the route passes through forest)

Route	Area	Length of Walk (km)	Grade	Page Nº
Walking to the Moon	Vilaflor	13.5	3	247
Northern Exposure	La Orotava	11.8	4	49
A Glimpse of Rural Life	La Orotava	7.5	2	56
The Guanche Way	La Orotava	15	3	61
Black Caves & Broken Cottages	Los Silos	17.5	4	103

APPENDIX 8

Coastal Walks

Route	Area	Length of Walk (km)	Grade	Page Nº
Taste of the Caribbean	Los Realejos/Puerto de la Cruz	5	1	132
The Virgin's Badlands	Guimar	6.2	1	145
A Merchant's Highway	San Juan de la Ramble	5	1	138
Way Out West	Buenavista	5.6	1	127
The Red Mountain	El Medano	7	2	206
The Yellow Mountain	Costa Del Silencio	9	2	211

APPENDIX 9

Caminos Reales (a substantial section of the route is along a camino real – see page number 5)

Route	Area	Length of Walk (km)	Grade	Page Nº
Walking to the Moon	Vilaflor	13.5	3	247
The Guanche Way	La Orotava	15	3	61
Into the Valley	Santiago del Teide	14.2	3	72
From Forest to Caves	The Anaga Mountains	12.4	3	22
Hamlets & Hillsides	The Anaga Mountains	13.3	3	30
To the End of the Island	The Anaga Mountains	11.7	4	38
Black Caves & Broken Cottages	Los Silos	17.5	4	103
A Merchant's Highway	San Juan de la Rambla	5	1	138
Up Country	El Palmar	10.5	3	95

Route	Area	Length of Walk (km)	Grade	Page Nº
The Lost World	Vera de Erques	5.5	3	189
Cereal Killers	Guia de Isora	7.2	3	183
Above Barranco del Infierno	Ifonche	7.2	3	153
Road to a View	San Miguel de Abona	9	3	199
King of the South	Arona	7.4	3	169

APPENDIX 10

Family Friendly Walks (walks 3hrs and under with something to see/do before, during or after)

Route	Area	Time	Additional Interest	Page Nº
Volcano Surfing	Teide National Park	2hrs 30mins	Running down a volcano	226
A Rockin' Good Route	Teide National Park	1hr 30mins	Rock formations	235
Take it to the Wall	Teide National Park	3hrs	El Portillo Visitor Centre	231
A Glimpse of Rural Life	La Orotava	2hrs 20mins	Trout farm	56
Pools & Pines	Santiago del Teide	2hrs 15mins	Ponds with wildlife	80
An Explosive Landscape	Chio	2hrs 10mins	Lava fields	86
Following the Lava	Garachico	1hr 55mins	Swimming in rock pools	120
Taste of the Caribbean	Los Realejos/Puerto de la Cruz	1hr	Pirate lookout from old fort	132
The Virgin's Badlands	Guimar	1hr 50mins	Pyramids of Guimar	145

Route	Area	Time	Additional Interest	Page Nº
Way Out West	Buenavista del Norte	50mins	Beach & rock pools	127
Road to a View	San Miguel de Abona	2hrs 55mins	Museum, abandoned village & caves	199

APPENDIX 11

Routes Near Resort Areas (within 20km)

Route	Resorts Within 20km	Page Nº
Cereal Killers, Guia de Isora	Alcalá, Callao Salvaje, Costa Adeje, Los Gigantes, Playa de la Arena, Playa de San Juan, Playa Paraiso, Puerto de Santiago	183
The Lost World, Vera de Erques	Alcalá, Callao Salvaje, Costa Adeje, Los Gigantes, Playa de la Arena, Playa de Las Americas, Playa de San Juan, Playa Paraiso, Puerto de Santiago	189
Hell's Ravine, Adeje	Alcalá, Callao Salvaje, Costa Adeje, Los Cristianos, Palm Mar, Playa de Las Americas, Playa de San Juan, Playa Paraiso, Puerto de Santiago	162
Northern Exposure, La Orotava	Puerto de la Cruz	49
A Glimpse of Rural Life, La Orotava	Puerto de la Cruz	56
The Guanche Way, La Orotava	Puerto de la Cruz	61
Taste of the Caribbean, Los Realejos	Puerto de la Cruz	132

Route	Resorts Within 20km	Page Nº
Road to a View, San Miguel de Abona	Costa Adeje, Costa del Silencio, El Medano, Golf del Sur, Los Cristianos, Palm Mar, Playa de Las Americas	199
Holiday Mountain, Los Cristianos	Callao Salvaje, Costa Adeje, Costa Del Silencio, Los Cristianos, Palm Mar, Playa de Las Americas, Playa Paraiso, Puerto de Santiago	175
King of the South, Arona	Costa Adeje, Costa Del Silencio, Los Cristianos, Palm Mar, Playa de Las Americas,	169
Red Mountain, El Medano	Costa del Silencio, El Medano, Golf,del Sur	206
Yellow Mountain, Costa del Silencio	Costa del Silencio, El Medano, Golf del Sur, Los Cristianos, Palm Mar	211

APPENDIX 12

Routes Vertigo Sufferers Should Be Aware Of

Route	Area	Notes	Page Nº
Climbing the Walls	Teide National Park	Unavoidable vertiginous sections	220
The Ultimate High	Teide National Park	Route not precipitous, but descent is by cable car	239
Northern Exposure	La Orotava	Unavoidable vertiginous sections	49
Hamlets & Hillsides	Anaga Mountains	Unavoidable vertiginous sections	30
Forest to Cave	Anaga Mountains	Unavoidable vertiginous sections	22
To the End of the World	Anaga Mountains	Unavoidable vertiginous sections	38
Up Country	El Palmar	Some ridge sections may be a problem for serious sufferers	95
Black Caves & Broken Cottages	Los Silos	Steep descent may be an issue for serious sufferers	103
Above Barranco del Infierno	Adeje	Unavoidable vertiginous sections	153

Route	Area	Notes	Page Nº
The Deserted Valley	Ifonche	Unavoidable vertiginous sections	158
King of the South	Arona	Unavoidable vertiginous sections	169
The Red Mountain	El Medano	Omit the path to the summit, the rest is fine	206
The Yellow Mountain	Costa Del Silencio	Omit the path to the summit, the rest is fine	211

APPENDIX 13

Our Favourite Walks

Route	Area	Distance (km)	Time	Page Nº
Climbing the Walls	Teide National Park	10	5hrs	220
Northern Exposure	Teide National Park	11.8	4hrs 25mins	49
Pools & Pines	Santiago del Teide	6	2hrs 15mins	80
Forest to Cave	The Anaga Mountains	12.4	3hrs 30mins	22
To the End of the Island	The Anaga Mountains	11.7	4hrs 50mins	38
Up Country	El Palmar	10.5	4hrs	95
Black Caves & Broken Cottages	Los Silos	17.5	6hrs 20mins	103
A Taste of the Caribbean	Los Realejos/Puerto de la Cruz	5	1hr	132
Road to a View	San Miguel de Abona	9	2hrs 55mins	199
King of the South	Arona	7.4	3hrs	169

APPENDIX 14

GPS Coordinates for the Start Points of Routes

Route	Latitude	Longitude	Page No
A Glimpse of Rural Life, Aguamansa	28.21480	-16.30123	56
A Merchant's Highway, Las Aguas	28.23687	-16.38359	138
A Rockin' Good Walk, Teide National Park	28.13400	-16.37841	235
Above Barranco del Infierno, Adeje	28.08221	-16.41530	153
An Explosive Landscape, Chio	28.17078	-16.45749	86
Black Caves & Broken Cottages, Los Silos	28.21874	-16.49002	103
Camino de la Virgen de Lourdes, Santiago del Teide	28.29440	-16.81528	85
Cereal Killers, Guia de Isora	28.20757	-16.77234	183
Climbing The Walls, Teide National Park	28.13428	-16.37632	220
Exploring the Red Mountain, El Médano	28.04131	-16.54274	206
Exploring the Yellow Mountain, Golf del Sur	28.02241	-16.61106	211
Following the Lava, Garachico	28.37289	-16.76415	120
Forest to Cave, Anaga Mountains	28.31880	-16.16802	22

Route	Latitude	Longitude	Page No
Hamlets & Hillsides, Anaga Mountains	28.55554	-16.24834	30
Hell's Ravine, Adeje	28.12625	-16.72377	162
Holiday Mountain, Los Cristianos	28.02490	-16.42504	175
Ifonche to the Deserted Valley, Ifonche	28.12209	-16.69004	158
In Ancient Footsteps, Masca	28.30432	-16.84048	110
Into The Valley, Santiago del Teide	28.30684	-16.80243	72
King of the South, Arona	28.06058	-16.40826	169
Northern Exposure, La Orotava	28.21480	-16.30123	49
Pools and Pines, Erjos	28.19071	-16.48272	80
Road to a View, San Miguel de Abona	28.05868	-16.37231	199
Take it to the Wall, Teide National Park	28.30446	-16.56676	231
Taste of the Caribbean, Los Realejos/Puerto de la Cruz	28.39547	-16.59378	132
The Guanche Way, La Orotava	28.21477	-16.30123	61
The Lost World, Vera de Erques	28.17744	-16.74602	189
The Ultimate High, Mount Teide	28.25942	-16.60344	239

Route	Latitude	Longitude	Page No
The Virgin's Badlands, Guimar	28.17917	-16.22265	145
To the End of the Island, Anaga Mountains	28.34111	-16.09582	38
Up Country, El Palmar	28.20447	-16.51029	95
Volcano Surfing, Teide National Park	28.30380	-16.56631	226
Walking to the Moon, Vilaflor	28.09616	-16.38058	247
Way Out West, Buenavista del Norte	28.22226	-16.52244	127

GLOSSARY OF TERMS

AEMet - Agencia Estatal de Meteorología.
Ahumado – smoked.
Almendra – almond.
Almendrados – almond biscuits.
Arepa – Venezuelan fried corncake, usually filled with savoury ingredients.
Autopista – motorway.
Balo – type of cactus shaped like a football.
Barranco – ravine.
Bejeque – aeonium.
Bodega – vineyard or wine bar/cellar/shop.
Brezal – moor, heath, tree heather.
Bruma – low cloud.
Buenas tardes – good afternoon.
Buenos días – good morning.
Caldera – crater.
Calima – hot wind blowing in from Africa and usually filled with sand particles.
Calvario – a site where crosses or depictions of Christ on the crucifix are found.
Camino – road, path, route or way.
Camino Real – lit. royal road, an old merchant trail.
Canarios – people born in the Canary Islands.
Cardón – type of cactus.
Casa rural – country house, often available to rent.
Cazuela – lit. cooking pot, stewed meat and vegetables.
Cerveza – beer.
Chozo – stone or wooden shelter.
Cistus – rockrose.
Costeros – lit. coasts but usually referenced in connection with weather alerts where it means high waves.
Coto de Caza – hunting zone.
Cueva – cave.
Curado – matured for more than 105 days.
Dorada – brand of beer.
Drago tree – Dracaena Draco subtropical tree with multi-headed crown growing naturally only in the Canary Islands, Cape Verde and Madeira.
Elevation – height above sea level.
Era – threshing circle.

Ermita – chapel.
Escaldón – gofio flavoured with stock and sometimes including meat and potatoes.
Espacio Natural Protegido – conservation area protected by law.
Finca – farm or smallholding.
Fresca – fresh.
Fuente – fountain or spring.
Geomorphic – study of the landscape and its features.
Gofio – toasted and ground grains.
Guagua (pronounced wah-wah) – local buses
Guanche – earliest settlers to the Canary Islands, thought to have arrived on the islands around 1000BC.
Iglesia – church.
Jablé – pumice.
Kiln – oven.
Laurisilva – subtropical laurel forest.
Lavadero – laundry.
Lomo – ridge.
Malpaís – lit. badlands, an area of rough and non-eroded volcanic fallout.
Menu del Día – daily menu.
Microclimate - a local atmospheric zone where the climate differs from the surrounding area.
Mirador – viewpoint.
Mojo rojo – a piquant sauce usually made from sweet red peppers.
Mojo verde – a piquant sauce usually made from coriander or parsley.
Montaña – mountain.
Papas arrugadas – small, salty boiled potatoes usually served with mojos, a Canary Islands speciality.
Pahoehoe – lava that has solidified in the shape of twisted rope.
Parador – Spanish government owned hotels.
Pista – trail or path wide and even enough for farm or forest workers vehicles.
Pollo al Ajillo (pronounced po-yo al a-hee-yo) – garlic chicken.
Puchero – traditional Canarian stew.
Puerto – port.
Pyroclastic – deposits of explosive, pumice-rich volcanic debris.
Recreation zone – picnic area.

Reserva Natural Espacio – areas with special or fragile eco-systems where it's forbidden to collect materials other than for scientific research purposes.
Salto de Pastor – ancient art of traversing ravines using a long pole, practised by the Guanche.
Selfie – self portrait photo.
Semi curado – matured for more than 35 days.
Scree – broken rock fragments.
Sendero – a walk or path.
Tabaiba – euphorbia (spurge), diverse group of plants common in the Canary Islands.
Tajinaste – echium.
Tasca – café/wine bar/tavern.
Tinerfeños – people born in Tenerife.
Web cam – camera streaming live images via the internet.
Zona Recreativa – picnic area.

Index

A

Above Barranco del Infierno	152-157,160-161
Adeje	151,152,**164**
AEMet	9
Afur	20, **30-37**
A Glimpse of Rural Life, Aguamansa	**55-59**
Aguamansa	46,47,**55-59**,66
Aguamansa restaurant	59,**66**
Aguere Hotel, La Laguna	20
Alcala	181,182
Alta Montaña Hotel, Vilaflor	219
Altavista Refuge, Teide National Park	241,**243**
A Merchant's Highway, San Juan de la Rambla	**138-142**
Anaga	**17-44**
Anaga lighthouse	40,42-43
An Explosive Landscape, Chio	**86-90**
Arenas Negras picnic zone	88
Arenas Negras, Teide National Park	**226-230**
Arguayo	68,69,71-77
Aripe	186
A Rockin' Good Walk, Teide National Park	**235-238**
Arona	167,172
Arona Gran Hotel	177

B

Baracán	100-101
Bar Fleytas	69,81,**84**
Barranco Afur de Tamadite	32
Barranco Cuescara	195
Barranco de las Casas, Arona	172
Barranco del Drago	201-202,**204**
Barranco del Infierno	151-152,**162-166**
Barranco del Rey	160,**172-173**
Barranco Salte del Encerradero	36
Bar Tropical, Arguayo	69,**77**
Black Caves & Broken Cottages, Los Silos	**103-109**
Bolico Ridge	**82**,84
Brasas de Chirche restaurant	188
Buenavista del Norte	**127-131**

C

Calima	9
Café Los Roques	225
Camino de Chasna	62,**249,252**
Camino de las Vueltas	34
Camino de la Virgen de Lourdes, Santiago del Teide	85
Camino de Los Guanches	62
Caminos Reales	5
Casa Alvaro, Chamorga	44
Casa Carlos, Anaga	37
Casa del Capitán	201,**204**
Casa Juan Luis, Vera de Erques	195
Casas Moradas	106
Casas de Tafada	42
Centinela Mirador	198,201,**203-204**
Cereal Killers, Guia de Isora	**183-188**
Cha' Domitila	75,77
Chamorga	19,**38-44**
Chibusque restaurant, Guimar	149
Chinamada	19,**22-29**
Chinyero	68,74-78,84,**86-90**
Chirche	**183,186,188**
Chirche Mirador	**186,188**
Chio	88
Climbing The Walls, Teide National Park	**220-225**
Clothing	12
Compass	15
Corona Forestal	75
Costa del Silencio	**211-215**
Costa Salada Rural Hotel	**20-21**
Cruz del Dornajito	**60-65**
Cruz del Carmen	16,**20-29**
Cruz Vieja	**32-35**
Cuevas Negras	108

D - E

Degollada del Cedro, Teide National Park	233
El Burgado restaurant, Buenavista	**130-131**
El Calvario	74,102
El Dornajo restaurant, Ifonche	151,**155-156**
El Fortin	135
El Médano	**206-210**

El Navio Rural Hotel	182
El Palmar	92-93,**95-102**
El Patio rural hotel, Guincho	94
El Portillo restaurant, Teide National Park	229
El Portillo Visitor Centre, Teide National Park	228,233
El Puertito	147,149
El Rincón de Roberto, Vilaflor	253
El Rosario	141
El Tanque	84,**123**
Erjos Pools	68,**79-84,103-109**
Escaldón	19-20
Estancia de los Ingleses, Mount Teide	241
Exploring the Red Mountain, El Médano	**206-210**
Exploring the Yellow Mountain,	**211-215**

F - G

Finca Salamanca Rural Hotel	143
Flashpoint Bar	210
Flora	18,47,68,93,119,143,151, 168,182,198,218,246
Following the Lava, Garachico	**120-125**
Footwear	12
Forest to Cave, Anaga Mountains	**22-29**
Fuente de Hermano Pedro cafe, Vilaflor	246,253
Fuente de Tamaide	203
Garachico	94,**118-119**,125
Gofio	19
Golf del Sur	211-215
Gran Melia Palacio de Isora Hotel	182
Guanche	18-19,24,**174**,204
Guanche Way	**60-66**
Gui de Isora	181,185
Guimar	143

H- K

Hamlets and Hillsides, Anaga Mountains	**30-37**
Hermano Pedro	245
Heat	9
Hell's Ravine, Adeje	**162-165**
High seas	9
Holiday Mountain, Los Cristianos	**175-179**
Hotel rates key	5

Ice Age	18,42
Ifonche	151-152,158
Iglesia de la Concepción	20
In Ancient Footsteps, Masca	110-116
Into The Valley, Santiago del Teide	71-77
Isla Baja	129
King of the South, Arona	169-174
Kompass maps	15

L

La Caldera, La Orotava	47,50-51,53-66
La Casona del Patio, Santiago del Teide	69,77
La Casona de Rastro, Los Realejos	135
La Cueva restaurant, Chinamada	19-20
La Escuela Restaurant	140,142
La Florida	46
La Fortaleza, Teide National Park	231-234
La Gordejuela	136
La Hoya	75,202-203
La Laguna	20-21
La Orotava	49
La Quinta Roja hotel, Garachico	94
La Romantica	136
Las Aguas	138-142
Las Aguas Restaurant	142
Las Cañadas del Teide	7
Las Carboneras	19,24,27
Las Fuentes	189,193-194
Las Manchas	75-76,78,88
Laurisilva	18,42
Llano de Los Viejos	29
Llano de Ucanca, Teide National Park	237-238
Lomo del Medio	203
Los Bailaderos	92-93,97,99
Los Bailaderos restaurant	97
Los Cristianos	177
Los Escurriales, Vilaflor	250-251
Los Gigantes	93,113,116
Los Órganos	48-54,57
Los Pedragales	98
Los Roques, Puerto de la Cruz	135,137
Los Silos	105,109

M

Malpais	100,**143-149**
Maps	**15**
Marítimo Hotel, Puerto de la Cruz	134-135,137
Masca	70,98,100,**110-116**,
Masca Barranco	**110-116**
Mercedes Forest	**20**
Meson del Norte restaurant	**98**
Microclimates	8,**68**
Mirador Aguaide, Anaga	**27**
Mirador de Centinela	198,**199-200**
Montaña Amarilla	**211-215**
Montaña Blanca, Teide National Park	229,**241**
Montaña de la Mar, Guimar	**148**
Montaña Grande, Guimar	**148**
Montaña Guajara, Teide National Park	194,**220-225**,237
Montaña Guaza, Los Cristianos	167-168,**175-179**
Montaña Roja, El Médano	178,**206-210**
Montaña Tejina	190-192,**194**
Monte del Agua	102,**106-107**
Morras del Corcho, Guimar	**148**
Mouflon	**15**
Mount Bilma	74,**76**
Mount Teide	

    3,4,42,46,49,50,52,56,61,63,65,68,72-74,80,82,84,87-89,92,96,99,
100,155,171,194,214,**217-221**,229,232,234,237,**239-243**

N – P

Nautica Nivaria water taxi	41,**43**
Nivaria Hotel, La Laguna	**20**
Northern Exposure, La Orotava	**48-54**
Otelo restaurant, Adeje	151,**164-165**
Paisaje Lunar, Vilaflor	**247-253**
Parador de Cañadas del Teide	218,222,225,236
Picnic zone	47,50-51,57,69,88
Pico Viejo	82,84,87,89,237,**242**
Pinolere	**46**
Playa de El Fraile, Buenavista	**130**
Playa de Las Arenas, Buenavista	129,**131**
Playa de la Tejita	**210**
Playa de San Juan	**271**
Playa Sur Tenerife Hotel, El Médano	**208**

287

Playa Tamadite	34-35
Plaza del Adelantado, La Laguna	20
Pools and Pines, Santiago del Teide	68,79-85,
Puerto de la Cruz	46,50,63,**134**
Punta Brava	63,**134-135**
Punta del Hidalgo	23,**24-29**

Q – S

Quatro Esquinas Hotel, San Miguel de Abona	198
Quinta Roja Hotel, Garachico	94
Rainfall	7-9,12,18,217
Rambla del Castro	132-137
Red Mountain, El Médano	203,**206-210**
Road to a View, San Miguel de Abona	199-204
Roque Bermejo	19,**38-44**
Roque Chinchado, Teide National Park	236
Roque de Fuera	35,42
Roque de las Bodegas	35
Roque del Condé	167-168,**169-174**
Roque de Taborno	24,26
Roque de Tierra	42
Roques de Garcia, Teide National Park	16,224,**235-238**
Route difficulty rating	5
Rural hotels	5,9,20,47,70,94,198
Rural Hotel Victoria, La Orotava	47
San Cristobál de La Laguna	21
San José de Los Llanos	81-82,84
San Juan Del Reparo	120-125
San Miguel de Abona	196-204
San Miguel Rural Hotel	198
San Pedro Mirador	125,**133-137**
San Roque hotel, Garachico	84
Santa Cruz	29,40,43
Santiago del Teide	68-90
Seasons	8
Shoes	12-13
Siete Cañadas, Teide National Park	222-225,228,229

T

Taganana	19,**30-37**,40
Tajinaste	68,93,218,244,246
Take It To The Wall, Teide National Park	231-234

Tamadite	32,34-35
Tasca Taguara, Ifonche	155
Tasquita de Nino, San Miguel	204
Taste of the Caribbean, Los Realejos	132-137
Teide Cable Car	243
Teide National Park	12-13,15,62-64,152,**216-243**,245,250
Teno Rural Park	92,116
Tesegre restaurant, Las Carboneras	27
The Deserted Valley, Ifonche	158-161
Theft from cars	16
The Guanche Way, La Orotava	60-66
The Lost World, Vera de Erques	182,**189-195**
The Ultimate High, Mount Teide	239-243
The Virgin's Badlands, Guimar	145-149
TITSA bus service	4
To The End Of The Island, Anaga Mountains	38-44

U – Z

UNESCO	20
Up Country, El Palmar	95-102
Valentín restaurant, Las Carboneras	27
Valle de Arriba	68-78,81-82
Valle de Guerra	20
Vento, Arona	172-173
Vera de Erques	182,**189-195**
Vertigo	4,273
Vieja Bodega restaurant, San Miguel	204
Vilaflor	62,218-219,222-223, 244-253
Villalba Hotel, Vilaflor	218
Virgen de Candelaria	148
Visitor Centre	19,**226-230**
Volcano Surfing, Teide National Park	226-230
Walking poles	13-14
Walking To The Moon, Vilaflor	247-253
Way Out West, Buenavista del Norte	127-131
Weather	4,6-10, 12, 18, 47, 68, 92, 118,143,151,167,181,197,217,245
Yellow Mountain, Costa del Silencio	211-215

WALK THIS WAY WILL RETURN WITH ANOTHER GREAT HIKING DESTINATION...

MAY OUR PATHS CROSS AGAIN SOMEWHERE ALONG THE TRAIL.

ALSO AVAILABLE FROM REAL TENERIFE

The Real Tenerife: The Insiders' Guide - a comprehensive native's eye view of the fascinating island of Tenerife; its people, places, language, fiestas, food and culture. Includes hotel & restaurant recommendations; must-see destinations; top 10 things to do; top beaches; favourite off-the-beaten-track locations and much, much more. *Available from Amazon on Kindle and in paperback.*

Real Tenerife Island Walks – comprehensive, self-guided walking notes to our Walk This Way routes in PDF format, sent as email attachments. NB All of the PDF walks are contained in Walk This Way.

Available online (www.therealtenerife.com) in PDF format emailed to your inbox.

Real Tenerife Town & City Guides – detailed guides to Tenerife's most compelling town's and cities (Santa Cruz, La Laguna, Puerto de la Cruz & La Orotava) including walking routes taking in the best of what to see; detailed descriptions of sights, parks, gardens, plazas, galleries, museums and points of interest; as well as recommendations on where to eat or enjoy a coffee and some relaxation.
Available online (www.therealtenerife.com) in PDF format emailed to your inbox.

Real Tenerife Island Drives - a combined trail finder and guide book written for anyone who intends to hire a car on Tenerife. Island Drives details a series of six, scenic drives around the island that take you away from the tourist resorts and into the real Tenerife. Includes information on places to visit along the routes; recommended restaurants and picnic areas along the way.
Available online (www.therealtenerife.com) in PDF format emailed to your inbox and on Amazon Kindle.

Printed in Great Britain
by Amazon